1225

MW01530887

A Year on the Farm

Other books by Sally Wise

*A Year in a Bottle: How to make your own
delicious preserves all year round*

Slow Cooker: Easy and delicious recipes for all seasons

*Out of the Bottle: Easy and delicious recipes for making and
using your own preserves*

From My Kitchen to Yours: Easy and gluten-free recipes

Leftover Makeovers

Sweet!

Slow Cooker 2

The Complete Slow Cooker

The Small Kitchen

Sally Wise

A Year on the Farm

Recipes and stories from my
Tasmanian tree change

ABC
Books

The ABC 'Wave' device is a trademark of the Australian Broadcasting Corporation and is used under licence by HarperCollins*Publishers* Australia.

First published in Australia in 2014
by HarperCollinsPublishers Australia Pty Limited
ABN 36 009 913 517
harpercollins.com.au

Copyright © Sally Wise 2014

The right of Sally Wise to be identified as the author
of this work has been asserted by her in accordance with the
Copyright Amendment (Moral Rights) Act 2000.

This work is copyright. Apart from any use as permitted under the
Copyright Act 1968, no part may be reproduced, copied, scanned,
stored in a retrieval system, recorded, or transmitted, in any form
or by any means, without the prior written permission of the publisher.

HarperCollins*Publishers*
Level 13, 201 Elizabeth Street, Sydney, NSW 2000, Australia
Unit D1, 63 Apollo Drive, Rosedale, Auckland 0632, New Zealand
A 53, Sector 57, Noida, UP, India
77–85 Fulham Palace Road, London W6 8JB, United Kingdom
2 Bloor Street East, 20th floor, Toronto, Ontario M4W 1A8, Canada
10 East 53rd Street, New York NY 10022, USA

National Library of Australia Cataloguing-in-Publication data:
Wise, Sally, author.
A Year on the Farm / Sally Wise.
978 0 7333 3280 7 (paperback)
978 1 4607 0113 3 (ebook)
Cooking. Condiments. Jam. Preserving.
Includes Index.
641.852

Cover design by Hazel Lam, HarperCollins Design Studio
Cover images: Rustic kitchen © Paul Poplis/FoodPix/ Getty Images;
chicken and apple tree by Lina Ostling/ Getty Images; author photo by Chris Crerar;
all other images by shutterstock.com
Internal images by shutterstock.com
Typeset in 11.5/14pt Bembo by Kirby Jones
Printed and bound in Australia by Griffin Press
The papers used by HarperCollins in the manufacture of this book are a natural,
recyclable product made from wood grown in sustainable plantation forests.
The fibre source and manufacturing processes meet recognised international
environmental standards, and carry certification.

5 4 3 2 1   14 15 16 17

This book is dedicated to my incredible family, whose love of fine produce, preserving and cooking is a constant source of inspiration.

Contents

By Way of Explanation

I have long wanted to write a sequel to *A Year in a Bottle* and for the last year I have been well situated to do this, living in these valleys of incredible abundance.

A Year on the Farm is a book about a tree change from a seaside existence, a whole new way of life with a view to a productive future. It follows our first year at our property in Molesworth, mapping the seasonal fruits and vegetables as they passed, and the recipes that we developed along the way. It tells of the school we set up, the people we met, the animals on and around the farm, and our quest for produce.

The back of the book reiterates basics about preserving, and extends those sections from *A Year in a Bottle*. I have learned a great deal through experimentation and have simplified many of the methods so there is more helpful information, and more tips and tricks for achieving optimum results. The troubleshooting charts have also been updated and expanded.

There are hundreds of new recipes, and a handful that originated in *A Year in a Bottle* have been modified so they are more easily prepared. I also provide recipes to show how best to use preserves in everyday cooking, not just as a jam on toast or a scone, or a pickle with meat — or worse, to leave them sitting unused on the shelf.

There are many recipes for cordial syrups. These are very easy to make and far better than serving people, especially children, additive-laden cordials. Homemade, they can provide nutrients in an easily consumed, acceptable, digestible form.

I have given the methods best suited to bottling each individual fruit. After decades of experimentation I've worked out the specific temperature to coax the best from each of the respective fruits, by way of appearance and the retention of nutrients.

This last year has certainly been a grand adventure with inevitable challenges along the way. It has most definitely been a learning experience, one of the richest of my life, and I wouldn't have it any other way.

Introduction

My family and I lived at Eaglehawk Neck, an idyllic corner in the southeast of Tasmania, for over 15 years. Our small brick cottage was where my husband Robert and I brought up our youngest three children and watched them grow into adults with careers and lives and families of their own. The house was set on a steep hillside. The property was a mixture of wetland, rainforest with massive trees and a large cleared area around the house.

From our front balcony we could look out over the ocean to tiny Clydes Island, around past the famous Tessellated Pavement and beyond past the surf beaches and round to the Blowhole. It was an enchanting spot where wildlife abounded. By day wallabies fed near the back door, unafraid, catching the hulls of seeds that dropped to the ground from the parrot feeders we set out each morning. The bird life was a constant moving kaleidoscope of colour and personalities. In summer the cool afternoon sea breezes shielded us from the soaring, intolerable heat, and in winter we never saw a frost. The colder months were my favourite — the sea roared and thrashed itself against the massive cliffs, dislodging boulders and changing the seascape in its fury, moving the sand and throwing mounds of seaweed onto the beaches.

However, there was no denying that we were getting older and our children expressed concern for us, encouraging us to think about moving closer to town. It was a great pity: I loved the place. However, I acknowledged their point — these days our legs complained about the trudge back up the hill from our weekend walks down to the picturesque Lufra Cove.

There were other reasons too, that crept into mind from time to time.

For as long as I can remember, I have wanted to have a little cooking school. Nothing grand, just a handful of willing participants having fun in a warm and hospitable kitchen. Here I'd indulge my favourite types of cooking: preserving, which always gives me that warm sense of plenty, and leads to pantry shelves full of treats for the leaner months; slow cooking, which I love for its nostalgia and convenience; baking with yeast, making sweet treats, gluten-free cooking, which helps the many people who cannot tolerate wheat, oats, rye and barley; and my area of special interest, convict and colonial-era cookery.

It would be a school for the everyday person who just wants to learn, or who simply loves to cook. The school would showcase the abundant wonderful produce we have in Tasmania, increasingly available from farmers' markets and farm-gate stalls. The island is a delight for the casual or more serious forager — berries, herbs, apples, pears, quince, edible flowers and more are ripe for the picking along riverbanks and down country lanes.

I had tried setting a school up at Eaglehawk Neck but the logistical obstacles defeated me. No suitable land was available, and sufficient tank water would be an issue. Potential participants may well have found the trip from Hobart daunting and chosen instead to bypass us on a day trip to Port Arthur.

This speculation stemmed from the fact that, for as long as I can recall, I have loved to cook. Even more than that, I have a compulsion to cook. Perhaps the seeds were sown in my grandmother's kitchen, where she obviously revelled in baking for family, who frequently came to visit. The aroma of cooking, her good nature, the sense of hospitality, the happiness she showed when sharing the food she had made — I'm sure they all played their part. She often chatted about her childhood, showed me photos of her parents' bakery and the delights they used to bake in early Hobart.

As I grew up I longed for the day when I'd have my own kitchen. As we did back then, I snipped out recipes from magazines and pasted them in scrapbooks to have at the ready. One day I'd be an exceptional cook, I decided. I had no aspirations to be a chef, as it was rare in those days for women to enter the field. I simply wanted to be able to bake on my own ground without restraint.

To my horror, after I was married and valiantly invited guests for lunch, dinner or a sumptuous morning tea, I found that very few of the recipes worked for me, and failures were more common than not. However, I'd waited so long that I decided to persevere until they were successful at last. It was only in recent times and with a visit to the now-operational school that a lovely young journalist expressed in words what I have done for so long — I 'deconstruct' the recipes, ingredients and method, and then put them back together again to obtain the results I'd envisaged.

And so the years passed, always baking, preserving, cooking in one form or another and blissfully happy doing so. Robert has always said that he knows where to find me no matter what — happy, sad, bored or angry, I'd be in the kitchen.

In time, preserving became a way of life for the whole family. Each summer saw an orgy of preserving strike the kitchen and such was the abundance from fields and orchards that we had the luxury of experimentation, inventing lots of recipes along the way.

It had turned out to be all that I had hoped for — perhaps above all else, being able to share what we cooked with extended family and friends that reminded me of my grandmother's kitchen so many decades before.

Although a mere home cook, time and circumstance led to my becoming the person for the Jams and Preserves talkback segment on ABC radio, which served to fuel my passion for preserving all the more.

At the instigation of listeners and especially presenter Chris Wisbey I finally put a book together with the recipes about preserves that I'd accumulated over the years. It did surprisingly well and other cookbooks followed.

It was from there that the desire to set up a little cooking school gained momentum. What had been little more than a pipe dream became almost an obsession. Matching this to our circumstance of moving closer to the city, the dream became more established and firmer plans undertaken.

And so began the process of looking around for a new home.

Robert and I had set our sights on the Derwent Valley. Its central township of New Norfolk is steeped in history and is picturesque in the extreme, especially down by the river, where elderflowers, blackberries, and rosehips grow wild. The valley beyond the township is also rich in history, with stories of bushrangers, and many hop fields, berry farms and more. Autumn sees the multitudinous poplar trees burst into a mass of brilliant yellow leaves, and serene willows line the banks of the Derwent River, dipping their branches into the cool clear water.

Another reason to move was that our daughter Stephanie and her husband Nat live in the township with their two children Jacob and Charly. Four of the other children and grandchildren would be closer as well, meaning we could see them more often.

But in the manner of would-be new home-owners everywhere, we spent two years visiting property after property and found each wanting in one way or another — too big, too small, overly expensive, too many repairs to be done. Each time, we retreated despondently to the Neck. However, mentally at least, we were breaking ties that bound us there.

On one cold Saturday morning in May 2012 we contacted a real estate agent about a property at Molesworth, a tiny township near New Norfolk, a former hop and berry-growing region and about 30 minutes north from the centre of Hobart.

It didn't appear to have much appeal from the photos on the website and the short drive off the main road towards the property confirmed my reservations.

'I hate this type of bush!' I grumbled as we drove along a dirt road lined with scrappy wattle trees and shrub, not at all like my beloved forest at the Neck.

Wisely, Robert kept quiet. However we rounded a bend in the road, and there emerged the most wonderful sight — a house made of western red cedar (to which I have always been quite partial) and alongside it, a small matching chalet. There was a cute cubby house (for the grandchildren) and, on all sides, rambling, lush green paddocks. There was even a small orchard of fledgling fruit trees.

Things improved more as we drove in through the gates. As Robert set off to explore a huge shed, with a mezzanine floor no less, the look on his face said 'Perfect!'

Meanwhile I combed through the house with our daughter Stephanie. Much bigger than our house at the Neck, it had a study (just for me), and a commandant's cottage-style den (for Robert). No more squabbling over whose paperwork belonged where or who lost what of whose.

The gardens did look a mite overgrown and neglected, but we were assured that there was unlimited bore water with a good pump, and a sprinkler system all set up. Bringing them into shape would be a simple thing — just add water, I thought to myself.

However, the overriding factor was that little chalet. It had been used as a daycare centre, and, it was rumoured, more recently as a home hairdressing salon, but in my mind it was already the long-dreamed-of cooking school — once it had been rescued from the ghastly internal coat of yellow paint and had several broken windows replaced. It would take a lot of elbow grease and not a little cash, but it would be so worth it. The dream was at last within reach, the main elements were all there.

Within two days we had signed a contract to purchase, and thank goodness we did, as a few days later one of the former owners asked the vendor if they could buy it back from them.

And so the adventure began. I am not by nature a patient person, so I wanted to get things up and running immediately.

Not so simple, I found. The broken windows and yellow paint were just the beginning. There were electrical problems and drainage issues, the source of a nasty musty smell. The stove looked suspiciously grimy and would need replacing sooner than we'd thought.

Outside, the paddocks needed something to graze them. Stephanie and Nat's friend Jordan had two alpacas that needed a place to graze. He would happily bring them here. It's not uncommon for alpacas to thrive in this region — in fact, there is an alpaca farm only about a kilometre away from our property.

And so all the ducks, comparatively speaking, seemed to be in a row. With an expectation of an easy ride to the finish line of getting the school up and running, we set about arranging to move into our new home.

As with all such moves, it was difficult to leave behind a much-loved family home with all its happy memories. At the Molesworth property there would be no feeding of the wildlife. It is fenced to keep them out, for the sake of the vegetable gardens. Most of all, I'd miss the possums that I fed Anzac biscuits to each night. I had no fear that they would fend for themselves quite effectively, but I'd miss their company.

I'd certainly fret for the awe-inspiring coastline, the cliffs and quiet and picturesque little Lufra Cove at the bottom of the hill. We would miss our friends, but we promised to keep in touch and they to visit.

What would our new neighbours be like? Would we be accepted as part of the community?

Leaving was bittersweet: heart-wrenching on the one hand, but full of hope and optimism on the other, in that the dream of the cooking school was looking more like a reality.

Cook's Notes

When foraging for produce, be sure that you know that the fruit or vegetable has not been sprayed or polluted in any way. For example, in some places blackberries may be sprayed with poison as they are considered to be a pest. I never pick any produce from roadsides, as they will have been polluted with exhaust fumes from passing vehicles.

The rule of thumb is to always be sure of your source, and to ensure that the produce is untainted.

Recipes for cooking and baking in this book are designed to be flexible — for instance, egg size does not really matter. I just use average-sized eggs, whatever our chooks happen to lay for us on any given day. I often substitute duck eggs, which make magnificent cakes, and you don't need to make adjustments to other ingredients in the recipe.

With butter, you can use either salted or unsalted.

If anything other than plain white sugar is needed, this will be specified, as in the case of meringue-style mixtures, where caster sugar is used because it dissolves faster when beaten with the egg whites. Even then, if I have run out, ordinary white sugar will still give a satisfactory result.

In this book if a recipe specifies an oven temperature, it is for a fan-forced oven. If your oven is not fan-assisted or fan-forced, increase the temperature by 20°C.

July 8

And so here we are, in our new home. The seemingly endless boxes of goods and chattels and clothing are piled in every room. To my disappointment the baby grand piano that my grandmother left to me in her will cannot fit through the doorway and so must be placed in the chalet. A little disconsolately, still homesick for the Neck, I begin unpacking. Within a few minutes however, daughters Stephanie and Courtney arrive to help and before we know it, the mood is lifted as the ample cupboards are filled with neatly packed belongings.

Robert and son-in-law Nat have retreated to the garden and are making plans to bring the overgrown berry patch into some sort of order. They seem to spend a lot of time in the shed, prioritising projects for the not-too-distant future.

Despite the tedious work of unpacking, it is plain to see that it will indeed be a place where our family can visit more easily and regularly. As for the grounds, to me it seems like a little piece of paradise. I admit that the Neck was becoming somewhat encroached upon by the surrounding forest, and its aspect was quite dark and gloomy by comparison. Here, the open fields allow in the sunshine, even on a cold winter's day, it is cheering, to be sure.

The cold, several degrees lower than the comparatively balmy winter days at the Neck, is unfamiliar, but there are ample heaters and the scenery on and around the property is breathtaking. Still, I anticipate it will be some time before I can get back into the swing of preserving, though normally I would carry on right through winter.

We plan to work on the vegetable gardens to ensure that we have homegrown vegetables as soon as humanly possible. I will also need to find where best to source winter vegetables for preserving. It is thought that preserving is only for the summer and autumn months, but you can preserve all year round, and I love the hearty vegetables that make excellent pickles — onion jam and marmalade, pickled cabbages and spicy onions.

Citrus fruits, especially lemons, are readily available; the lemon tree near the back door is smothered in them. The enthusiastic preserver need never be idle.

July 10

The house is still awash with boxes and random furniture in strange places. It is much larger than our cottage at the Neck, and the cold in such open spaces is intense. Still, the wood heater does an incredible job of warming our home so that it's comfortable. This is no small feat, given the fact that not only is the house rather large, but in the loungeroom and dining area, the very attractive wooden ceiling is very high.

I admit to being a bit worried about this move, having seen movies where houses were bought and all sorts of things go wrong. Lack of heating would be the worst, I think. We'd even surreptitiously driven past one day before the final inspection date to check if smoke was coming out of the chimney. I was pleased to see a plume steadily rising from the flue as we drove past.

The bedrooms have electric panel heaters, which we make good use of and which give us a false sense of temperature security. When I opened the curtains this morning I was literally gobsmacked. What is this? The paddocks and gardens are white with thick frost as far as the eye can see. The ramshackle railway sleepers that serve as surrounds for the ailing vegetable gardens look as if some unseen hand has painted them thickly with stark white paint.

The wood heater had gone out in the night and the main part of the house was accordingly icy, but that is soon remedied. Suitably warmed by an ample hot breakfast and noting that the winter sun has broken through the mist, we decide to explore our new surroundings.

It's years, decades in fact, since I've experienced frost and never one such as this. At Eaglehawk Neck we never had a single frost on our property in our 15 years there. Here on this cold, cold morning our boots crunch the grass still crisp with ice. However, it's undoubtedly every bit as beautiful as we remembered when we first set eyes on it. The landscaped gardens at one time had been carved out lovingly and edged with rock walls. A large elm tree, now almost barren of leaves, holds promise of cool shade in the summer and I can already imagine the abundance of fruit we'll harvest from the fledgling orchard, hopefully apples, plums, peaches, figs and cherries at least.

The berry patch also holds great promise — it appears to harbour raspberries, loganberries, perhaps boysenberries, blueberries and gooseberries (and at present a mammoth crop of weeds). The former owners told us that the patch bears exceedingly well in summer and I am certainly hoping so. My idea of prolific bearing is buckets and buckets of huge, flavoursome berries that I'll be able to use in the planned cooking classes.

The day passes with visits from family who help to unpack yet more boxes. It's an opportunity to put the stove through its paces. It looks a bit grimy but that's not too much of a worry and I plan to cook a roast leg of pork with crisp crackling for dinner. I'll make a spice rub for the rind of the pork so that the crackling will be incredibly flavoursome as well as have its characteristic crunch.

This electric stove in the house does not comply at all well to requests to change its temperature and instead bakes at full pelt. I've had a stove like this once before, in rented accommodation during our first years of marriage. To be able to cook becomes a bit of a guessing game, with much turning on and off of the oven to ensure food cooks as it should. The hotplates are not so bad and are up to the task of cooking vegetables at least.

I decide to go out to the chalet and use the stove out there. It's very old, but often an old stove is a good, reliable one, and I was told that it's great for roasts. When I turn it on it smells ominously strange and soon grease is oozing out from around and under the door and across the floor. So much for that option then, though I do try for a while in a very well-covered dish. This stove also suffers from the problem of no temperature control, or precious little, though it's better than the one in the house. Well, this is supposed to be an adventure, I guess.

Dinner is successfully cooked at last without too much hassle and is even quite edible. It's become obvious though that both stoves will need replacing. I had sort of expected this from the start, but it will have to be done sooner rather than later.

Spice Rub for Pork Roast

3 teaspoons ground coriander
3 teaspoons ground cumin
1 teaspoon sweet paprika
1½ teaspoons salt
1 teaspoon sugar

Mix all the rub ingredients together. Brush the pork rind with vegetable oil and then sprinkle over the spice rub and massage into the surface.

Bake the pork as usual — the rind will be tasty as well as crisp and crunchy.

I sometimes double the spice rub and make hasselback potatoes to accompany the pork. This amount of spice mix will be sufficient for 4 medium-sized spiced potatoes.

To make **Hasselback Potatoes**, peel, then cut a flat surface on one side. Place cut side down on a board and with a sharp knife make 4mm slices about three-quarters of the way through. Drizzle oil evenly over the potatoes and sprinkle with the spice rub mix. Roast for about

4

40 minutes until cooked through and crisp. If there is room in the roasting pan, cook alongside the roast during the last 40 minutes of the pork's cooking time.

Makes enough for 2kg leg or shoulder of pork

July 12

I can't stand being without a vegetable garden, though I make no claims to being a greatly successful gardener. Even so, I usually manage to have a vegetable patch that produces at least some pickings for our table every day.

With this in mind I decide to tackle the neglected small vegetable plots that have haunted me as I look out my study window. As the abundant weeds are pulled, I am very pleased to find that the soil is easy to work, quite sandy and loamy. What a dream this is compared to the stodgy black clay of vegetable gardens I've endured in the past. It strikes me as an anomaly that it was clay by the sea, but sandy here.

Furthermore as the earth is uncovered and dug over, the neglected ground yields a barrowful of potatoes and, quite amazingly, many small red tomatoes. There will be something for the table after all. The potatoes prove to be pink eyes, that great Tasmanian favourite. A waxy potato with little pink eyes from which they derive their name, they are at their best in December and grace summer tables in many tasty dishes. They are ideal for potato salads, as they are not given to crumbling.

It's hardly time for cold salads, but I will serve them as my nan did — boiled with their skins on, then rolled in butter, salt and chopped mint. I could make hot potato salad, loaded with cream, bacon, cheese and onion. It's a favourite, but not so great for keeping Robert's cholesterol level down.

The tomatoes I can roast in my fickle oven, drizzled with a little olive oil and balsamic vinegar, with just a sprinkle of salt and sugar. A few stray beans I've found can supplement the feast.

Although these plots are small, it doesn't take much to provide quite a bit of food for the table and so I will plant them out with winter vegetables in a few days' time.

July 14

Some decisions need to be made, and soon. There is quite a bit of maintenance to be done on the house itself, but my heart always turns towards the chalet and in my mind's eye I can see the school up and running, making the most of and showcasing the reputedly wonderful produce of the region.

What, then, is going to be the priority? This must be decided soon and a plan implemented accordingly. House, gardens, paddocks? Robert, a recycling education officer for Veolia Environmental Services, will retire in a few years' time and he wants to convert the far paddocks into a small berry farm.

The orchard here obviously needs work. For some reason ornamental trees have been planted in among the fruit-bearers. I have no problem with ornamentals in their place, but an orchard is a fruit-producing venture and so the impostors must go, or at least be transplanted.

After a discussion with Stephanie and Nat, we decide that the school should be top priority. I'd love to apply for a grant of some sort, but what the school will be and what it is now are poles apart, and it may be difficult to explain my vision to others.

The house itself will have only the necessary repairs and maintenance undertaken for the time being, and the orchard and extensive gardens will follow the school overhaul. In the meantime, minimal tidying and maintenance work will be continued in the existing garden.

Little did we know just how much would actually need to be done.

July 15

It strikes me that pineapples must be in season somewhere in the northern states as there are some magnificent specimens on offer at the supermarket today. We have to pay a pretty hefty price for them here in Tasmania, mind you, and so I've always treated them with the utmost respect, using every possible morsel.

A year or so ago I invented a recipe for the peels and cores after being aghast at how much needed to be cut off the get to the precious, sweet, soft flesh inside. I'd been asked to develop a recipe for a pineapple relish, but so much waste!

This is how the recipe for pineapple cordial syrup came into being. It is delicious served one part syrup to four parts water or soda water. It is very nice as part of a cocktail such as Blue Moon or just with a splash of gin or vodka. You could serve it as a coulis over a slice of cheesecake even, or use it to flavour the cheese filling.

The relish is very nice served with pork or ham, or as part of a hamburger with the lot.

My supplies of both of these preserves has run dry, I tell myself by way of justification, so I'm happy to make a batch of both, content that no part of the precious pineapples will go to waste.

Pineapple Relish

1kg chopped fresh pineapple flesh
2 small onions, peeled and chopped
250g chopped red capsicum
2 teaspoons finely grated fresh ginger
juice of 1 lime
1 red chilli, seeded and chopped
2 cloves garlic, crushed
2 cups sugar
2 cups vinegar
1 teaspoon salt
1 teaspoon mustard
1 teaspoon turmeric
¼ cup vinegar (extra)
3 teaspoons cornflour

Place all ingredients (except the extra vinegar and cornflour) in a large pot.

Bring to the boil, stirring frequently, then reduce heat to medium and cook for 1 hour, stirring occasionally.

Mix together the extra vinegar and cornflour and stir some or all into the simmering relish if needed to make a spreadable consistency. Keep in mind, however, that the relish will thicken slightly as it cools. Cook for a further 3 minutes, stirring constantly.

Pour into sterilised bottles and seal immediately.

Makes about 1.5kg

Pineapple Cordial Syrup

> 1.5kg pineapple cores, peel or a whole pineapple
> 2 cups water
> sugar
> juice and zest of 1 large lemon
> 2 teaspoons tartaric acid

Chop the pineapple roughly and place in a food processor. Process until the pieces are quite fine. Pour into a saucepan with the water. Bring to the boil and barely simmer for 15 minutes.

Strain though a colander, then the resulting liquid through a finer sieve, pressing down to extract maximum juice.

To each cup of liquid (there will probably be about 3 cups) add 1 cup sugar. Bring up to the boil and simmer for 1 minute. Remove from heat and stir in the lemon juice and rind, along with the tartaric acid. Leave to cool. Strain through a fine kitchen sieve, then pour into bottles.

To serve, use 1 part syrup to 4 parts water or soda water.

In warmer climates or in summer keep in the fridge.

Makes about 1.5 litres

I once long ago made pineapple jam. When my dad lived with us he was quite partial to it. He forever scorned the use of pineapple in savoury dishes, as indeed he did with rice, both of which he declared were 'just for puddin's'.

I know many people do love this old-fashioned jam and so for that reason the recipe is included here. It's really nice as a filling for little tarts, especially topped with a spoonful of whipped cream. You could even top with a little meringue mixture and bake for 15 minutes at 100°C.

Pineapple Jam

1kg pineapple flesh, diced, without peel and cores
juice of 2 lemons
1kg sugar

Place all the ingredients in a large bowl and stir to combine. Leave to stand overnight, then pour into a large saucepan or jam pan and bring to the boil, stirring.

Boil briskly over a medium–high heat until the setting point is reached (see page 393). Leave to stand for 5 minutes, then pour into warm sterilised jars and seal immediately.

For **Pineapple and Ginger Jam**, at the end of cooking time, stir in 250g diced glacé ginger.

Makes about 1.8kg

July 18

Robert is rather fond of digging — always has been — and today he is in his element. It's just as well as it's been discovered that the musty odour in the chalet is due to earth resting up against the end wall. Therefore it's a matter of some urgency that a drain is dug to prevent further damage to the outside of the building, and to help rid us of the musty smell inside. No use painting anything, he tells me, if the moisture problem is not fixed first. I am champing at the bit, anxious for the bright yellow to be banished, but it will not to be so for quite some time.

One of the doors to the chalet doesn't work and many windows are cracked, letting the rain in and so they will need replacing. The heat pump works, however, which is just as well as it's freezing cold. There is a great deal to be done by way of cleaning and scrubbing before a paint brush goes anywhere near it. Light fittings are broken and the closer we look, the more we realise needs to be done.

Stephanie and Nat are stalwarts as they work alongside us, providing the encouragement and incentive to continue when our old bones get weary and our spirit for the overwhelming task ahead falters.

July 20

Last week it occurred to me that the neighbours seem to be keeping their distance. Are we really that scary? I fret for my friends on the Tasman Peninsula terribly — Tony, Dave and Denise, Deirdre, Mervyn, wildlife carers Lesley and Richard, and many more besides.

I miss people dropping in and I wish the neighbours here would. Still, there's no time to be morbid about it as there is so much work to be done, every which way we turn.

Actually, I think perhaps I have been a bit quick to judge as this week I've had a dozen eggs left at my door or by the letterbox and today a huge bag of Granny Smith apples. Maybe one day I'll find out who left them for me.

We only brought two chickens and three ducks with us from Eaglehawk Neck and they are so stressed by the move, plus it is winter after all, that there are no eggs in sight. It is so very good to have true free-range eggs to cook with again — the colour of the yolks is astounding.

And *homegrown* Granny Smith apples, what a treat! It just so happens that the garden here has plenty of year-round mint for the picking. Most of my preserves are still at the Neck house, and I could do with the light relief from cleaning, which I loathe, with an excuse of doing some preserving, which I adore.

Mint jelly, I decided, would be just the thing. I don't just use this to accompany roast lamb; it's fantastic as a glaze and to baste roast pork, ham or lamb, and adds a magnificent flavour to the gravy as well as the meat itself. By using different herbs in place of the mint, you can have a whole array of flavours suited to any dish you care to make.

Then I remembered something my grandmother used to make: Apple Ginger. It was so delicious, a bit like ginger marmalade but without the lemon skin that so many people dislike. Yes, certainly that would be more than useful.

There *were* rather a lot of eggs too — could I, would I, have the time to make pickled eggs? They're jolly good with various vegetable pickles, meat, bread and cheese, and some of Robert's homemade beer would top it off nicely — the perfect Ploughman's Lunch.

John's Pickled Eggs

I'd not definitely decided to do pickled eggs — maybe I should just savour them fresh, boiled, scrambled, made into omelettes or in cakes. However, as is the way of incidental happenings in Tasmania, today I met a man called John at a community expo.

He began to speak about his love of preserving and how he had just been pickling eggs. His wealth of information was astounding — he had travelled extensively and had applied his own flavours by way of spices to his pickled eggs. I'd only preserved mine very plainly in the past, but inspired by John, I decided to be more adventurous.

He said ginger was a common addition, even in England; cinnamon was good, as were a pinch of nutmeg and cardamom.

He also gave a few good tips for the novice egg-pickler. Eggs should not be freshly laid — let them sit for a few

days before boiling them as it makes them much easier
to peel.

I've found that the best way to boil eggs is to place
them in cold water in a saucepan with a splash of white
vinegar (this helps to keep the egg intact should the
shell crack). Bring to the boil, then reduce the heat and
cook for 5 minutes. Remove from heat, drain off the
water and cover with cold water. Leave for 5 minutes,
then peel the shells. It seems to work best if you tap the
shells all over lightly on the bench top, then peel from
the pointy end down.

This whole conversation with John led to the creation
of the following recipe, which, given all John's advice,
I know will be delicious. For English pub-style eggs,
substitute the white or cider vinegar with dark malt
vinegar.

> *12 eggs, hardboiled and shelled*
> *4 cups white or cider vinegar*
> *8 allspice berries or 1 teaspoon ground allspice*
> *6 cardamom pods, bruised, or ½ teaspoon ground*
> *   cardamom*
> *½ cinnamon stick*
> *3 teaspoons grated fresh ginger*
> *1 bay leaf*
> *½ teaspoon salt*

Place the cooled, peeled eggs in a sterilised jar.

Bring the vinegar, spices and salt to the boil in a
saucepan, then reduce the heat and simmer for 10
minutes. Allow to cool, then strain through a fine
sieve. Pour over the eggs, making sure they are entirely
submerged.

Makes 1 dozen

Apple and Mint Jelly

The first version of this recipe appeared in *A Year in a Bottle*. Since then I've found that the jelly can be made successfully with Granny Smiths, Bramleys or Sturmers.

500g cooking apples
390ml white or cider vinegar
500g sugar
Pinch salt, optional
5 to 6 tablespoons chopped mint

Remove any stalks from the apples, then chop them (no need to peel or core).

Pour the vinegar over them, then bring to the boil and cook until the apples are very soft.

Sieve the mixture, then add the sugar to the resulting puree.

Bring back to the boil, stirring, and cook for 8 to 9 minutes.

Remove from the heat and stir in the chopped mint.

Allow to stand for 5 minutes before pouring into warm sterilised jars and seal immediately.

Makes about 700ml

Apple Ginger

1.5kg apples
500ml water
1.5kg sugar
3 teaspoons ground ginger
60—90g crystallised or glacé ginger, finely chopped

Peel, core and roughly chop the apples, then place the flesh in a saucepan with the water. Bring to the boil and cook gently until soft, stirring often.

Add the sugar and ground ginger and bring back to the boil, stirring. Boil over a medium heat until the setting point is reached (see page 393). Stir in the crystallised ginger and bring back to the boil for 1 minute.

Remove from heat and leave to stand for 5 minutes, then pour into warm sterilised jars and seal immediately.

Makes about 2.5kg

July 22

At first glance the bush — a mix of scrappy wattle trees and bracken — that lines the country lanes here at Molesworth had held little appeal, and I was homesick for the sound of the ocean and the trees of the forest at Eaglehawk Neck. But once I lifted my head enough to actually take note, my initial misgivings were swept aside. I was assured by the locals that the hillsides would soon become a blaze of bright yellow as the wattle trees came into bloom in spring. And in autumn, the landscape would transform with the poplars yellowing, an iconic Derwent Valley sight.

A neighbour also told us that there were amazing rock formations and little waterfalls woven through the bush reserve on the hillsides opposite, to be enjoyed by anyone who goes for a casual stroll.

Today on our wanderings through the bush we come across an unexpected treasure — a small plot of abandoned olive trees. I'd already picked the last of the olives from the two trees in our garden, but now I had more — enough for a batch for brining.

Now, the art of preserving olives had long escaped me. It seemed such a complicated business of soaking and rinsing, pricking/slashing and brining — very tedious. Worst of all, it included the use of caustic soda — surely it couldn't be good to consume this?

However, one day in the winter of 2008, a visit to Salamanca Market in Hobart gave food for thought. An elderly Italian gentleman was selling his homemade olives straight from a huge barrel. I asked him how they were done (they were so delicious) and he told me they were simply soaked in brine.

'No pricking or slashing them, no caustic soda?' I asked.

'No,' he replied, 'you just soak them in brine for a few months.'

That was as far as he was prepared to go, but it did offer a glimmer of hope that there was an easier way than what I'd come across before. When I pressed him for details about the strength of the brine, he became a bit evasive.

'Just make it strong enough so an egg in its shell floats on the top,' he said. A bit inexact, I thought.

A year later I was asked to give presentations at a Gardening Australia expo. During one such demonstration, I spoke about olives and how the man at the market hadn't really been specific about the amount of salt. An Eastern European man in the audience literally jumped to his feet and, waving his arms in his enthusiasm, shouted out, 'I know exactly how much salt to use. I preserve all my own olives! For each 10kg of olives you use 1kg salt. Place the olives and salt in a barrel and cover with water, mix well. The olives will be ready in about a month.'

And so the mystery was solved. Now with my new-found source of untamed olive trees, I have great hopes of delicious olives for our table this year.

Oh yes, both gentlemen who told me about the olives claimed it made no difference what variety you used. However, I would ask a grower to make sure I got the best results.

Preserved Olives

This recipe can be scaled back if you have a smaller number of olives.

5kg olives
500g cooking salt
5 litres water

Place the olives and salt in a food-safe container. Mix well and cover with cold water. Mix until the salt is dissolved. Make sure the olives are entirely covered with the salt solution. If they tend to float, crumple a piece of baking paper and press into the container, making sure there are no air bubbles underneath.

Place the lid on the container and leave for 3–6 months until ready.

Makes 5kg

July 23

I can stand it no longer: I simply must do more preserving of some description.

I'm addicted, I know. I love the process, the results and, best of all, sharing them with others when they come to visit, giving them a little jar of this or that to take home when they leave. It definitely will be a feature of the cooking classes I have planned — there must always be samples for participants to take home to enjoy later.

I've been able to pick up some locally grown onions, as well as good-quality Queensland oranges at the local supermarket. Some former owner here has optimistically planted an orange tree, but it's a poor specimen at best and it looks unlikely to survive, let alone bear fruit.

A year or so ago, before we left the Neck, I developed a recipe for Orange and Onion Marmalade. I love it, delicious as it is served with meat or cheese. A dollop of this added to a warming winter casserole is simply sensational, and it is also delicious served with a hearty steak.

Orange and Onion Marmalade

45g butter
2 tablespoons olive oil
10 large onions, peeled and finely sliced
6 cups brown sugar, lightly packed
3 teaspoons finely grated orange zest

6 level tablespoons Dijon mustard
¾ cup orange juice
1¾ cups white vinegar

Heat the butter and oil over gentle heat, add the onions, and sauté until soft. Add the sugar, orange zest, mustard, orange juice and vinegar. Cook, stirring occasionally, for 2 hours or until thick. Pour into warm sterilised jars and seal immediately.

Makes about 600g

This recipe used precious few of the 3kg of oranges I'd purchased. Hating waste and needing no excuse to continue anyway, I decided to make some orange vinegar. This is best made with blood oranges, but any sort will do. I first came across the concept when judging one year in the Tasmanian Fine Food Awards. It was so exceptionally delicious that I immediately came home and invented a recipe so that I could have some in my pantry at all times.

It is simply exquisite used as a salad dressing or can be splashed over lightly steamed green beans. If you have a mind to make savoury cabbage with onion, bacon and apple, it is magnificently enhanced by a tablespoonful of orange vinegar added at the end of cooking time. A little trickle is a nice addition to old-fashioned coleslaw.

Blood Orange Vinegar

1kg blood oranges
1 litre good-quality white vinegar
sugar

Mince the whole oranges and place them in a bowl with the vinegar and stir to mix well. Cover the bowl with cling wrap and leave to stand at room temperature for 7 days. Strain through a colander, then the resulting liquid through a fine sieve. For each cup of vinegar add ¾ cup sugar. Bring to the boil, stirring, until sugar dissolves. Pour into sterilised bottles and seal immediately. Leave for at least 1 month before using.

Makes 1.25 litres

I simply love making cordial syrups and think it a travesty against good nutrition to purchase additive-laden, poor-quality commercial equivalents, especially as they are so easy to make. Citrus cordials are particularly good as they are not cooked at all, so all the essential oils from the skins are captured in the bottle. They are delicious served hot by adding almost boiling water, and in summer, with chilled water or soda water.

Today, inspired by the leftover oranges and lemons hanging on our own tree, I've decided to make an orange and lemon syrup I've affectionately named St Clement's Cordial, in memory of one of my favourite children's nursery rhymes.

St Clement's Cordial

4 oranges
2 lemons
1.5kg sugar
1 tablespoon tartaric or citric acid
4 cups boiling water

Finely grate the zest from the oranges and lemons. Cut the oranges and lemons in half and juice. Place the zest and juice in a bowl with the sugar, tartaric acid and boiling water. Stir until the sugar dissolves.

Leave to stand until cool (overnight for preference), then strain through a sieve and pour into sterilised bottles. Seal. Store in the fridge after opening.

Makes about 2 litres

July 25

There's some light relief today from the hard work in the chalet; of necessity really as the grass is getting out of hand. This is a new thing for us. We only had to mow the grass about once a year at the Neck as the constant grazing by wallabies and other wildlife kept the growth in check.

However, it's not all bad. The former owners have left us the ride-on mower. It is, as they say, an old 'un but a good 'un — at least I hope so. Still, the thought of riding such a mechanical beast is a bit daunting but Stephanie loves the task and rides off into the distance, rugged up warmly with woolly hat and scarves to ward off the cold. It's no small job — it takes about 3 hours to mow just the area around the house.

The berry patch needs attention also. It has to be weeded and last year's canes stripped out in preparation for next season. Stephanie and Nat set to work on that as well, using a fancy plaited method that I've not seen before. Apparently it promotes an abundant crop and makes it easier to determine which canes need removing at the end of the season. It looks very neat.

While they work away outside, I feel a little guilty for being inside in the warmth. Mind you, it's lovely spending time with the grandchildren Jacob and Charly and besides, I've been able to pick a small bag of crabapples from a long-abandoned tree that I came across a few days ago down by a creek.

In *A Year in a Bottle* there are recipes for crabapple lemonade and cheese, jam as well. I have enough apples now to make some paste, which doesn't need as much cooking as the cheese but is equally nice.

I decide to pickle and spice some of them as well. These little bundles of flavour are delicious served with pork or ham, and are far superior to apple sauce.

Crabapple Jelly

> *2kg crabapples*
> *1.5 litres water*
> *sugar*

Wash the crabapples and place them in a large saucepan or jam pan with the water and bring to the boil. Then reduce the heat to a simmer and cook until the crabapples are soft. Pour the mixture into a colander, capturing the juice in a pot below. Take this juice and pour it through a colander or sieve lined with 2 thicknesses of muslin.

To each cup of the resulting liquid add 1 cup sugar. Bring to the boil and cook over medium heat for about 20 minutes or until setting point is reached (see page 393).

Pour into warm sterilised bottles and seal immediately.

Makes about 1.5 litres

Some years ago I made a crabapple and chilli jelly, which was quite delicious. As the jelly set in the jar, I pushed in a small bird's eye chilli, which looked really attractive in the finished product. This jelly can be served with pork or even lamb. If you prefer a regular sweet crabapple jelly, you can leave the chillies out.

Crabapple and Chilli Jelly

1.5kg crabapples
60g bird's eye chillies
water
sugar
10–12 extra chillies (optional)

Wash the crabapples and place them in a large saucepan. Wash and roughly chop the chillies and add to the pan. Cover with water and bring to the boil, then reduce the heat to a simmer and cook until the crabapples are soft. Pour the mixture into a colander, capturing the juice in a pot below. Take this juice and pour it through a colander or sieve lined with 2 thicknesses of muslin.

To each cup of the resulting liquid add I cup sugar.
Bring to the boil and cook over medium heat for 12–15
minutes or until setting point is reached.

Pour into warm sterilised bottles and seal immediately
if you are not adding a chilli to the jar. If adding one
to each jar, leave the jars unsealed for about 5 minutes,
then insert the chilli so that it sits decoratively in the
middle of the jelly and seal immediately.

Makes about 1.4 litres

Spiced Crabapples

SPICED VINEGAR
400ml cider vinegar
8 cloves
2 bay leaves
1 stick cinnamon
6 cardamom pods
8 coriander seeds
6 allspice berries

SPICED CRABAPPLES
1 cup Spiced Vinegar
500g sugar
1kg crabapples, washed and stalks removed, each pricked twice
with a fork

To make the Spiced Vinegar, combine all the
ingredients in a large pot. Bring to the boil, then
immediately remove from the heat, cover with a lid
and leave to infuse for 2–3 hours. Strain the vinegar
through a kitchen sieve.

To make the Spiced Crabapples, combine the spiced
vinegar and sugar in a saucepan and bring to the boil,
stirring to ensure that the sugar is dissolved.

Add the crabapples to the liquid and barely simmer till
just tender.

Strain off the liquid, then place the crabapples into sterilised jars. Return the vinegar mixture to the heat, bring back to the boil and cook briskly for a further 5 minutes. Pour the mixture over the crabapples, then seal.

Makes about 1.5 litres

Crabapple Paste

1kg crabapples
1 cup water
sugar

Wash the crabapples and place them in a large saucepan with the water. Bring to the boil, then reduce the heat and simmer until the fruit is soft. Press through a sieve or food mill. For each cup of purée add 1 cup sugar. Bring back to the boil, stirring, and simmer over very low heat until a paste-like consistency has formed. It is important to stir very frequently. It will probably take about 40 minutes to reach this point. Pour into small jars and seal immediately. Serve as part of a cheese platter.

Makes about 550g

July 27

Since we moved here there have been so many reasons for happiness, not least of which is having little gumboots lined up at the door once more. Seven-year-old Jacob and five-year-old sister Charly visit almost every day, now that we live so close by.

In the relatively short space of time we've been here I've noticed a curious relationship developing. Jacob is autistic and sometimes has trouble controlling his moods. For an autistic child the world can be a scary place and relationships difficult to manoeuvre.

Della, our old beagle, moved with us from Eaglehawk Neck. She had been a champion show dog that we bought when she came out of breeding. She is very lovable, but, being part of a kennel of dogs all her life, had not related to us quite the same as other dogs had done. Still, she was sweet-natured and we adored her. After she was desexed, her once-svelte figure turned into one of immense proportions.

Della and Jacob have formed an incredible bond. Sometimes Jacob arrives distraught or moody and sits in the car, not wanting to be with others young or old, not knowing how to cope with life at all. Della will without fail waddle with tail wagging up to the car and within a few minutes the two of them can be seen wandering off companionably through the paddocks in search of gemstones (Jacob's passion) or for wallabies and other wildlife to befriend.

If Stephanie should visit without the children, Della sits forlornly beside her car, as if willing Jacob to materialise. I am sure they must have some marvellous adventures, or so Jacob tells me. He has now built a cubby house of chicken wire and straw in the far paddock, where they spend many afternoons.

A small slip of a ginger cat is often seen a small distance behind them. Jacob has told me that the cat shows him where the wallabies hide and where it sleeps at night, in the depths of a hollow bush.

I sometimes wonder at Jacob's heightened ability to interact with the natural world, and am glad that he finds a space and place that accepts him for the wonderful little man he truly is.

July 28

There were pears at the gate this morning and once again I wonder about the anonymous donor and why they didn't come in. Mind you, Della can manage a bit of a bark here and there, and for a person who is fearful of dogs it might be a bit off-putting. I am very thankful to get these pears — they are obviously homegrown and are small and sweet. This makes them perfect for bottling and other preserves, and soon I set to work filling numerous jars for the Fowlers Vacola. Pears bottled in a light or medium sugar syrup are delicious served for breakfast, as a dessert or simply to top a teacake before baking to lift it to a whole new level.

Bottled Pears

Pears tend to discolour once they are peeled and cored. You can help prevent this by soaking them in water that has a little lemon juice added. Try using 2 tablespoons lemon juice per litre of water. I find the best way to avoid this is to fill one jar at a time with the pears, covering them immediately with the preserving syrup.

To preserve, follow the basic method on page 385. Bring the temperature up to 90°C over 50 minutes, then hold at this temperature for 1 hour.

However, as I have so many pears I have the luxury and opportunity for a little experimentation.

Our son Alistair is a pastry chef who, after years overseas working for Gordon Ramsay, has come back to Tasmania. He loves the produce here and had always planned to set up his own little patisserie, and now with wife Teena and five-year-old Matilda, owns and operates the very successful Sweet Envy in North Hobart.

Alistair has told me about mustard fruits, a delicious preserve to serve with meats or cheese. They were a speciality of Angela Hartnett, the then manager of the famous Connaught restaurant in London, where he worked for a year or two.

Now it seems the opportune time to give them a try once more. I had attempted this last year but wasn't satisfied with the result. An absolute necessity is mustard essence — not easily acquired, in fact, only in Italy, so I'd substituted mustard oil. Both are hot and flavoursome, but the essence is by far the more pungent. However, the oil was not the proper ingredient, and the pears were less than impressive.

In the meantime my friend Deirdre had been to Italy and had brought back two small bottles of the essence for me. Perfect: one for Alistair, one for me.

Once more I went through the process, following the instructions in the recipe to the letter. I am always inclined to be heavy-handed with ingredients and this was no exception, plus I think I lost count of the number of drops I added. Only 10, it was supposed to be, but a few more surely couldn't hurt. Mind you, when I'd taken the lid off the bottle and sniffed it, as you do, it had taken my breath away and burned off all my nose hairs, I'm sure.

Within a few days the mustard pears were ready. I proudly took a jar into Alistair, happy to show I'd done it properly this time.

He didn't taste them there and then, but a few days later placed a whole pear in his mouth and it apparently nearly blew his head off — they were way too hot.

So it's back to the drawing board as I had to throw the whole batch out once more.

August 5

The grass is growing at incredible speed and needs mowing at least once a week. It's time that I learn to drive this ride-on mower. Stephanie has manned it for me until now but it's really my responsibility, so I must brave it out. I am not much good with a car I'm told, so this new piece of drivable machinery fills me with trepidation.

I should perhaps mention here that I am renowned for being clumsy and accident prone; I have been since childhood. I notice a small stick in the grass and give it little thought, continuing to ride right on over it. A few minutes later I pay the price — the mower starts blowing black smoke and smells terrible. The stick had been connected to a larger bit of branch and I've stripped the belt. That is quickly replaced but it still runs very badly and will need repairing.

I've now mowed patches for hours with the push mower, but still the main area looks like it will overtake the house, so obviously it was time to call in the local grass slasher.

My spirits have been much lifted at his admiration of the beauty of our property — he could totally understand why we bought it and at such a bargain price. I told him about my initial reservations regarding the bush along the roadside.

'Yep,' he said, 'it's so stony and scrubby up there that an echidna would need a packed lunch to pass through. This place of yours is like an oasis.'

Well spoken. For all the challenges that face us, it's so totally worth it and his words spur me on with renewed energy.

August 12

This week alpacas Charlotte and Clarence have come to stay. Their owner needed somewhere with ample feed for them and we seriously needed something to graze the grass in the paddocks. The vegetable garden needed manure and alpacas obligingly defecate in one place for easy collection, so all things considered, we anticipated a reciprocal beneficial arrangement.

My only experience of alpacas had been with those that belonged to a friend on a farm at Broadmarsh — and that was at shearing time, a process they objected to most strongly and so would hurl foetid grass-seed laden mouthfuls of spit at anyone within reach.

'See how that spit hits so hard it goes right into the wood?' the shearer said as he pointed to grass seeds embedded in the wooden fence posts.

So it was with some caution that I approached the 'mindership' of Clarence and Charlotte. This was reinforced when I went to pat Clarence and Charlotte and they nearly bowled me over, quite unnecessarily aggressive, I thought, towards one who was only trying to be kind. She was, I was told belatedly, extremely protective of Clarence. I was unsure why and the answer made me wonder about the art of animal communication.

Clarence, a desexed male, had been brought to Tasmania from South Australia. For a time they were agisted at a property where Clarence was unmercifully bullied by another, stronger male. Did Charlotte sense this and become his protector? Even now, whenever anyone approaches him, she rushes to his side and places her neck across his back. Clarence is very shy and a little aloof, no doubt as a result of his harrowing life experience.

Now they've settled in, Charlotte has taken it upon herself to become the keeper of the paddocks. Anything that dares step inside is rounded up and unceremoniously chased away. The only exception is our three ducks. For some reason she tolerates them but certainly not the two chooks Whiskey and Brandy, who get sent squawking and feathers flying into the safety of the chook run.

Charlotte has turned out to be the comic of the farmyard. She will come running up to us at full pelt, threatening with guttural mutterings and snorts as if to spit, and then stop in an instant and instead 'kiss' us on the cheek several times before prancing away across the paddock.

Robert decided one day this week to change the water in two of the old bathtubs they use for drinking. He thought that the bore water would be fine, but Charlotte and Clarence had other ideas. The water is high in iron and tastes a bit like rust, not suitable for human consumption, but ideal for the garden and for animals to drink. Charlotte strongly disagreed with Robert's viewpoint on this. She stood at the fence line and stared at me as I went back and forth between the stove and sink in the house. She kept this up for a good two hours, not moving. Eventually I took the hint and carried down to her a large container of fresh water from our rainwater tank. With a kiss on the cheek to thank me, she danced off across the paddock, satisfied no doubt that she was able to communicate what she wanted — or more likely, that she was able to manipulate me.

August 20

The trees of the small orchard are still a bit of a mystery. We have no real idea what is what as almost all of them are now devoid of foliage. It's evident that there are loquats, olives and figs, but that's about the extent of it. As spring approaches summer and blossom starts to appear on trees, vines and bushes, we guess at the fruit that we might hope to have at our table and to preserve in the warmer months.

Friends and family are venturing opinions, gardening books are being consulted at length and so we soon expect to have peaches, apricots, greengages, loquats, medlars, cherries, apples, figs and olives, blueberries, raspberries and loganberries as well as currants red, white and black.

The former owner assured us that there are two greengage trees and I was especially pleased as it's hard to buy them retail. However last summer I was pleased to see some at farmers' markets and farm-gate stalls and they are so well worth the eating. Their flavour is unlike any other plum — it is as hard to describe as the flavour of quince — to what can you compare it? Nothing — it must be tasted to be experienced and its attraction is then understood. The ripe plum takes on a purplish tinge, at which stage the plum is bursting with flavoursome juice.

My grandmother used to make literally buckets of jam from them each summer — her signature dish, so to speak. Others in the family thought her greengage-jam making a bit excessive, but inevitably came round looking for another jar when they ran out.

I've tried bottling them and they are delicious to be sure, but some of the flavour, if not lost, is changed a little by the preserving process.

Perhaps my fondest association with this fruit relates to a picnic last winter at Eaglehawk Neck. Our friend Mervyn often came to visit and we decided one day to go on a bush walk and picnic, taking with us a loaf of crusty fresh bread, a toasting fork, butter and a jar of greengage jam and the makings for billy tea.

The place we had in mind as our destination is one of Tasmania's hidden secrets. It is quite well known to residents and sometimes tourists stumble across it as they continue along the beach adjacent to the famous Tessellated Pavement.

In our case a short walk from the house down to Lufra Cove and north-eastwards brings you to Clydes Island. You can climb up there if you have a mind for it. It's a bit of a scramble up a steep rocky outcrop, but the view is worth it. There are two graves on the island, one reportedly of the local Lufra Hotel's original owner.

However, this day we planned to go further to the left before the island, following a somewhat overgrown path that leads to a ledge several metres wide, carved out by the sea, in the middle of two cliff faces. During the frequent wild weather, piles of boulders and fossils are tossed up there by the ocean as if they were mere pebbles. The sea still bashes at the face of the cliffs unmercifully on a stormy day — it is well worth the trek to see this in action. On a calm summer's day when the ocean is quiet, there is an alternative beauty with a breathtaking view for hundreds of kilometres up and down the coastline.

When the day designated for our picnic arrived it was blustery but sunny, ideal conditions for walking in my opinion, and holding the promise of a great deal of sea spray on the cliff ledge. The walk was spectacular, but there was no chance of reaching Clydes Island as the small channel that separates the island from the mainland was a raging torrent with the ocean pouring through, sucking the seaweed back and forth as it went — a spectacular sight, but certainly to be experienced only from a distance.

After about an hour's walk we reached the ledge. In a sheltered hollow between some large boulders we made a campfire and cooked a simple but incredibly good feast of toast, butter and greengage jam, followed by sweet billy tea, flavoured with a gum leaf we had picked along the way.

With the waves pounding on the cliff face flinging a fine mist up and over us, I'm sure there never was a more spectacular setting for such a simple meal and one that will certainly never be forgotten.

The greengage jam recipe to follow is my nan's, and comes with her hints on how best to make it. I remember preparing it with her as a child — it was her pride and joy, and the reason for the massive tree in her garden.

Any sort of plum can be substituted for the greengages — yellow cherry plums are very nice — but nothing compares to the unique and wonderful greengage plum.

Greengage Plum Jam

My nan would have told you not to worry about taking the pips from the plums, a tedious process at the best of times. Leave them in as the fruit breaks down, and once you add the sugar and it boils away to setting point, the pips will rise to the top and can be skimmed off with a slotted spoon. You'll miss a few, she assured me, but they give the jam flavour in the jar and besides, it's a mark of authenticity.

If you add the lemon juice in this recipe it will help extract the pectin (as acid does) and your jam will set better and reach setting point sooner.

> 1.5kg greengage plums
> ½ cup water
> juice of 1 large lemon or ½ teaspoon citric acid, optional
> 1.25kg sugar

Place the greengages, water and lemon juice in a saucepan and bring to the boil. Reduce the heat and simmer until the plums are soft.

Return the mixture to the heat, add the sugar and bring to the boil, stirring. Boil briskly for 20 minutes, by which stage it should have reached setting point (see page 393). The jam should be poured into clean sterilised jars (as full as possible) and sealed with a lid immediately.

Makes about 2.25kg

August 25

There's still a huge amount to be done in the chalet and the work can go ahead at last. Already it smells better with the drain taking the water away from the edge of the building. And so finally the time has come to paint. I've spent days with Stephanie painstakingly going over colour charts — we want the interior to be clean and bright, yet warm and welcoming. Huge tinfuls of paint are bought and along with Steph and Nat we set to work.

In the past, I've never really got the hang of painting. Whenever I have tried, I am banished by others and today it's obvious that there's been no improvement in my technique. The others tease me as being the only person they know who can spray paint with a brush. I am covered from top to toe in a fine spray of paint, and splodges in most places. I have paint patches on my knees, all of which would be OK if only more went on the walls. The floor has to have drop sheets to protect it from my assault on the walls and window ledges.

Despite all this the transformation in the rooms is nothing short of incredible. Gone are the ghastly yellow walls with even brighter skirting boards and trims, the colour scheme obviously a relic of the days when the chalet served as a childcare centre.

New tiles are obviously needed in the hand-wash area and behind the dishwasher, but Stephanie and I decide that perhaps some of the original tiles in the bathroom and around the kitchen sink could simply be painted. It would save a huge amount of money, so tomorrow I'll need to put that into action by purchasing the special paint.

September 2

I really, really want to make the garden beds around the chalet more suited to the theme of the school. At present there is nothing on two sides except a horrible strappy plant. Robert rather likes them and would like them left as they are, but I can envisage lovely little garden beds, walking out from the school kitchen to pluck this and that to add to the dishes we are cooking. A few straggly cactuses fill a tiered set of blocks that I have earmarked for growing parsley.

Robert grumbles but retreats to the shed and I begin to pull out the offending plants. My goodness, these grassy things must have roots that go to China! Eventually, Nat ties ropes around them and drags them out with their four-wheel drive. I suppose they will grow back, but with careful weeding and mulching, perhaps not. For the time being, they are gone at last and within days I will have the whole area planted out with edible flowers, herbs and vegetables.

September 25

After a few weeks' work, the chalet definitely has a different feel to it. It won't be much longer before we start thinking about advertising the classes.

With our heads down for the chalet renovations, we've not had a great deal of time to take stock of our surroundings and the animals that live here with us.

Admittedly the alpacas are hard to ignore as they wander almost regally through the paddocks.

It was primarily because of the high-spirited Charlotte that we became more aware of the cat in the paddock. We had seen a flash of ginger fur in the distance at times, and one day we saw Charlotte break into the chook pen where the cat was sheltering and chase it up over the fence. The poor thing had taken up residence with the ducks, sleeping with them at night, and, desperate for company, playing with them during the day. The ducks flick beaks full of water from their bath out onto the grass for the cat to chase and he in turn catches the drops and romps with them, jumping on their backs, only to be playfully flicked into the air with a flap of wings and a toss of their heads.

We were not really inclined to take on another cat as we had our rather pampered indoor cat Ardy, but what can you do? So I started feeding him. He looked so pathetic, all skin and bone, a mere slip of a creature, obviously undernourished. I contacted the homeopathic vet who made up a vitamin powder to mix into his food.

At first the cat would stay far away and only come to the food bowl after I'd left and shut the gate. With a little more courage each day he came progressively closer until, after a few weeks, I could finally pat him. It was as if I'd unleashed a well of affection. He revelled in the patting and petting, but wouldn't let me pick him up, turning into the proverbial feral hellcat whenever I tried.

One day I decided to attempt it one last time. As if sensing this, he turned and looked directly into my eyes, then snuggled into my shoulder and purred as if his little heart would break. And there I stood, foolish old woman, with tears rolling down my face, so happy that he had come to trust me at last.

Charlotte has come to realise that he is part of the family. Tom, as we have named him, can now weave in and out around her legs with never so much as her looking like kicking him, let alone chasing him over the fence.

Since then Tom will ignore his food in favour of a cuddle and now lets grandchildren Jacob and Charly pick him up as well. I am sure there never was a happier cat.

October 5

I've had this notion of buying some goats to help keep down the grass — well, we have so much feed, why not? Charlotte and Clarence are simply not gaining much ground in this respect. We have researched until we are blue in the face — this is all new to us. How do you look after them? What breed? Milkers or desexed males?

On a whim a few days ago I rang an animal shelter. I'd love this place to become a haven for abandoned or unwanted animals. It just so happened that they had two goats that needed to be adopted — two males, desexed. They couldn't be separated as they had bonded well, so it was challenging to place them. Luigi and Mario, they'd been named — how could I refuse? I used to live with a wonderful Italian family back in my teenage university days. Maybe this is an omen!

Luigi has a permanently stiff leg from being struck by a truck, but isn't in any pain and doesn't need medicating according to the vet.

They are very approachable, even walk on a lead and are great with children, we were told. Better and better news. And so, after persuading long-suffering Robert that it was a good idea and extracting a promise that he would build them a suitable shed, I went to visit them at the animal shelter — a getting-to-know-you, I'm-going-to-be-your-new-mother situation.

I've adopted animals before from one place or another and it hasn't always worked out entirely well, and once you are the owner you're in it for the long haul.

Maybe it was with this subconscious thought that I made this fateful visit. When the carer took me into their pen, the goat with the limp was very obviously tame, though he did fix me with his suspicious glittering eye. However, the other, Mario, took one look at us and yes, friendly he was but maybe not so tame. He jumped up on the carer and she politely pushed him down. He then jumped up on me, both hoofs, dung-covered, on my chest. Pity I had to go shopping like this afterwards!

'How are your fences?' the girl kindly asked.

'Good,' I said naively, 'they are about one metre high.'

'Oh dear,' she said. 'We've had to build the fences to eight feet here just for the goats. They climb, you see. That's how Luigi got his limp — hit by a truck when he climbed over the enclosure fence at his former home.'

Now, to fence five acres to a height of eight feet was going to be impossible. The words of a neighbour when I had proudly announced we were getting goats came back to haunt me.

'Good luck with that,' he'd said. 'I'll put another rung or two of wire on the fence then', no doubt fearing for the promising fruit crop on his trees.

I left the animal shelter abashed and ashamed, as it had become obvious that we really weren't in a position to give the goats the home they so desperately needed.

October 10

There is great excitement afoot today — the Carmichael stove is due to arrive.

For as long as I can remember I have wanted a wood-burning, slow-combustion stove. There is something about the smell of wood smoke, the aroma of the baking, the sense of warmth emanating from it.

I'd hoped to get sponsorship for just such a stove, and indeed was offered one by a stove company. As they say, there is no such thing as a free lunch, let alone a free stove, and the conditions were so stringent that I decided to paddle my own canoe.

Stephanie is an eBay whizz and soon found a stove on offer. We learned weeks ago now that such stoves are in high demand and quick to disappear. Bidding is strong as more people appreciate their worth.

Some we saw were in dire need of repair. I'd gone to see one near Huonville in southern Tasmania, travelling half a day to get there, only to find it in pieces and its innards covered in rust. A less than auspicious start. The lovely man who was selling it assured me that all the pieces were there or replacement parts could be made or purchased, but I simply wasn't that brave.

From all the photos on ebay, from conversations with the owner, it seemed that the Carmichael Stephanie had found was the one for us. Loath to part with the treasure he'd lovingly restored, the owner was able to provide information galore about the stove and promised that he would ensure it came to us intact and in prime condition. This was from country NSW.

Bidding was a new phenomenon for me. I would be hopeless, but Stephanie was a dynamo with the computer keys and, ignoring my pleas of 'Bid now, bid NOW!' she waited until the last second, punched a key and won the prized Carmichael.

We waited for the day of its arrival with bated breath. Its owner had kindly travelled for five hours to deliver it to a Sydney freight company depot for a mere $100.

And now it is here, fastidiously wrapped in strong plastic, padded against possible damage from buffeting on the journey and securely tied to a strong wooden pallet.

Getting it through the door has been quite an endeavour — Nat needs to remove doors and hinges, hotplate covers and more, but finally it is pushed through. We needed to cut up one of Robert's prized pine logs from the garden to roll it across the floor, but still, it was done and now sits resplendent on the bed of tiled hearth made in its honour.

I am ecstatic — it is all I'd hoped it would be. It has a couple of little dings that we already knew about, but this only adds to its character. Once installed it will play a large part in the functioning of the school. There is nothing so incredibly delicious as a loaf of bread baked in a slow-combustion stove. It has to be experienced to be believed — the crust is always crisp, the texture inside soft and moist.

The installer is also much impressed with our prize and soon everything is up and running. Come hell or high water, this stove will chug on. No power failure will affect it, no shortage of gas, even flood would only temporarily cramp its style. For a mere few pieces of wood for each baking session, I know it will serve us well and welcome all those who come to the school.

October 15

A skill inherent in, or more likely learned by, children of our household is tree-spotting. Not just any tree for the sake of it, but food-bearing trees — be it fruit, flower or berry, trees apparently neglected or unappreciated despite what they could bear. Our six children became experts and on family drives in the country would often spot just such specimens in a paddock, along the banks of a creek or down country laneways.

When we lived on the Tasman Peninsula, our Courtney was chief pepperberry tree spotter. From an early age it became apparent she was very long-sighted and often we would drive through the bush at the back of the township of Taranna. Hidden quietly among the trees and ferns of the undisturbed wetland environment were concealed pepperberry trees. Robert and I could never see the tiny berries, not even the trees with their distinctive leaves, but Courtney could spot them every time. We'd pull out the ladder and pick as many as we needed, along with a generous amount of the leaves.

The berries are a wonderful fragrant pepper. I've steeped them in vinegar to use to dress a simple salad and even in gin, which was pretty amazing. The leaves I dehydrate, then crumble and use to sprinkle over homemade flat breads or dinner rolls. (To dehydrate the leaves, place in paper bags with the tops loosely closed and store in a dark, dry place for three to four weeks.)

Now that we've moved to Molesworth, I know there will be plenty of spotting done, though whether this will be of pepperberries remains to be seen.

We already know of yellow cherry plums, quinces, pears and apricots and I'm sure there will be many other delights ripe for the picking.

Even today, Stephanie, who lives a few kilometres away, has just rung to tell me that she's spotted several huge elderflower trees in bloom down by the river. Early tomorrow morning they will be investigated and tonight I'll think about what I'll be able to make with them.

October 20

The elder, a tree I'm especially fond of, is known to have been used for four thousand years. It is reportedly the oldest herb cultivated by man. Nearly all old herbal books refer to the elder as 'the medicine chest of the country folk'.

Traditionally it has been used as a detox, to build the immune system by clearing toxins through the lymph glands.

It is reportedly good for helping with respiratory problems; in fact elderflowers were used to treat asthmatics in the days before 'modern' medication, and as an expectorant to clear catarrh. In spring, elderflower concentrate, also known as elderflower cordial, was used to relieve the symptoms of allergies to pollens.

Quite aside from all that, it is a very attractive tree — a mass of tiny flowers in huge sprays, so delicate and so fragrant. This morning, as soon as Stephanie drops Jacob and Charly at school, we head down to the river where several trees thrive, fed and watered by the constant water supply.

Some of these trees are so large they must be decades old. Their heady scent fills the morning air. I'm sure passers-by must wonder what we are doing. We fill three tubs with the blossom, ample to make the family favourite of sparkling elderflower, and enough for a serious bout of experimentation.

For years I have tried to make elderflower cordial syrup but any recipe I've tried spoils quite quickly in the bottle, within a matter of weeks. I expect the shelf life of a cordial to be at least several months.

And so the experiments begin. I look up a few recipes, but hold out little hope for them given past experience. Suddenly it dawns on me that perhaps I could adapt my lemon cordial recipe. After all, that is a really good 'keeper'.

And so the recipe to follow comes together. By the way there's also the recipe for Sparkling Elderflower and Lemon and it is a truly delicious 'soft drink', all natural. In temperate climates you will often find elderflower trees in older-style gardens, even botanical gardens. They are easily recognised by those sprays of delicate tiny white flowers that drop from their stalks if not handled carefully.

There are many commercial versions of elderflower cordial and other drinks on the market now, but it you can find elderflowers and make your own, the flavour is infinitely better and the recipes here are both recipes that require very little effort.

Be sure to use just the flowers for these recipes, not any of the stalk (just snip the flowers off with a pair of scissors). The stalks will give the syrup a grassy taste, not altogether pleasant.

Elderflower Cordial Syrup

1.5kg sugar
4 cups boiling water
1 rounded tablespoon tartaric or citric acid
juice and zest of 1 small- to medium-sized lemon
12–15 elderflower heads

Mix together the sugar, boiling water and tartaric acid and stir until the sugar is dissolved. Mix in the lemon juice and zest and the elderflowers and leave until the mixture is cold.

Strain through a fine sieve or a colander lined with muslin. Pour into sterilised bottles and seal immediately.

Store in a cool, dry dark place.

Makes about 1.75 litres

Sparkling Elderflower and Lemon

> *6 elderflower heads*
> *3 cups sugar*
> *4.5 litres water*
> *2 lemons, chopped*
> *2 tablespoons white or cider vinegar*

Snip the tiny flowers from the elderflower heads and place in a food-safe bucket with the rest of the ingredients. Stir to mix well, then cover the bucket with a tea towel.

Allow to stand for 48 hours, then strain through a fine nylon kitchen sieve or a colander lined with muslin and pour into PET bottles and seal immediately. (Empty soft-drink bottles are ideal, or you can buy new ones from home-brewing suppliers.)

The sparkling elderflower will be ready in 1–2 weeks. Store at room temperature during this time. Once it develops its 'fizz', refrigerate before opening.

Makes about 4.5 litres

October 31

I look forward to a visit from my good friend Steve, former manager of an ABC shop in Hobart. He is looking to go into a cafe venture and would like to learn a few really good recipes to include on his menu, especially those that can showcase fresh seasonal produce. A few of his friends will come along with him.

The night before their visit I decided to make more raspberry cordial syrup just because supplies were getting low and I still had ample fruit in the freezer.

I serve them some during the few hours they are here and they pronounce it amazing. Suddenly it occurs to me that I'd neglected to add the tartaric acid and vinegar, so thought it must have been deadly dull on the palate and reach for these ingredients to add belatedly.

'NO!' they protest, 'it's simply delicious as it is.'

'Could we use this in milkshakes?' they ask.

'No,' I start to say, then realise that maybe you could. I had thought it would curdle as is usually the case with my regular syrups, but without the added acid, this may well not happen.

I pour about 2cm of the syrup into a glass and top it with milk and wait with bated breath … Nothing, no curdling and really delicious! A milkshake made from it with a little added ice-cream would be sensational. And so a new recipe is born.

I had, actually, on a whim, reduced the amount of water, so the raspberry flavour was intensified. All in all a winning combination, quite by accident.

I think it would be really nice made with any sort of berry. Loganberry springs to mind as a lovely alternative, blueberry maybe, or a combination of any or many berries of the season — yes, a 'fruits of the forest' milkshake — how good would that be?

Use whatever you have to hand, fresh or frozen, and enjoy an exquisite drink that, again and importantly, is not only nutritious and delicious but free of artificial additives.

Raspberry Syrup

1kg raspberries
3¼ cups water
sugar

Place the raspberries and water in a saucepan and bring slowly to the boil. Barely simmer for 5 minutes. Strain though a fine sieve, then for each cup of the resulting juice add 1 cup sugar. Bring back to the boil and barely simmer for 1 minute.

Pour into warm sterilised bottles and seal immediately.

Use 1 part syrup to 4–5 parts milk or water or soda water.

To make a **Raspberry Milkshake**, place 300ml milk, 1–2 tablespoons syrup and a scoop of vanilla or berry ice-cream in a milkshake maker or similar and process until frothy. You could, if you had them to spare, add some extra fresh or frozen raspberries, or a little yoghurt.

The syrup can also be used as a topping for ice-cream or as a coulis to pour over a slice of cheesecake or panna cotta.

Makes about 2 litres

November 3

Last weekend final major practical preparations were put in place for the cooking school. The purpose-built cupboard doors arrived, and the electrical fittings were in place at last. Unwanted furniture was sent off to the local secondhand dealer and final general cleaning and finishing touches got underway.

In the cool of the late Saturday afternoon the sound of a clarinet floated down the valley — a slow melodious sound, answered, it seemed, by the call of a bird.

By now we have started to meet many more people in the community. We had met Terry the fire chief on a few occasions, a wonderful, helpful neighbour who watches out for fire risks around the properties in the valley. Terry and Rosemary are well-known, gifted musicians and I thought it must be their music we heard on the wind.

A few days later the mystery was solved when Terry called in. It has been his son playing the clarinet in the bush.

'Have you seen doves at your house?' he asked.

I hadn't seen hide nor feather of them, but apparently Terry and Rosemary shared their land with them.

The male dove had been seeking a mate and had returned home sad and mournful, calling out in the bush to attract a female. So haunting was his lament that Terry's son had taken his clarinet out to mimic the answering call of a female dove. His ploy obviously succeeded for just this evening as I went to the kitchen window there were a pair of doves contentedly foraging for food under the massive elm tree just outside.

They are joined in close proximity by a kookaburra and a plover, and several green rosellas, an unlikely band of brothers, but seeming to share the space, at peace with one another.

It is a real education here with the bird life. At Eaglehawk Neck the most common birds in our garden were green rosellas and currawongs, not always delighted at sharing the air space above our property. The squabbles among the rosellas were monumental — whirling dervishes of colour and ill humour as they fought over the bowls of seed we put out for them each day. Here they feed on the grass looking for seed of some sort with never a sign of being fractious with each other or any of the other birds. Perhaps amiability is linked to the natural environment in which they find themselves.

November 5

Spring marched towards summer and I watched with pride when first the blossom then the leaves started to appear on the fruit trees. This preserving season is shaping up to be marvellous. Each morning I'd admire the crop as I sat at the kitchen bench, and could fairly see my jam pans and preserving bottles full to overflowing.

That is, until one morning recently when I woke to find that all the leaves were gone. It just so happened that it was a Saturday morning and Peter Cundall's gardening talkback was on the radio. A listener had just rung in with exactly the same problem as mine, and Peter pronounced it to be the work of possums.

I am very fond of possums as a general rule. At Eaglehawk Neck I baked Anzac biscuits especially to feed to them each night when they came onto our front deck. In return the mother would let me pat the baby in her pouch. This went on for years, very amicably.

Now it seemed they had a darker side, yet I still didn't want to harm them — to shoot them as some do would be unthinkable. Peter went on to relate a remedy recommended to him by Tino Carnevale; namely, to rub Vicks Vaporub around the trunk of each tree. Possums hate the smell apparently.

So off to the supermarket I went a day or two later, but as is the way when Peter Cundall dispenses advice, it was taken to heart by a large number in the community and the shop was out of stock. Not to be deterred I noticed a couple of jars of generic-brand menthol rub way over the back on a top shelf, hidden from general view. I climbed up, not a pretty sight and somewhat hazardous, but I soon had them in my hand.

Now smeared with the magic product, the trees have new leaves once more. I'm happy for the peaceable solution, though I don't know how long the smell that offends them so much will last. It's a bit of a conundrum. I know they can be a pest, but as I arrived home one night, one of them wandered complacently across the top of the gate in front of me — so cute! I knew there could be no other but a peaceable way and that there were a whole new set of rules and adaptations to learn in our chosen new environment.

November 14

What a misery of a day this has turned out to be. On a quick trip into New Norfolk, I went past a garage sale sign. I love garage sales where you can often find all sorts of interesting cooking gear. On the way back from dropping off an operation manual to the ride-on mower repairer, I called in at the sale and asked them to keep aside an absolute bargain, a Fowlers preserver — complete with bottles, lids and so on — for a mere $50. I promised to return tomorrow morning with payment and to pick it up, and the old gentleman promised to find me dozens more bottles under the house.

Lovely old couple, I thought, until the woman of the house rang an hour or two later and told me she'd sold it all to someone else. I was furious at first, then realised that more likely I'd not made myself clear enough.

The only antidote to such frustration was to do some cooking, something comforting to soothe my mood. There were still plenty of lemons from the tree and oranges in the fruit bowl on the kitchen table. I also had a tub of yoghurt past its best-before date in the fridge. Soon I'm distracted from the loss of the preserver and the success of the following recipe lifted my spirits no end.

Yoghurt Citrus Buttercup Cakes

125g butter, melted
1 cup sugar
1 tablespoon orange juice
1 tablespoon lemon juice
grated zest of 2 oranges
grated zest of ½ lemon
1½ cups self-raising flour
¾ cup yoghurt
2 eggs
1 teaspoon baking powder

CITRUS ICING
180g icing sugar
grated zest of ½ orange
grated zest of ½ lemon
1 teaspoon butter, softened
about 1 tablespoon orange juice

Preheat the oven to 160°C. Grease a 12 x ½-cup muffin pan or line with baking cases.

Combine all the ingredients in a bowl and beat for 2 minutes with an electric beater. Spoon into the muffin tins, filling them to two-thirds full.

Bake for 12–15 minutes or until cooked through. Test by inserting a metal skewer in the middle; it should come out clean.

Remove from the oven and cool on wire racks before icing.

To make the Citrus Icing, sift the icing sugar and mix with the zests and butter. Gradually add the orange juice until you get a spreadable consistency.

Makes 12

Robert, on a recent trip to the west coast, came across a collectibles store and bought me two really old nut-loaf tins. I used to make these round date and nut loaves when we were first married and they were in vogue. There is really nothing quite so delicious as a plateful, nicely buttered, at community gatherings. I decide to revisit my old recipe.

If you don't have these nut-loaf tins, you can simply use empty soup tins with the top and bottom cut out. Before putting the mixture in though you will need to firmly wrap a double thickness of foil around and over the base, and do the same to serve as a lid for the top once the tin is filled. Be sure to grease the foil where it will come into contact with the mixture.

The loaves can be a bit dry (hence the butter when serving), so I think my old recipe could be improved. I'm very pleased with the result — it's every bit as good and better than the ones I used to bake so many decades ago.

Round Date and Nut Loaves

200g chopped dates
125g sultanas
60g raisins
90g chopped walnuts or pecans

60g butter, diced
1 teaspoon bicarbonate of soda
1¼ cups boiling water
2 cups plain flour
½ teaspoon baking powder
1 egg, whisked

Preheat the oven to 160°C. Grease 2 nut-loaf tins (with their bases fitted) or 3 x 400g soup cans.

Place the dates, sultanas, raisins, nuts, butter, bicarbonate of soda and boiling water in a bowl and stir to combine until the butter is melted.

Mix in the combined flour and baking powder, then add the egg, folding together until smooth.

Pour into tins until they are two-thirds full, then place greased lids or foil over the top and secure well.

Bake for 40–50 minutes or until cooked through. Turn out onto a wire rack to cool completely. (You may need to run a knife around the outside of the loaves to loosen them.)

Serve cold, sliced and buttered, or warm as a dessert with custard and ice-cream.

Serves 6–8

By now my anger is almost spent but, thoroughly in the mood for baking, I decide to make some little apple tartuffins. The reason I have so named them is because they are a cross between a tart and a muffin. There is no need for rolling pastry as with tarts, but they contain more fruit than a muffin would. Today I'll use apple or maybe apple and rhubarb; the recipe is also great for Christmas (or anytime) with fruit mince as the filling.

Apple Tartuffins

2½ cups plain flour
2 teaspoons baking powder
½ teaspoon bicarbonate of soda
½ tsp ground cinnamon
¾ cup sugar
grated zest and juice of 1 large lemon
1 cup milk
2 eggs
125g butter, melted
¾ cup stewed apple (or any stewed fruit, slightly sweetened)

Preheat the oven to 160°C. Grease a 12 x ½-cup muffin pan or line with muffin papers.

Whisk together all the ingredients, except the fruit, until smooth. Fill the muffin pans until one-third full, then top with 2 teaspoons stewed fruit, then top with more muffin batter until two-thirds full.

Bake for 15 minutes until cooked through and golden.

Cool on a wire rack and dust with icing sugar to serve. Alternatively, ice with lemon icing (see recipe for Citrus Icing, page 44, using lemon juice only).

Makes 12

November 22

I have always wanted to find a source of good meat but I'm not sure how to access it in this new region, so temporarily I've had to compromise and buy meat from the local supermarket. Today, however, a solution has come my way from an unexpected quarter.

A bit of a smelly aroma had been permeating the yard for a week or two.

'The septic needs pumping out,' pronounced Robert, and so this service is duly ordered.

The amiable, well-spoken young man, Jay, who arrives to perform this somewhat onerous task, turns out to be an enigma. Chatting over a cup of coffee, he tells me he's actually a butcher by trade. He works in the waste-management industry to support his twin infant daughters whom he clearly adores. Born and bred a country boy from the Bothwell area of the Midlands, he doesn't mind the job at all. It means he's able to be out and about on the truck, not confined to an office, which he feels he would never be able to tolerate.

On the subject of every aspect of meat, from the rearing of the beast, to the paddock to the cooking and serving on the plate, he offers advice on how to respect the animal. He tells us about cuts of meat in a way I've never heard explained before — the importance of the animal not being stressed, and how it should have lived an agreeable life on clean, green pasture.

'This,' he says, 'applies to wildlife such as wallaby as well. You must never eat wallaby that has fed on bracken as they are wont to do, as it taints the meat to the point of being inedible.'

Any question I care to ask, he answers. For instance, why would one of two goat loins I'd purchased at a farmers' market be tender, while the other, in the same packet, cooked at the same time by the same method, be quite tough?

'The tougher one may well have seen the other one killed,' he replies, 'and this would stress the animal and toughen the meat.'

His brother and father are still butchers, and provide only the best of meat to their customers, more as a hobby than a full-time business.

'Can I access some of this meat?' I ask, hardly daring to hope.

'Yes,' he says, 'I think that could be arranged.'

I put it to the back of my mind when he leaves; after all, people are busy and he may not remember.

I truly have never met a butcher with such a passion for his trade, with so much concern for the animals and the food on the plate.

In the end it turned out that the septic wasn't really in need of pumping and settled down again of its own accord. Whatever its hiccup, it has been well worth the cost to meet a man of Jay's calibre.

November 29

Today some ladies, members of the Willow Court Committee, came for a meeting. They know about my passion for colonial food and we were exploring the possibility of a function featuring some of the recipes in the not-too-distant future.

Willow Court was an institution for the criminally insane, though it didn't start out that way. Nor was that its purpose in later times. Many people with a disability lived there in less than desirable conditions.

The site is steeped in history, and the settlement actually predates Port Arthur. More details and relics are progressively being unearthed and there is interest in the paranormal aspects of the buildings, some of which are being restored.

I believe that food reveals a great deal about history, and the food that was available at the time, how the everyday person lived. What was fed to inmates also reflects the level of care for those who lived there more generally.

To this end there is some discussion about the event planned for 19 January: a 'Meet the Matron' play, to be followed by a simple meal of colonial-style soup and bread.

This seemed like a good idea, and I was swept away by their enthusiasm for the Willow Court project. I've been referred to as an 'ideas' person, and while this may indeed be true, the notions and plans are not always practical in their application.

The ladies at times asked if I would like to be involved with the event to raise funds for the ongoing restoration of the site.

'Oh yes,' I reply enthusiastically, and proceed to expound my theory about food being a quintessential part of a successful event such as they have in mind.

Could we do convict/colonial food then? Yes, not too hard, I thought. 'Sure,' I say, getting swept up in the idea and reaching for Paul Hamlyn's book *Colonial Cookery*. This book had come into my possession quite recently, a gift from a friend.

'Here we are!' I say, as I rifle through the book without thinking too much. 'How about sheep's head and/or calves' foot broth?'

Great idea, they agree. With colonial-style bread? Why not? Surely I could cook that, I thought.

Maybe I should have thought more about it. As it is said, 'First take your sheep's head' (not to mention calves' feet). Where are they to come from? I think belatedly.

Local abattoir, of course. Problem: I had once gone to purchase meat from an abattoir and had to make a hasty retreat — I nearly fainted at the overwhelming sense of death and doom.

Now, how this will work out I don't know, but it surely won't be me who accesses those necessary ingredients. Yet if I don't, I will look more than a bit foolish in the face of people's great expectations of the colonial broth-and-bread day.

As it later turned out, the event had to be cancelled, but we will revisit it one day soon. In the meantime I've found a way to access a sheep's head without having to set foot in the dreaded abattoir. A local farmer will collect it for me. I'm still not sure about the eyes looking at me from a boiling cauldron of soup, but in the name of research for the subject, I think it will need to be done.

December 1 and 2

Stephanie and I are in Melbourne to give a preserving workshop at The Essential Ingredient. We've come over a day earlier to do some shopping.

The class goes without a hitch, with lovely people in attendance, and soon we need to leave to catch the plane. Not before we embark on a shopping spree in the shop of course! After all, we still need many items for the school. For instance, we badly need cake forks, so we purchase ten and pack them in our hand luggage. (We had not paid for luggage to save on costs.)

With our carry-on small cases, we arrive at the security line and here we come across some unforeseen problems.

We're asked about having knives or forks in our carry-on luggage (all we'd brought to save on costs, and we'd severely under-estimated the extent of our shopping spree).

'Yes, we have some forks,' says Steph. 'But only little baby ones.'

To check them into luggage, we're told, would cost us $70, to post them, even supposing there was a way to do this, would be mightily expensive too.

'We're starting a cooking school,' I try to reason. 'That's what they're for.'

'She writes cookbooks,' Stephanie throws into the ring.

This strikes a chord with the airport worker, who tells us to pull them out and they will see what they would need to confiscate.

Thankfully it all ends well and we are allowed to bring them home after all. A few small cake forks they may have been, but we'd carefully chosen them for their style and size, so perfect for the cooking school.

However, we will be wiser and more aware the next time we buy equipment of any shape or size when returning from interstate.

December 4

I've been invited to give a presentation about the cooking school at Tourism Tasmania in Hobart, who want to know more about the school and how it will operate, who I anticipate will attend, what sort of topics we will cover, and so on. It's a marvellous opportunity for any new tourism business. It's a bit unnerving, given the fact that speeches are not my forte.

I've made some labna, spelt bread rolls, slow-cooked corned silverside with various pickles, scones and jam and cream, and a large rhubarb and raspberry cheesecake. I feel better already; cooking is such a destresser. For good measure I've thrown in a couple of bottles of sparkling rhubarb and raspberry, and elderflower.

I ask Robert to leave out the trolley as it had turned out to be quite a load. Nerves under control, all goes well until I arrive at the multi-storey carpark and go to pack the trolley for ferrying the food into the Tourism office.

This trolley has in times past been the bane of my existence, though it behaves perfectly well for everyone else. It's the handle, you see — it needs to be pulled up and always defies me at the worst possible moment, and this is just such an opportunity for it to be temperamental. Try as I may, it remains steadfastly stuck in the down position. I load the filled crates as best as I can and then tie the securing rope through the handles of the drink cooler bags to hold them in place.

I make my way to the lift, looking like the hunchback of Notre Dame. The cooler bags are not actually secure at all, and flop alarmingly over the side. Once in the lift a kindly backpacker takes pity on me and asks if I'm OK.

'No,' I say, 'I can't work this handle!'

He kindly offers assistance and (of course) the handle works like a dream for him. Embarrassed and nonplussed but at least and at last upright, I scuttle away.

Speech delivered, it's time for morning tea. The food I've brought is duly placed on the table for serving. A helpful lady opens one of the bottles of sparkling rhubarb and raspberry. It can be a bit tricky anytime, and today the trip from the carpark has done it no favours.

The bottle's bright red contents immediately froth up and over — not just the table, but onto the new carpet in the boardroom. Disaster. Thankfully, as is the case with most things natural, the stains come out easily with plain water, but it's not the best moment.

All turns out well — the food and even what remained of the offending drink are received well, its intrinsic wonderful flavour somewhat erasing the memory of the accident.

A rhubarb and raspberry cheesecake is to be the *piece de resistance*, in that it actually epitomises all that the school will represent by way of showcasing the best of fresh seasonal produce. The rhubarb has been carefully selected from the flourishing patch under the kitchen window. With the luxury of such an abundance, it's possible to choose the stalks with best colour and the size that looks likely to carry the best flavour. The raspberries from our berry patch too can be chosen to the purpose — deep scarlet for sweetness to counteract the tartness of the rhubarb, thus reducing the necessity for the addition of a hefty amount of sugar. It means that a perfect balance can be achieved that will complement the creaminess of the cheese-based filling. At least this was the plan, and it appears to have worked a treat, as the cheesecake is very well received indeed.

The recipe is of course included here. It will be delicious even if you don't grow your own fruit, but keep in mind when purchasing that a deep colour of rhubarb and raspberry will ensure a stunning appearance as well as flavour. I'd avoid buying rhubarb with green stalks as they will look less attractive in the finished product.

Rhubarb and Raspberry Cheesecake

150g crushed plain sweet biscuit crumbs
70g melted butter
1 bunch (6–8 stalks) rhubarb
200g raspberries
½ cup sugar (or to taste)
3 teaspoons cornflour, mixed to a paste with ¼ cup cold water
4 teaspoons gelatine
½ cup hot water
500g cream cheese, softened
½ cup icing sugar
juice of 2 lemons
395g tin sweetened condensed milk

Grease a 20cm round springform tin.

Mix together the biscuit crumbs and butter and press evenly into the base of the tin. Place in the fridge to set (this will only take a few minutes).

Remove any tough or stringy pieces from the rhubarb, then cut into 1cm lengths and place in a saucepan with the raspberries and sugar. Bring to the boil and simmer gently until the rhubarb is just tender. Add the cornflour paste and stir until thickened. (Add extra sugar if needed.) Remove from the heat.

Sprinkle the gelatine on the hot water and whisk until dissolved. Mix into the rhubarb and allow the mixture to cool completely.

Whisk the cream cheese with the icing sugar, lemon juice and condensed milk until smooth. It's easiest to do this in a food processor. Pour on to the biscuit crust and leave to stand for 5–10 minutes until it begins to set. Dollop spoonfuls of the cooled rhubarb mixture over the top, then swirl through with a knife to give a marbled effect.

Place in the fridge to set.

Serves 8–10

December 6

Today is the day that I must finally admit defeat with the brassicas — broccoli, cabbage, kale and cauliflower — well, at least for the time being. They are all riddled with caterpillar holes. I know I should spray with something or derris dust them, but I am always loath to and am consequently slow to get to it.

After an hour there is a huge pile of leaves and young decimated plants sadly wilting in the sun.

On the other hand, the tomatoes look as if they are picking up. This is a novel notion for me as at Eaglehawk Neck, with the lack of sun, they took months to reach flowering point, and green tomatoes were the inevitable result more often than not. I did get cherry tomatoes to ripen occasionally.

The sun here during the day is scorching; I can only water the garden until about 10.30 a.m., otherwise, with this heat, it'll just burn the grass and garden beds.

I am very pleased to note that the garlic is ready to pull. I'm used to tiny little bulbs that I'm ashamed to say I've no patience with peeling, and so have thrown them out or fed them to the chooks. Here, despite the late planting and incredible frosts, they are a respectable size. I even have enough to preserve.

Stephanie arrives with huge plaits of her garlic, about five times the size of mine, I might add. Never mind, next year I'll do better. The garlic has to be washed and laid out to dry completely, then it can be plaited. The stalks are left on naturally — a chemical within the plant feeds the bulbs and prolongs the keeping time for up to six months or more.

So our plaits, large and small, are now hanging at the entrance to the chalet. It smells a bit like a salami factory but there are worse aromas about to be sure, and it looks a treat.

Over the years on ABC Radio talkback I've had many questions about preserving garlic. People have told tales of their several kilos of garlic, carefully preserved in oil, going rancid, a dangerous situation, so it has to be discarded.

For peeling garlic, which is such a pain, here is an easier method. Take two stainless steel bowls (same size) and place the unpeeled garlic cloves in one. Upturn the other bowl over the top and shake like crazy. The skins will simply peel off of their own accord.

Freezing Garlic

I think this is the best and easiest way to preserve garlic. Just peel the cloves and place in freezer bags. They are a little soft and mushy when you take them out, but this can be a good thing as there is no need to crush them for recipes. The flavour is the same as fresh garlic.

Garlic Preserved in Vinegar

The taste of this garlic is not quite the same as fresh garlic — a bit sweeter and with a softer aroma. It is served in some Middle Eastern countries on its own or used in cooking.

520ml white wine vinegar or distilled malt vinegar
45g cooking salt
1kg fresh garlic

Put the vinegar and salt into a saucepan and bring to the boil. Gently simmer for 5 minutes, then remove from the heat and allow to cool completely.

Peel the garlic cloves and blanch in boiling water for 1 minute. Drain and place in sterilised jars. Pour in the cooled vinegar. Some of the garlic will most likely want to float to the surface but it must be submerged completely. To do this, press a piece of crumpled baking paper into the top of the jar and press down into the vinegar, ensuring that there are no air pockets underneath.

The garlic will be ready in 5 weeks.

Makes about 1.5kg

December 7

Paul has rung from the ABC — can I go in for talkback radio tomorrow? So now I am madly cramming Christmas recipes into a folder and hopefully into my head.

I love to take morning tea in for Chris Wisbey and any staff who are about. I especially love the fact that listeners ring in with their favourite family recipes and hints. From my perspective, I like to pass on any hints I might have discovered too. I am really excited to pass on an especially good one this time. It concerns my sparkling fruit drinks.

This came about through many queries I've had, one in particular — won't the drink become more alcoholic during prolonged storage? Well, to be frank, I didn't know — I've never noticed this to be the case, but then my method for measurement wasn't exactly accurate. Anything alcoholic always makes my cheeks go bright red and tingle and this has never happened with these fruit drinks, no matter how long they've been in the bottle.

I consulted brewing experts and again the answers varied. Therefore I decided to try freezing the drinks once they have developed their bubbles. Of course you need to make sure that the bottle is not too full or you will have a nasty accident as I did with one of sparkling strawberry, but in the end I was delighted to discover that when thawed, the drinks retained their sparkle with no risk of the alcohol content increasing. I've since taken it a step further and made icy poles with it. They have proven to be very popular with the grandchildren — fruit tingle icy poles, we call them.

Another thing I discovered this year is that you can use frozen fruit (e.g. berries) to make the sparkling fruit drink so that they can be made all year round. It's a far superior option to commercial soft drinks.

There are many variations, so you are limited only by your imagination and the fruit available to you. However, I have found that it does not work with apples and pears, in fact the results were quite disastrous as they seemed to grow all sorts of sinister things in, on and through them. Rather strangely, this is not the case with crabapples, which make a delicious sparkling fruit drink.

Sparkling Fruit Drink Basic Recipe

875g fruit, diced (or left whole in the case of berries, except
*   strawberries which should be roughly chopped)*
875g sugar
1 lemon, chopped
4.5 litres cold water
200ml cider or white vinegar

Place all the ingredients in a food-safe bucket, mix well, then place a tea towel over the top and leave to stand at room temperature for 48 hours.

Strain through a fine nylon kitchen sieve and pour into PET bottles and seal immediately. (Empty soft-drink bottles are ideal, or you can buy new ones from home-brewing suppliers.)

The sparkling rhubarb will be ready in 2 weeks, maybe less. Open carefully — it's best to refrigerate it before opening.

Makes about 4.5 litres

I notice today that Tom, the ginger cat, is getting fat, quite portly in fact. He now comes into the house all the time and even deigns to stay overnight, which is far better for the local wildlife. Mind you, I wouldn't mind if he kept the possums off the trees.

He now eats several meals a day — the best of dried food, sachets of cat food, lamb kidneys and milk. I would have thought that the milk wouldn't be good for him, but he seems to be thriving on it. Oh yes, and he loves a little egg here and there.

The egg thing took a bit of an undesirable turn today. As I was separating eggs into the mixmaster bowl to make a pavlova for the ABC, I found Tom on the bench about to lick the egg whites out of the bowl. I am thinking he possibly lived on eggs when he was a stray. It suddenly occurs to me that when we thought our chickens weren't laying, it was during the time Tom was living with them in the chookhouse.

Since we've been feeding him, we have eggs once more. I'd thought it was strange seeing as we had continued to have duck eggs, possibly because their shells were too hard for him to break.

Tom is now a wonderful companion, rather like a dog, and likes nothing better than to be carried around the yard endlessly. He gives me a sharp nip when I have the audacity to put him down to move a hose.

Ardy the house cat takes great exception to Tom's presence so we now play musical cats.

'Is Ardy out of the bedroom?' is my common call to Robert or his to me. If the answer is affirmative, Tom has to wait until Ardy is coaxed in there. We shut him in so that Tom can roam inside through the house at his leisure. Once or twice they have come face to face and it wasn't pleasant. I am hoping for better in time as the in-cat, out-cat routine is a bit wearing.

The day heats up — 32 degrees in Hobart tomorrow and at least 5 degrees hotter here. I fear for the new seedlings I've planted — how can they survive?

In the evening we water everything in sight. We will go to the ABC in the morning and then head down to the Eaglehawk Neck property to tend to the garden there to reduce the fire hazard.

I anticipate that the crop from the Molesworth orchard will be somewhat leaner than I'd hoped this year. There will be enough for eating and the apples are looking promising, but the possums are ravaging the other fruits, even though they are far from ripe. It seems the Vicks Vaporub has lost its deterrent power. It's very evident that we will need to fence the orchard and certainly replace the trees that are struggling despite our best attempts at watering them. The searing heat we've experienced some days makes it plain that some of these trees just won't survive the summer. We've had discussions with the local nursery and decided that we will plant as replacements more apples and certainly apricots. Cherries as well — and fruits that are harder to buy commercially, like medlars and Kentish cherries.

Cherries will be bottled and also used to make liqueurs. I especially like to make my own cherry brandy or Kirsch for Black Forest Cakes — it's amazing what a difference the pure homemade product will make. For the time being we will content ourselves with what little we can get, which will amount to some eating cherries and later the apples.

December 8

ABC day — when will I ever get over my nerves?

We are up watering again, since 5 a.m. actually. It is already steaming hot.

My pavlova, as Murphy's Law would have it, is a sunken, shallow specimen. I have no back-up plan so am going to be forced to take it anyway.

A fact of life for me is that some of my best recipes come from my worst failures. If ever there was a moment for this to apply, it's now, though I'm not quite sure how.

I cut off the edges and when I do, the centre is fine, a lovely rich marshmallow, so I decide on a new way to present it. I spread a layer of whipped cream over the base, then break the edge pieces of pavlova into chunks and place them strategically over it. In between I place pieces of freshly picked strawberries, then cover the whole lot with more of the cream and top with berries. I make a berry coulis–style sauce for spooning over at serving time.

It looks pretty good considering, and I think the ABC staff like it. Upon reflection, I guess it was a bit Eton Mess-ish. Anyway, it was good enough to make the cut onto the ABC website, so there you go — a new recipe is born.

In a case like this, should I ever want to make the dish on another occasion, the challenge is how to duplicate it. After a bit of experimentation, here's how you do it.

Eton Mess Cake

PAVLOVA
6 egg whites
2¾ cups castor sugar
2 teaspoons white or cider vinegar
2 teaspoons cornflour
3 tablespoons boiling water

COULIS
500g mixed berries (fresh or frozen)
½ cup sugar, approximately

CHANTILLY CREAM
500ml cream
3 teaspoons icing sugar
400g fresh strawberries, sliced

Preheat the oven to 130°C. Line a 30cm x 30cm baking tray with baking paper.

To make the Pavlova, place all the ingredients in a very clean bowl, boiling water last. Beat with an electric beater until very stiff. To test this, remove the beaters and tilt the bowl. If it doesn't move, carefully turn the bowl upside-down. If it keeps its shape and still doesn't move, it is ready.

Pile onto the baking tray, spreading out to cover to within 3cm of the edges.

Place in oven at 130°C for 15 minutes, then turn the oven down to 90°C and cook a further 40 minutes. Remove from oven and leave to cool at room temperature.

To make the Coulis, place the berries and sugar to taste in a saucepan and heat until sugar dissolves. Leave to stand for 2 hours to cool completely. Purée with a stick blender and then sieve to remove the seeds.

To make the Chantilly Cream, whip the cream and icing sugar together until firm peaks form (though not too stiff or it may turn to butter).

To assemble, remove the pavlova from the baking paper — it will inevitably break up, but that's fine. You will need to have pieces about 4cm x 8cm, but that's approximate. Place a layer on the base of the serving dish, then join and spread with the cream.

Place more pieces of pavlova over the top, leaving 8mm spaces between. Drop the sliced strawberries in these spaces, along with extra cream. Layer in this fashion until all the pavlova pieces and strawberries are used, then spread the remaining cream over the top and sides. Decorate with remaining strawberries.

Serves 8

As is often the case with the Jams and Preserves talkback, it develops a life of its own as listeners ring in. This week is no exception — halfway through, the conversation turns to the subject of sassafras beer. I remember hearing about this early Tasmanian drink from old-timers, and the recipe can be found in cookbooks of the early and mid-1900s.

As can so often happen, a listener, Ken, rang in with a recipe from two of his late aunts. This recipe is pure gold and many listeners request it be written up for the ABC website.

I am really keen to make it — can't wait, in fact. Finding a sassafras tree is a prerequisite, not to mention hops, but this is the Derwent Valley after all. I am sure it will be possible.

When the promised letter arrives from Ken, it actually contains two recipes. I have converted the measurements to metric.

Ken's Sassafras Beer 1

60g hops
1 cup treacle
a handful of sassafras leaves
1 kerosene tin (about 18 litres) water
1.25kg sugar
1 cup raisins

Boil all the ingredients together for 20 minutes. When cool, add 1 small bottle yeast (about 1 cup), leave overnight, then strain and bottle (put a raisin in each bottle).

Makes about 18.5 litres

Homemade Yeast

a small handful of hops
1.1 litres water
1½ tablespoons flour
1½ tablespoons sugar

Boil the hops and water together for 20 minutes, then leave to stand until the hops sink to the bottom of the pan. Strain and cool.

Blend the flour and sugar together with some of the hop liquor and mix well. Bottle, cork and tie securely.

Makes about 1.2 litres

Ken's Sassafras Beer 2

4 sprigs sassafras
4 cups sugar
a handful of hops
3 tablespoons ground ginger
¾ kerosene tin (about 13.5 litres) water

Boil all together, then strain and cool. Add 1 cup yeast, then bottle and leave to work.

Makes about 14 litres

December 9

Driving into New Norfolk this morning it's obvious that berry season is now in full swing. Tickleberry, the berry farm set on the fertile river flats, has cars lined up waiting to buy the first of the summer raspberries along with fresh peas and pink-eye potatoes they have on offer. They are also supplied by a farm near the township of Plenty, and so it's time to seek out all that's available in the valley. Our own patch is a bit behind the rest as our property is at a slightly higher altitude.

There will definitely be loganberries before long at some of the nearby properties. Decades ago we used to visit a loganberry farm a mere stone's throw down the road at old Andy Arnold's place. His farm was a sight to behold, with well-tended rows of loganberry canes over acres and acres of land. The farm is long gone now, unfortunately.

There will be mulberries soon though, then blackcurrants, redcurrants and whitecurrants, gooseberries, tayberries and so many more. What a smorgasbord of exquisite flavours at our fingertips!

I am especially partial to capturing their flavour not only in jam, for which there is limited use in our house other than for toast and baking, but all the more so for berry drinks, whether it be in the form of sparkling brews to enjoy on hot summer days, or the everlasting cordial syrups that both children and adults enjoy so much.

With gooseberries there will pies and tarts to be made. I will be bottling them too so that both of these delicacies can be enjoyed through the depths of next winter.

December 10

It's becoming clear that we seriously need to do something about the driveway here if it's to be used as parking for the school. We invite the contractor and his family for dinner along with Stephanie and her family. Neighbours drop in and are invited to stay for dinner.

This morning I found very inexpensive legs of lamb at the supermarket, so we put two on to roast. We need to cook two more for lamb wraps for a picnic we have planned so we light the wood-fired pizza oven and trial baking them in that fashion. My goodness, they are delicious — smoky and crisp and golden. I'm hoping that over the Christmas break we may be able to have even more friends, family and neighbours around for a pizza evening, as we often did at Eaglehawk Neck.

This is, I admit, something I really miss. I would put out the call to friends on the peninsula when we fired up the pizza oven that Robert had crafted. It was huge, at least a metre square inside, and once fired up would cook each pizza in less than a minute — with crisp bases, a soft, fluffy interior, and the topping cooked to perfection.

I could always count on many people coming along and made a bucketful of sangria to accompany the pizzas. I know it's not a traditional match, but no-one ever seemed to mind. It provided the opportunity for me to add some jars of preserved fruits (such as gooseberries for their tang), cherries and small amounts of liqueurs I'd made the summer before.

In the morning I would mix up a 40-cup flour batch of pizza dough and leave it to rise several times over. Just before friends arrived, I'd cut off 125g portions and roll each into a ball, leaving it to rise on a central kitchen bench. Single-serve pizza trays were at the ready.

Along the benches were all manner of toppings. The system was that guests would take and gently flatten a ball of dough on a tray, add toppings of their choice, then take it up to the pizza oven where Robert would bake it for them.

This went on for hours and in the cool of the evening, the remaining sangria was heated so that it became, more or less, a warming mulled wine that was jolly good.

I really, really miss those times. Hopefully we can do similar things here before much longer.

I've included the recipe for pizza for about four people. You can multiply it out to 40 cups of flour with the corresponding amounts of other ingredients. I am told I could use far less yeast and I dare say that's correct, but as the dough is always so deliciously light and fluffy, I'm loath to change it.

Pizza

This recipe can be used to make a family-sized pizza that can be cooked in an electric or gas oven, which will take 15–20 minutes, or in a well-heated outdoor clay pizza oven, which will take 5–10 minutes.

If preferred, you can use this recipe to make 2 smaller pizzas.

DOUGH
4 cups plain flour
4 teaspoons instant dried yeast
2 teaspoons salt
3 teaspoons sugar
¼ cup vegetable, canola or light olive oil
2 cups warm water, approximately

SAUCE
500g diced tomatoes (fresh, tinned, bottled or frozen)
1 rounded tablespoon tomato paste
2 cloves garlic, peeled and crushed
½ teaspoon brown sugar
½ teaspoon salt
3 teaspoons chutney (any sort)
1 sprig fresh or ½ teaspoon dried rosemary

thinly sliced meat such as salami, ham, pepperoni, cooked
chicken, bacon
vegetables such as chopped capsicum, tomato, onion, crushed
garlic, roasted pumpkin, even pineapple, fresh herbs
seafood such as mussels, calamari, crayfish, anchovies, scallops
150g mixed grated tasty cheese, mozzarella and parmesan

To make the Dough, in a medium-sized bowl, mix the flour, yeast, salt and sugar. Make a well in the centre and pour in the oil and water and mix to a soft dough, adding a little extra water if needed. Cover with a tea towel and leave to rise in a warm place for about 1 hour or until approximately doubled in size. At this stage you can take the dough to the following step, or just turn it over with a spoon and let it rise again (several times if you like).

Turn dough out onto a lightly floured surface and knead until smooth. Shape into a ball and leave on the floured surface to rise for 15 minutes, covered with a tea towel.

To make the Sauce, combine all the ingredients in a saucepan, bring to the boil then simmer gently for about 20 minutes or until it is reduced to a thick purée. Cool before using. Remove the rosemary sprig.

Preheat the oven to 200°C. Grease a 35cm pizza tray.

Press the ball of dough out with the fingers to the size of the tray. Spread immediately with the cooled sauce, followed by a little grated cheese, then the toppings of your choice. Always put meat toppings on first, with the exception of bacon, which should go on top of the cheese. Be careful not to overload the pizza or the crust will be soggy after baking.

Bake the pizza until the cheese is golden and the crust is golden brown and crisp.

December 11

I've been invited to do a book signing at Patchwork Café in New Norfolk today. They stock not only my books but also Stephanie's homemade preserves.

Before long, two ladies take the time to sit down and chat over coffee and cake. They tell me about plants to grow in the area. I am told that jostaberries love the climate of Molesworth and thrive on the icy chill of winter. They even tell me where I might find the plants — at the Bushy Park Market, which I plan to visit soon.

Jostaberries are a cross between a gooseberry and blackcurrant, and came to my attention not long after gooseberries became scarce due to a mould that almost wiped them out here in Tasmania several years ago. Jostaberries make excellent jelly, probably my favourite. The flavour is very much like blackcurrant but there are definite undertones of gooseberry, so the jelly is beyond delicious. You can make jam with them, though they do need topping and tailing. I often make cordial syrup that doubles as a coulis that is a good addition for your pantry shelves.

Bottling Jostaberries

You can bottle them as for currants. It's a bit tedious removing the stalk and tail end but if you use scissors for the task it's not too bad. If you choose to do so, use the basic method (see page 385) and bring the temperature up, over a period of 45 minutes, to 85°C, then hold for 1 hour. Alternatively if you have a thermostat-controlled preserver, turn on set to this temperature and leave for one-and-three-quarter hours.

Freezing Jostaberries

To freeze so that they are free flowing, spread in a single layer on a tray and freeze, then store in freezer bags or containers in the freezer.

Alternatively, for solid pack, place in sealed freezer bags or containers in the freezer.

Jostaberry Jam

> *1.5kg jostaberries*
> *2 cups water*
> *1.5kg sugar*

Top and tail the jostaberries and place in a large saucepan or jam pan with the water. Bring to the boil, then simmer until the berries are tender.

Add the sugar and bring to the boil, stirring. Boil briskly over a medium—high heat until setting point is reached (see page 393).

Leave to stand for 5 minutes, then pour into warm sterilised jars and seal immediately.

Makes about 2 litres

Jostaberry Jelly

> *1.5kg jostaberries*
> *2 cups water*
> *sugar*

Place the jostaberries and water in a large saucepan and bring to the boil, then reduce the heat and simmer until the berries are very soft.

Line a colander with muslin and pour the mixture into this to collect the juice.

To each cup of juice add 1 cup sugar.

Bring to the boil, stirring and then cook over medium heat (briskly) until setting point is reached (see page 393), about 20 minutes.

Pour into warm sterilised jars and seal immediately.

Makes about 1.8 litres

Jostaberry Cordial

1kg jostaberries
1.2 litres water
sugar
3 level teaspoons tartaric or citric acid
2 tablespoons white or cider vinegar

Place the berries and water in a large saucepan and bring to the boil. Simmer very gently for 5 minutes. Strain through a colander, pressing down to extract maximum juice, and then pour the resulting liquid through a fine kitchen sieve.

For each cup of liquid add 1 cup sugar. Bring to the boil, then reduce the heat immediately to a bare simmer and cook for 1 minute more. Stir in tartaric or citric acid and vinegar, pour into sterilised bottles and seal immediately.

The cordial will keep at room temperature but in warm weather or climates it would be best to keep it in the fridge. In either case, refrigerate the bottle once it is opened.

Makes about 2 litres

December 13

The raspberries are ripening painfully slowly. Others in the valley have an abundance of luscious ripe raspberries for sale. The canes are loaded and today three berries were ripe — what a treat! I hope that by January and the preserving classes we will be able to pick and preserve from our own patch. There are plenty of ripe loganberries here already, which make incredibly tasty jam, jelly and (my favourite) cordial syrup.

We have managed to find plenty for what we need on a property at nearby Lachlan.

Freezing Loganberries

To freeze so that they are free flowing, spread in a single layer on a tray and freeze, then store in freezer bags or containers in the freezer.

Alternatively, for solid pack, place in sealed freezer bags or containers in the freezer.

Loganberry Jam

1.5kg loganberries
juice of 1 lemon (optional)
1.5kg sugar

Place the loganberries and lemon juice in a pot and bring slowly to the boil. Cook for 10 minutes over a gentle heat.

Add the sugar and bring back to the boil, stirring. Boil briskly over a medium–high heat for about 15 minutes or until setting point is reached. Stand for 5 minutes, then pour into warm sterilised jars and seal immediately. Refrigerate after opening.

Makes about 2kg

Loganberry Jelly

2kg loganberries
juice of 1 lemon (optional)
600ml water
sugar

Place the berries, lemon juice and water in a large saucepan and bring slowly to the boil. Simmer for 10 minutes, then strain through a colander lined with muslin.

For each cup of liquid, add 1 cup sugar. Bring to the boil, stirring, then boil briskly over a medium–high heat until setting point (see page 393) is reached.

Pour into warm sterilised jars and seal immediately. Refrigerate after opening.

Makes about 2 litres

Loganberry Cordial Syrup

1kg loganberries
1.1 litres water
sugar
2 tablespoons cider or white vinegar
2 level teaspoons tartaric or citric acid

Place the berries and water in a large saucepan and bring to the boil. Reduce the heat and simmer very gently for 15 minutes.

Strain through a colander, and then strain the resulting liquid through a kitchen sieve lined with a layer of muslin (or even a clean tea towel will do).

For each cup of liquid, add 1 cup sugar. Bring to the boil, then reduce the heat immediately to a simmer and cook for 2 minutes more. Stir in vinegar, tartaric or citric acid, pour into sterilised bottles and seal immediately.

To serve, use 1 part syrup to 4–5 parts water or soda water.

For adults, add a splash to a dry sparkling white wine. It can also be served over (or stirred through) ice-cream or poured over panna cotta, yoghurt or cheesecake.

Makes about 2.75 litres

December 14

Son-in-law Nathaniel works for a printing company and as coincidence would have it, as so often happens in Tasmania, a gentleman in his office was asking him about gooseberries. He had so many of them apparently, almost growing wild on his property. Did he think I would like some and if so, how much? If not, what could he do with them? Jam, maybe?

No need for him to make jam, none whatsoever. I will take as many as he cares to give me. These gooseberries are all the more desirable as they come from old, old bushes, so I know they will be packed with flavour.

They will need to be topped and tailed, which is tedious to be sure, but it's a small price to pay to be able to enjoy their exquisite flavour once more.

So tonight on the trip home from work on the bus, Nat is carrying a large bagful containing several kilos. All his generous work colleague asks for in return is a gooseberry tart, a simple thing indeed.

I have bottled gooseberries before, which, in our household of depleted numbers, is by far the best option. They look nothing short of stunning in the jars, and are a wonderful addition to the pantry shelves, with their promise of gooseberry tarts to be enjoyed over the winter months. I will also make a little jam to pass on to family and friends so they can enjoy this exquisite fruit.

Bottled Gooseberries

Use the basic method for bottling (see page 385). Bring the temperature up to 83°C over about 50 minutes, then hold at this temperature for 1 hour. Alternatively, if you have a thermostat-controlled model, set to temperature and leave for 1 hour 50 minutes.

Freezing Gooseberries

The gooseberries can be topped and tailed either before or after freezing for preserving. This is best done with a pair of scissors. If you leave this till after, it needs to be done before thawing. If they are to be made into jelly, this is not necessary.

They can be spread on a tray so that they are free flowing when you need to use them, or simply frozen in airtight bags or containers. Some people like to add sugar before the fruit is frozen, but this must never be done if there is a chance that you will be making them into jam or jelly later.

Gooseberry Jam

1.5kg gooseberries
1½ cups water
1.5kg sugar

Place the gooseberries and water in a saucepan and bring to the boil, then simmer for 10 minutes. Add the sugar and bring to the boil, stirring. Boil briskly for 15–20 minutes or until setting point is reached (see page 393). Pour into warm sterilised jars and seal immediately. Refrigerate after opening.

Makes about 2kg

Gooseberry Jelly

This is a delicious semi-sweet jelly that is wonderful served with scones and whipped cream, or as a glaze for tarts. It is also delicious served as an accompaniment to roast pork.

1.5kg gooseberries
3 cups water
sugar

Place the fruit in a large saucepan and bring to the boil, then reduce the heat and barely simmer until the fruit is very soft. Line a colander with muslin and pour into this, collecting the juice below.

To each cup of juice add 1 cup sugar. Bring to the boil, stirring, then cook briskly over a medium–high heat until setting point is reached (see page 393).

Pour into warm sterilised jars and seal immediately.

Makes about 1.7 litres

The gooseberry pie was duly made and well received. Gooseberries certainly make one of the best pies of summer and I well remember my grandmother baking them each year — the smell reminds me of summer.

Double-crust Gooseberry Pie

PASTRY
125g butter
125g sugar
1 egg, lightly beaten
250g plain flour
½ teaspoon baking powder
a little beaten egg white

FILLING
600g gooseberries, topped and tailed
about ¾ cup sugar
about 1 tablespoon cornflour, mixed to a paste with just a little cold water

To make the Pastry, cream the butter and sugar together, then whisk in the egg until well combined. With a metal spoon fold in the combined flour and baking powder and mix to a soft dough. Wrap in cling wrap and place in the fridge for at least 30 minutes.

To make the Filling, place the gooseberries in a saucepan, cover with water and bring to the boil over a gentle heat. Simmer only until the gooseberries are just cooked. Add the sugar and stir to dissolve.

Bring back to the boil and thicken with the cornflour paste, stirring constantly. The mixture should thicken to a custard-like consistency, though not too thick. You *may* need a little more cornflour paste but use with care

— too much will mean losing that wonderful gooseberry 'zing' and the mixture will by its very nature thicken as it cools. Check for sweetness and add more sugar if needed. Leave to cool.

Preheat the oven to 170°C. Grease a 20cm pie plate.

Roll out two-thirds of the dough on a lightly floured surface. Press into the pie plate. Brush all over with the lightly beaten egg white, then fill almost to the top with the cooled fruit. Roll out the other piece of dough and cut strips of pastry 8mm wide and place, lattice style, over the fruit.

Bake for 30 minutes until the crust is golden brown all over.

The pie is best left to stand for a couple of hours before serving, when it will then cut out beautifully and is delicious served with sweetened whipped cream and/or a homemade vanilla ice-cream.

I dust the pie with sifted icing sugar just before serving.

Serves 6–8

December 14

The weather is cooler today, thank goodness, so any watering I do won't be boiled away by the sun. Finally the pump man is to arrive, to attend to the idiosyncrasies of that aging pump in the shed. Lately it seems to have a will of its own and shuts down for no apparent reason.

We had been told it will take four hoses on at full rate, but this is by no means happening and our beautiful oasis is at risk of drying out. I fear for what the problem might be and how much it will cost.

However, things aren't so bad after all: we merely needed a switch, and it cost $110 to fix. Even more encouragingly, we are told it's a very good brand and should perform well for years to come.

December 15

The family are to visit for dinner tomorrow so will I make good use of the remaining gooseberries that are sitting in the fridge. Beautiful specimens — they are not green as is usually the case, but have progressed to a redder shade — they are bound to be sweeter and very flavoursome.

Rosemary called in with a bunch of Christmas flowers from her garden and asked if I knew how to make homemade yoghurt. Yes indeed, it is simplicity itself.

In this day and age of yoghurt-makers it is a simple thing to make your own yoghurt. Not long after we were married and in the days before the luxury of yoghurt-makers, my friend told me to place the jar on the electric blanket to set the yoghurt, an inexact science but apparently it worked for her. I never did try that method as soon after the first of the 1970s yoghurt-makers was released, a yellow-and-white (naturally) contraption in which you sit the jar, turn it out and leave for eight hours undisturbed. I still have and use it to this day.

You need to be sure that the yoghurt you buy to add to the mixture contains the necessary acidophilus culture.

Homemade Yoghurt

> *3 cups lukewarm milk*
> *3 tablespoons Greek-style yoghurt*
> *3 tablespoons skim-milk powder*

Whisk all ingredients together and pour into a litre jar with a lid or containers and put into the yoghurt-maker. Leave for 8 hours until set, then remove and cover the containers with a lid and refrigerate.

Once you have your yoghurt it can be flavoured with fruits or even some of the fruit cordial syrup you have made over summer. I like to make labna, yoghurt cheese, flavoured with the season's herbs. It can also be made just plain for use in cheesecakes and the like.

Makes about 750ml

Labna

3¾ cups Greek-style yoghurt
juice of ½ lemon
2½ teaspoons salt
2 teaspoons finely chopped fresh thyme (optional)
2 teaspoons finely chopped fresh mint (optional)
½ teaspoon snipped fresh chives (optional)
3 teaspoons olive oil
olive oil, extra

Combine the yoghurt, lemon juice, salt, thyme, mint, chives (if using) and olive oil in a bowl and mix well.

Boil a 30cm piece of muslin for 3 minutes. Drain, allow to cool, then lay it out in a large colander over a bowl. Pour the yoghurt mixture into this, and tie the top to form a bag. Hang this bag over the bowl to collect the whey and leave for 2 days in a cool place. If you live in a warm climate, or in summer in cooler climates, this may need to take place in the fridge. (The whey, I am told, is good for making sauerkraut, which I plan to try next winter when cabbages will be in abundance.)

Roll the resulting yoghurt cheese into walnut-sized balls and place in a sterilised litre jar. Cover with extra olive oil, making sure there are no air pockets, and add chillies, if desired. Seal and store in the fridge for 2–3 weeks.

Makes about 400g

Hint: The whey liquid can be used in bread dough.

December 16

The school is at the point where we have been advertising the classes and have had a great deal of interest through the website.

We need just a few final bits and pieces so that classes can begin in earnest. Today Stephanie and I go on one final shopping trip. We take my little old Peugeot, which is a bit optimistic really, as we have some rather bulky items to purchase, not least of which are three sets of stackable shelves for cooking equipment and ingredients.

It's a mystery how we do it, but we manage to squeeze them in, together with bathroom accessories, cake tins and everything from cleaning products to rolls of plastic bags. Stephanie in the passenger seat has parcels piled high on her, and the back-seat haul reaches the ceiling of the car. Still, it is done.

Once unpacked, the school is ready for business. We stand back and admire the handiwork of the past several months, very pleased indeed. What a transformation!

December 17

Laurelle and John come to visit today. They have a small luxury hotel nearby, Woodbridge on the Derwent, and have seen our advertisements for the cooking school. They would like to see what we have here, with a view to recommending the school to their patrons.

It turns out they are great foodies and we spend several hours testing and tasting gooseberry tarts and apricot shortcake, along with sparkling fruit drinks. I really want them to taste the sparkling elderflower but, despite the fact that a bottle or two said 'EF' on the lids, they turn out to be rhubarb. I really must mend my random labelling ways. I always think I will remember what I put in each bottle, but unfortunately and inevitably this is not the case.

A bottle of elderflower syrup comes to the rescue, the recipe I invented earlier this year, made from flowers of the trees down by the river.

I'd like to think that by the time they leave we have become friends, and they tell me they will indeed promote the school. I am very fortunate, considering my haphazard ways. They have been in business much longer than me, and have given me some invaluable tips that I will apply immediately.

December 18

Yesterday Denis from the Tasman Peninsula rang. For many years now he has picked blackberries for me from the fields behind Saltwater River. He also brings me raspberries, grown behind his garden shed, absolutely beautiful specimens. Most are frozen, but this does them no harm at all. Stephanie adores them for the blackberry jam she makes and sells — the pectin level is so high that the jam sets like a dream.

Our first meeting with Denis came from a chance visit to the Frog Hollow Nursery. Here we are told that a man down the road has around 10 kilos of blackberries in his freezer that he might like to sell to me. I am always in the market for the best of fresh berries, even if frozen, so I went to visit him immediately.

'Ten kilos,' says Denis, 'I've got 100 kilos!'

We quickly agreed to a price, took eight kilos with us and promised to return soon for the rest.

I thought that we had enough freezer space and returned a week or two later to purchase the rest. As Denis pulled them out and weighed them up, we realised that 100 kilos was a bit of an underestimation. They filled the back of Robert's ute, piled high — 198 kilos in all.

I was extremely happy to get them, but how to store them? We filled our freezers and barely made a dent in the pile. Our friend Tony turned on his freezer and we filled that. We took the rest somewhat optimistically to our son Andrew's freezer at Primrose Sands, which was quickly filled.

Getting desperate now, Andrew sought out his neighbour, who was down at the local RSL. Could he come home and let us store the rest at his place? He obligingly did, and so finally the last bag of blackberries was catered for.

Not a single berry went to waste between son Alistair's shop, Stephanie, Andrew and my obsessive cooking sprees.

Since then we have gladly taken all the luscious, untainted purple clumps of flavour that Denis can pick us. I always make a decent amount of blackberry jam to share with family and friends, and a double-crust blackberry pie, or even blackberry and apple, is always welcome. (Blackberry cordial syrup and sparkling blackberry are also very good.)

I've tried making blackberry chutney and didn't like it one bit. Such a shame to overpower their wonderful flavour with the likes of vinegar and spices.

The haul that Denis brought today was another freezer-full, the remnants of last autumn's pickings. It will tide us over until the new season begins in February. There will be ample to work and play with, to be sure.

Blackberry Jam

1.5kg blackberries
¼ cup water
juice of 1 lemon or ½ teaspoon citric acid (optional)
1.5kg sugar

Place the blackberries, water and lemon juice or citric acid in a pot and bring to the boil, stirring often. Cook for 10 minutes over a gentle heat.

Add the sugar and bring back to the boil, stirring. Boil briskly for 15–20 minutes over a medium–high heat until setting point is reached. Stand for 5 minutes, then pour into warm sterilised jars and seal immediately.

Makes about 1.75kg

Blackberry and Apple Jelly

1kg blackberries
600g apples
600ml water
sugar

Place the blackberries in a large saucepan or jam pan. Wash the apples and then cut them into 1cm pieces and add to the pan with the water. Bring to the boil and reduce the heat and simmer until the fruit is soft.

Line a colander with muslin and pour the mixture in, collecting the liquid below. Leave to stand for 2 or more hours if possible.

To each cup of liquid add 1 cup sugar. Bring to the boil and cook briskly over a medium–high heat until setting point is reached (see page 393).

Pour into warm sterilised jars and seal immediately.

Makes 1.7 litres

December 20

Tomatoes today, which must be dealt with. The owner of nearby hothouses has rung, trying to track down Stephanie, who purchases sauce tomatoes from him regularly. In the recent intolerable heat, a few of his tomatoes have ripened fast and so must be used quickly.

I know Stephanie will take many but tell Nick I'd like some as well. Nick has developed an amazing tomato farm with hothouses that produce nine months of the year. The quality is sensational. Equally good is the fact that he grows a hothouse full of the best quality basil — the aroma when you walk in has to be experienced to be believed. Oh, yes, it's going to be a good summer.

My own tomato bushes are doing quite well, despite the wild weather swings. Being at the head of the valley, winter fog is not the only thing that sweeps up the valley. Yesterday a wind roared through and, trapped in this little nook at the end before the rise into the surrounding hills, raged its way like a tornado around the garden before its fury was spent.

I was sure that the tomatoes and fruit trees would lose their flowers or fruit, but they seem to have survived intact. They surely must be hardy.

While I fear for my apricots, plums and greengages I remember the story of Tilly, the elderly mother of our friend Kaye, and who was a great lover of greengages, standing at the back door calling out to the fruit on her tree: 'Hang on! Hang on!' She was quite a character, and as I listened to the wind howl I understood her sentiments entirely.

However, there is no time to lose in collecting the tomatoes. I want to preserve them by every possible means as they are one of the mainstays of the pantry cupboard over winter.

I always start with bottled tomatoes as they can be added to all sorts of savoury dishes, but can also be held for later use in making all manner of relishes, chutneys and sauces, even jam.

Bottled Tomatoes

Put rings on bottles.

Chop tomatoes and place in bottles, filling to the neck. For each 500g tomatoes, add ¼ teaspoon citric acid.

Fill to the top with water or tomato juice.

Put lids and clips on bottles, or if using screwtop jars, screw the lids on, then release a quarter of a turn.

Place in a preserver or a large pot in which a rack has been set. Bottles should not touch each other.

Bring slowly to the boil (this should take at least an hour). Boil for 15 minutes.

Turn off the heat, screw down the lids if using screwtop preserving jars, and allow to stand for 1 hour before removing to a wooden board.

Leave to stand for 48 hours before removing lids and clips. Check that lids are concave.

Freezing Tomatoes

Freezing is also another good option, especially when you're in a hurry or you've run out of preserving jars. I simply throw the whole tomatoes into freezer bags and place in the freezer where they will keep very satisfactorily for several months. One advantage of this is that when you take them out, if you dip them immediately in water, the skins peel off in an instant.

For the moment, however, I will make tomato relish. This is a good staple recipe. If I want tomato sauce, I often just purée the mixture at the end and, hey presto, a really delicious tomato sauce.

Tomato Relish

2kg tomatoes, chopped
3 medium-sized onions, peeled and chopped
2 tablespoons salt
3 teaspoons mustard powder
3 teaspoons curry powder
500g sugar
3 cups white or cider vinegar
1 tablespoon cornflour
¼ cup vinegar, extra

Place the tomatoes, onions, salt, mustard powder, curry powder, sugar and vinegar in a large saucepan. Bring to the boil, stirring until the sugar is dissolved, and continue to boil for 1½ hours.

Mix the cornflour to a paste with the extra vinegar, add some or all to the boiling mixture and stir till thickened. Pour into sterilised jars and seal immediately.

Makes about 2kg

Tomato Chutney

This is really just a variation on a theme. With the addition of apples and garlic to the relish recipe, a

fruitier, thicker, more rounded flavour is achieved.
It's just a matter of personal preference really. I prefer
the sharp, fresh flavour of the relish.

2kg tomatoes, chopped
500g onions, peeled and chopped
300g cooking apples, peeled, cored and chopped
2 cloves garlic, peeled and crushed
2 tablespoons salt
1 tablespoon mustard powder
3 teaspoons curry powder
500g sugar
3 cups vinegar
1 tablespoon cornflour
¼ cup vinegar, extra

Place the tomatoes, onions, apples, garlic, salt, mustard
powder, curry powder, sugar and vinegar into a large
saucepan. Bring to the boil, stirring until the sugar is
dissolved, and continue to boil for 1½ hours.

Mix the cornflour to a paste with the extra vinegar,
add some or all to the boiling mixture and stir
till thickened. Pour into sterilised jars and seal
immediately. Eat at once or store in a cool, dry and
dark place for up to 1 year.

Makes about 2.2kg

I still have plenty of tomatoes and Stephanie's garden is producing
abundant cucumbers. Capsicums are plentiful too, so I can make a
batch of Tomato and Cucumber Relish. It is delicious with meats,
but I especially like it as a quick snack on top of grilled cheese on
toast.

Tomato and Cucumber Relish

1.5kg ripe red tomatoes, diced
500g onions, diced
⅓ cup salt
1 cucumber, cut into 8mm pieces
2 large red capsicum, cut into 8mm pieces
500g sugar
650ml white or cider vinegar
1½ teaspoons mustard
1 teaspoon curry powder
1 teaspoon turmeric
3 teaspoons cornflour mixed to a paste with 2 tablespoons
vinegar

Place the tomatoes and onions in separate bowls and sprinkle each with half of the salt. Leave for several hours, then drain.

In a large saucepan or jam pan, place the tomatoes, onions, cucumber, capsicum, sugar, vinegar and spices.

Bring to the boil, stirring, and cook for 1 hour over medium heat. If the mixture needs thickening, stir in some or all of the cornflour paste. Pour into warm sterilised jars and seal immediately.

Makes about 2.25 litres

Once all these are made I decide to semi-dry the rest in the blessed cool of the cooking school (air-conditioning). They will be delicious for entertaining over the holiday season on pizza, in salads and on antipasto platters.

My two ancient dehydrators are set on their way and within hours I have ample for what I need. It's essential to dip the prepared segments into vinegar before placing in the jars and covering with oil. The acid of the vinegar helps prevent spoilage. Even when the oil is poured in, you must be careful that there are no air pockets. As an extra safety measure I keep them in the fridge. The oil may solidify, but scooping out whatever you estimate you will need and sitting at room temperature for a few minutes easily remedies this.

Never be tempted to add garlic to the oil as this does not keep at all well and can quickly grow dangerous bacteria.

Semi-dried Tomatoes

Once the tomatoes are used, the oil can be used as part of a dressing or for sautéing vegetables, chicken or meats.

> *ripe red tomatoes*
> *white or cider vinegar*
> *olive oil*

Wash the tomatoes and cut into eighths or quarters, depending on their size.

If you have a food dehydrator, place the segments on the trays. If you are using the oven, place racks (such as cake coolers) over a baking tray lined with baking paper and place tomatoes on these.

Dehydrate until semi-dried in the dehydrator (this will be at its highest setting). With the oven go as low as possible, at least to 70°C. Open the door occasionally, or leave the door just slightly ajar, to allow built-up moisture to escape.

Dip the semi-dried tomato segments in white vinegar before placing in sterilised jars. Do not pack too tightly.

Cover with olive oil, ensuring that tomatoes are *completely* covered, ensuring that there are no air bubbles.

For **Dehydrated Tomato Slices**, instead of cutting the tomatoes into segments, cut into 6mm slices and dry as for semi-dried tomatoes.

Tomato Stock Powder

This is a very handy product to have on hand and is very simple to make. It is basically taking the dehydrating process just a little further.

> *ripe red tomatoes, thinly sliced*
> *salt*
> *sugar*

Sprinkle the tomatoes lightly with salt and sugar. Dehydrate as for semi-dried tomatoes, but taking them to the point of brittle dry. Place the dried tomatoes into a food processor and process until they form a powder. Store in an airtight container in the fridge or freezer.

Tomato Leather

Similarly, you can make a tomato fruit leather that can be cut into pieces and added to a pasta sauce.

> *ripe red tomatoes, chopped*
> *salt*
> *sugar*

Place the tomatoes in a large saucepan or preserving pan and bring to the boil, stirring often, over a medium–low heat. Cook until a purée forms, then add salt and pepper to taste. Purée.

Spread over fruit leather sheets and dehydrate in a dehydrator at 65–70°C. Alternatively, spread on baking paper-lined baking trays and dehydrate at 60–70°C in the oven. The leather is ready when the sheet can be torn but no beads of liquid are exuded. Roll and chop into pieces then store in an airtight container in the fridge for 3 weeks or freezer for 12 months.

December 21

Today is the day for the driveway repairs to begin. Unfortunately a particularly beautiful stretch of grass has to be torn up to make way for a drainage line.

'Can't make a cake without breaking an egg,' I'm told. 'It'll grow back again soon enough,' the backhoe operator assures me. And so the work begins, including the digging of a waterhole in the far paddock to provide another source of water for the animals.

While the men are thus engaged, I decide to take on the mowing once more. The orchard is badly in need of it. Mowing around the fruit trees is quite a challenge — do I go up and down or side to side or round and round the trees? I try a combination of all and instead of having nice neat mowing lines it looks like a mad drunk has taken charge of the machine. After several hours in the hot sun I am beastly careless — at least it's done.

As the grass is quite long from recent rain and heat, a contraption has been rigged to hold up the outlet part, instead of letting the grass fall to the side and underneath, which inevitably clogs it. It's a good idea, but the downside is that the cut grass, clover and random weed seeds and pollen get thrown in the air to come down on top of my head, in my eyes, ears, in my mouth even. And there's a terrible itching inside my bra from all those little sharp bits of seed. I'm not impressed. I have dreamed for years of having a ride-on mower but I am quickly becoming disillusioned.

It is, however, heart-warming to see that the orchard is starting to give up some of its secrets, which I discover as I'm not-so-merrily mowing. There are definite signs of olives, currants of all kinds as well as golden drop plums by the look of it. The orange tree has picked up a little and is covered in flowers. Its leaves are perilously dry, but I'm hopeful that the flowers are a good sign and not, as a niggling doubt tells me, an indication that it's dying.

The raspberries are ripening well but I am horrified to see dry dead tips on some of the canes. Robert tells me this is quite normal but I'm not so sure. It's very worrying. This is the one thing at least that I want to be able to pick for the school.

Today there is a basketful of cucumbers that need to have something done with them. They are picked fresh from Stephanie's garden. She certainly has a green thumb. Each day Jacob and Charly care little for breakfast of the regular kind. They head straight out the back door and pick whatever they fancy by way of fruit and vegetables. When Stephanie asks them would they like cereal or toast, Jacob's frequent response is a cheery, 'No thanks, Mum. I've had a salad!'

I've always loved bread and butter cucumbers. They are excellent in salads or cold meats, with cheese even. They retain their crunch because of the brining process and are a great standby in the pantry cupboard. They turn fresh homemade bread with cheese into a feast.

Bread and Butter Cucumbers

1.25kg cucumbers
2 large onions, peeled
½ cup salt
3½ cups white or cider vinegar
2 cups sugar
1 teaspoon curry powder
2 teaspoons mustard seeds
1 bay leaf
½ teaspoon dried chilli flakes

Cut the cucumbers and onions into 8mm slices. Place in a large bowl with the salt and barely cover with water and stir to combine. Leave to stand for a few hours.

Combine the remaining ingredients in a large saucepan and bring to the boil, stirring often.

Drain the vegetables in a colander and add to the boiling vinegar mixture. Bring back to the boil, then remove from the heat. Spoon into sterilised jars and seal immediately. Be sure to use all the vinegar, otherwise they may not keep well.

To make **Pickled Zucchini Slices**, substitute 1kg zucchini and 1 red capsicum for the cucumbers.

Makes about 1.5kg

December 25

In our family we do things a little differently. All the family comes for a Christmas-cum-family day on Boxing Day. I remember when I was a child the interminable disagreements and hurt feelings over who went to whose parents and when for Christmas, and vowed never to let that happen. So the very amicable arrangement is for everyone to go to their in-laws on Christmas Day and then come here on Boxing Day for a get-together.

Courtney has decided to come over today to help me with the cooking. She has in mind a gingerbread house, something we've not done together before. It's just as well we have so much bench and oven space in the school. We don't have a pattern or a template so go free hand, making huge sheets of gingerbread with which to form the walls.

We also make a thick butter icing and have at the ready several large bowlfuls of lollies for decoration. I cleared the cupboard of long-forgotten silver cachous and nonpareils along with all the usual and more contemporary sweets we've bought.

Courtney is a dab hand with anything of a craft nature — from sewing to knitting, crochet and more, making her own patterns as she goes, and this stands her in good stead for this major exercise. It's going to be one large house.

Here is the recipe. I made four times this amount, which was, as it turned out, a bit excessive. However, I will turn the leftover full and part sheets into crumbs in the food processor. I'll keep those for making biscuit bases for cheesecakes by adding two parts crumb to one part melted butter.

The following amount is sufficient for a small to medium house or will make four dozen small gingerbread men.

Gingerbread House

250g treacle
250g golden syrup
120g butter
1 egg yolk
1 tablespoon ground ginger
2 teaspoons bicarbonate of soda
500g plain flour
1 teaspoon baking powder
¾ cup milk

ICING
1kg icing sugar
125g butter, softened
boiling water
a few drops natural cochineal or desired food colouring

Melt together the treacle, golden syrup and butter over a low heat, then leave to cool to lukewarm. Whisk in the egg yolk, then fold in the combined and sifted dry ingredients with a metal spoon. Mix in the milk. Wrap in cling wrap and refrigerate for at least 30 minutes before using.

Preheat the oven to 150°C. Line 2 baking trays (30cm x 30cm approximately) with baking paper or grease well.

On a lightly floured surface roll out the dough to 6mm thick. Cut out 4 walls and 2 roof panels for your gingerbread house, cutting out doors and windows as desired. Or use a gingerbread man cutter to stamp out biscuits, pressing in currants and sultanas for eyes as decorations.

Bake for 12–15 minutes or until golden. Remove to a wire rack to cool completely.

To make the Icing, place the icing sugar and butter in a bowl and mix in enough boiling water to make a good spreading consistency. Add a few drops of cochineal to colour the icing pale pink. Join the house panels together with icing — you will need to be patient as you'll have to hold the joins together for a few moments until they cement together.

December 26

The day of the feast — a day of over-indulgence with food, but it's that time of year and how can you resist, with all those luscious summer berries, not to mention cherries and apricots?

I am still looking hopefully at the fruit trees. Although the orchard is young and has been virtually untended for quite a while, there are greengages to be seen, plus apples, medlars, even some peaches on a struggling tree.

When are loquats due to fruit, I wonder. The trees' foliage is good, but there is no sign of fruit. It's not a huge disaster as it's not a fruit I would go into raptures about, but a little jelly is good to keep on hand for glazing fruit tarts and I know some people are very partial to it. Loquat jam even — I'll give that a try should any fruit ever appear. The jelly is good as a glaze because it doesn't detract from the flavour of the fruit that it's covering. This to my way of thinking implies it's tasteless, which is my experience. Maybe the jam will be better, but first, the trees must fruit.

December 27

Good progress is being made with the driveway, transforming the entrance to the school before our eyes. Among all this activity Stephanie arrives with a bucket full of raspberries. She's been picking out at Tara's Home Stay at Richmond. Tara has an incredibly productive garden and is an enthusiastic preserver.

After a morning of picking in the sweltering heat, they have more raspberries than either of them can handle, and so some have come my way. It's the perfect opportunity to make some truly delicious tangy raspberry cordial.

Raspberry Cordial

500g raspberries
500g sugar
450ml water
3 teaspoons tartaric acid

Place all the ingredients in a pot, bring to the boil and leave to cool. Strain through a sieve, then bottle. Store in the fridge.

Makes about 1.5 litres

Jacob and Charly have a passion for icy poles, which I have been making from either the sparkling fruit drinks or fruit cordial. Today I make a jug of the raspberry cordial, adding water, and some of the pulp that has been strained out and pour this mixture into the icy-pole moulds. This gives the icy poles some texture; they are even more nutritious for the children and I'm not wasting a byproduct.

Did I mention that it's hot here? I mean HOT. At Eaglehawk Neck there were only a very few days of the year when I needed to wear actual summer clothing — trousers and a long-sleeved top or T-shirt were mostly fine. The trees shaded us from the morning sun and the sea breeze came in soon after lunch.

Not here, no way. By 9 a.m. I am looking for cooler clothes. By 11 I've stripped off more, by 2 o'clock I am desperately hot and head inside to the comparative cool and then by 3.30 to 4 p.m. it is beyond oppressive and won't generally cool until late in the evening, if at all.

As uncomfortable as it is at times, I wouldn't trade it really. The fruit and vegetables grow amazingly here. I've had to rethink the vegetable garden, though. The crops I grew at Eaglehawk — broad beans, spinach, kale, peas, Chinese greens and broccoli — all grow so fast they run to seed and the beans are dry in the pods. I find myself looking for cucumber, capsicum, chilli and aubergine plants. Apparently they will grow well in this corner of the valley.

December 29

The tomato bushes are looking quite good so today I decided to take a closer look, now that things have calmed down a little. In actual fact they had grown tremendously and were in dire need of tying to their stakes as many were sending their branches out along the ground.

'What to tie them up with?' became the burning question. I didn't want to go into the hardware store to buy special ties and certainly didn't want to spend the money for such a simple thing. Stockings, I thought, an acceptable alternative.

I don't seem to get out to functions much any more and I hadn't had need of stockings for some considerable time so I sacrificed them for the task of tying. It took every pair I had, duly cut into strips to cater for the tomatoes' screaming need. Hope I don't get an invitation to some high-class event in the near future!

Much to my amazement and delight, the bushes are absolutely smothered in tomatoes. I have several varieties in and will be interested to know how each one performs when it comes to flavour and texture. A very attractive bush is a currant tomato — hundreds of tiny little yellow beads of fruit. I imagine that they will be flavoursome, delicious little morsels to grace any salad. Bottled they would look astounding.

By the time I finished several hours later my hands were green. When I washed them the water turned bright yellow from the pigments from the leaves and abundant flowers.

Tom the cat keeps me company, though helpful he is not. He grabs at the scissors as I cut the stockings, jumps in the tomato bushes and when I move the never-ending hoses he pounces on them and weighs them down as I try to drag the sprinkler from one spot to another.

He has another form of torture for me if he feels I am not giving him enough attention. He races up behind me and grabs me by the legs, or more usually jumps up the back of my legs, digging his claws in. He likes to be carried around in my arms, often grooming himself as we go. He will tolerate my putting him down while I turn the tap on and off, so long as I pick him up immediately again afterwards.

Despite this, he really is adorable and thrives on affection. He appears so thankful we adopted him, as much as any cat can be.

For at least the hundredth time I find myself wondering about his past. I noticed a day or two ago when cleaning out Della's basket that Tom commandeered her pillow for a while, sleeping contentedly. Today we brought down a discarded but almost new basket Ardy had rejected when a kitten. I placed an old towel and a jumper of mine in there. Tom has been asleep there for hours now. It is truly heart-wrenching to see him. He seems so very happy to have a bed of his own. He asks little but gives such affection and light entertainment in return. We are so lucky he has come our way.

January 1

Today some of the family are to come out for a special celebration meal. Stephanie and Courtney exchange gifts in line with their shared passion for making confectionery. Stephanie is actually a watchmaker and gemologist by trade but is an excellent cook and has set up her own little business from home, Steph's Kitchen. She makes jams and preserves, biscuits and cakes to sell to businesses locally and interstate. However, she has always loved making confectionery and since purchasing *Liddabit Sweets Candy Cookbook* it has become even more of an obsession.

The sweets she makes are irresistible — s'mores bars, nougat, chocolate and toffee treats. In an attempt to curb my bad habit of going back to the packets for more, I chopped the last two bars up and made them into choc caramel muffins. Then I couldn't resist the muffins. So much for that idea.

One of the best things about the conversion of the chalet into a commercial kitchen is that it is magnificent for our own cooking purposes. Plenty of bench space, lots of stoves, air-conditioning even.

The girls decide to have a candy-making day in the not-too-distant future.

'What we really need is a candy hook for pulling the toffee,' they say. Of course! And so the search is on. I can't wait for this candy-making day. It harks back to when the children were small and used to make pulled toffee on a piece of marble on the bench top. They did extraordinarily well then. I can only imagine what we can do now with everything that is needed at our fingertips.

January 2

When we lived at Eaglehawk Neck, Robert built me a little stall by the roadside. Given as I am to baking and preserving endlessly, I would fill the stall if not every day, then at least once a week.

This was my plan for Molesworth but I'm afraid the stall has sat by the gate, sad and empty, for months now. The setting up of the cooking school and getting the garden into some sort of order has taken precedence, but finally the time has arrived when I can fill the stall once more.

Stephanie provides some of her preserves to stock the shelves, and I include a range of mine as well. This week there is elderflower cordial, a fresh batch made from the huge flowers from Steph's trees. They make a milder flavoured syrup than those down by the river. She and Robert prefer this; I like both. The first batch was more earthy and floral, whereas the latest batch is lighter in flavour and colour. Either way, they're jolly good.

I am much in love with the organic spelt flour from Callington Mill and am able to order it in 12.5kg bags through the Molesworth Fabulous Foods shop. This lovely, sweet, nutty-flavoured flour makes sensational bread, and is very good for anyone with a touchy tummy, though it's not gluten-free. I make 600g cob loaves for the stall and some flowerpot loaves.

I'm back to baking cakes, scones, muffins and biscuits as well to fill the shelves. Wherever possible I use fruit from the garden, such as today's apricot tartuffins, raspberry and loganberry cup cakes and apricot tea-cake loaves.

I'll be putting out fresh produce from the garden wherever possible — herbs and berries.

January 3

The rhubarb is doing remarkably well — I have some with stalks as thick as double a big man's thumb. Thankfully the rampaging possum that robs our trees at night is leaving it alone. I've planted it out in the bed on the sunny side of the cooking school. It seems to like it there much better than at Eaglehawk Neck where it saw little sunshine. Our friend Mervyn has added to our bounty by providing us with a variety that grows to an immense size. Our pride and joy rhubarb stalks look miniscule beside the monsters these are growing into. It's actually a very attractive combination and looks so striking against the backdrop of the boards of the school and the lush green grass of the lawn alongside it.

This abundant crop of rhubarb can be used in many ways. It lends itself well to many methods of preserving and is well worth capturing in a bottle for use when supply from the garden is lean.

Most of us have memories of rhubarb, an old-fashioned favourite that combines so well with other fruits such as apples and strawberries to make delicious desserts. In our household rhubarb and strawberry cobbler was often on the menu. Back then I used to make an old-fashioned evaporated-milk vanilla ice-cream to serve with it. These days I favour a simple buttermilk-based ice-cream made in my wonderful ice-cream machine. It's a perfect complement to the earthiness of the rhubarb.

Rhubarb and Strawberry Cobbler

1 bunch rhubarb (6—8 stalks), stalks diced
2 tablespoons cornflour
¾ cup sugar or to taste

2 punnets strawberries, hulled
1 teaspoon finely grated lemon zest
1 teaspoon finely grated orange zest
1½ cups self-raising flour
60g butter, melted
1 egg, lightly beaten
⅓ cup milk

Preheat the oven to 180°C. Grease a 20cm casserole dish.

Toss the rhubarb in the cornflour and sugar and place in the prepared dish. Cover the dish with foil and bake for 20–30 minutes. Stir in the strawberries and lemon and orange zest. Check for sweetness and add a little extra sugar if needed.

Mix together the flour, butter, egg and milk and drop dessertspoonfuls of mixture over the fruit. Bake, uncovered, for 20 minutes or until well risen and golden brown.

Serve with vanilla ice-cream or buttermilk vanilla ice-cream.

Serves 6

Buttermilk Ice-cream

¾ cup milk or buttermilk
1½ cups cream
½ cup sugar
2 teaspoons golden syrup
½ teaspoon vanilla-bean paste or vanilla extract

Place all the ingredients in a bowl or jug and whisk until combined. Pour into the pre-chilled ice-cream machine and churn according to the manufacturer's instructions. Spoon the ice-cream into ice-cream containers or trays and freeze. If your containers have no lids, cover the surface closely and tightly with cling wrap.

Makes about 600ml

Personally, I love to bottle bite-sized pieces of rhubarb that can later be used to decorate a fruit flan or go straight into a dessert. It looks so very attractive in the bottles on the pantry shelf, especially if a red-stalked variety is used.

For the last year or two we have also grown the green-stalked variety. These stalks are much thicker and have a stronger flavour.

I've learned recently that to peel rhubarb stalks (as is sometimes needed if the stalks are really stringy), do so from the base end upwards. And while rhubarb leaves are poisonous because of the oxalic acid they contain, they need not be wasted. They can be boiled up and used as a spray to kill aphids on roses. Robert and I tried this once not long after we were married, adding the recommended Lux soap flakes for good measure. I note these days that recipes for the spray do not include a generous amount of garlic as ours did. We proudly sprayed the roses and it did indeed kill all the aphids in record time.

Within days however the spray on the rose bushes developed a putrid odour that deterred any visitors — even neighbours crossed the street as they passed by our house. Maybe it was the fact that we sprayed in the middle of summer, or maybe the garlic was the culprit — either way it was not good and took a couple of weeks to disperse. No more aphids on the roses though.

Have you noticed how when you stew up red rhubarb the colour diminishes and the purée is more green than red? I used to make it for a café whose customers insisted that the rhubarb purée served with panna cotta be red. You can add red food colouring, but by far the better choice is to purchase some beetroot powder (spice shops generally stock it). A mere pinch of the powder will transform about 2 cupfuls of purée to a rich and natural scarlet, and the taste of beetroot is indiscernible.

Bottled Rhubarb

Follow the basic method (see page 385). Bring the temperature up to 88°C over the space of 50 minutes, then hold at this temperature for a further 50 minutes.

Alternatively, if you have a thermostat-controlled preserver, set the temperature to 88°C and leave for 1 hour 40 minutes.

Freezing Rhubarb

Simply cut the stalks into 2.5cm pieces and pack into freezer bags or plastic containers. You can add sugar before freezing if you like, up to 250g per kilo of rhubarb. However, if there is a chance you may use the rhubarb for jam later, then don't add sugar. You can stew it before freezing in plastic containers, leaving about 1.5cm headspace to allow for expansion as it freezes.

Dehydrating Rhubarb

Try making rhubarb fruit leather sheets. It's a good idea to include some apple to help to counteract the tartness of the rhubarb. Keep in mind that natural sugars are concentrated as the purée dries so little if any sweetening is needed; 1 teaspoon honey per cup of purée is more than ample. Once the sheets are dried, roll up, snip into short lengths and store in airtight containers or jars. Freeze them if not used within three weeks.

Rhubarb Syrup

For best colour use red rhubarb stalks. It doesn't matter if you use older, tougher stalks and there is no need to peel them.

Use as a cordial syrup: 1 part syrup to 4–5 parts water or soda water. Try adding to sparkling white wine for a delicious simple cocktail with a twist of lime or lemon.

For a mocktail use lemonade in place of the wine, along with a splash of lime or lemon juice.

1.5kg rhubarb, chopped
6 cups water
sugar
30ml cider vinegar
2 teaspoons tartaric acid

Place the rhubarb and water in a large saucepan and bring to the boil, then simmer for 15 minutes. Strain the mixture through a colander, then the resulting liquid through a sieve lined with muslin.

For each cup of liquid add 1 cup sugar. Bring back to the boil and simmer for 2 minutes. Stir in the vinegar and tartaric acid. Pour into warm sterilised bottles and seal immediately.

Store in a cool, dry and dark place. In warm climates it would be best to store in the fridge. Always refrigerate after opening, regardless of climate.

Makes about 3 litres

Today I have no time to make any jam, but there will be plenty later on if the patch keeps producing at this incredible rate. For jam, it's best to combine rhubarb with other fruits such as raspberries or cooking apples to lift the pectin content. It is lovely combined with ginger and/ or strawberry also.

January 3

The heat has arrived with even greater force. It started out quite cool this morning, but by lunchtime it was oppressive again. I've watered the garden as far as I can with bore water, but it's so hot that it's proving futile.

The wind came up this afternoon — my goodness, what a wind! The fire danger must be huge, matched as the wind is to this heat. I fear for the garden that I've carefully cossetted over the last few months. I think of the cool summer breeze of Eaglehawk Neck but our friend Dave, one of the neighbours down there, tells me that it is similarly hot and dry. Even with their advanced water storage and sprinkler system, they have still had to buy a large load of water.

There is no time for stressing, however. Produce is coming in thick and fast from the garden. There are buckets and buckets of tomatoes — red and yellow and even some green that have prematurely fallen from the bushes.

They are matched by an astounding number of zucchinis and cucumbers.

Recipes will need to be developed to incorporate these so they don't go to waste. The following recipe has proven invaluable.

Tomato and Zucchini Relish

If your zucchini have seeds in the middle, remove them before using in this recipe.

1kg tomatoes, chopped
1kg zucchini flesh, diced
3 medium-sized onions, peeled and chopped
1 apple, cored and diced
2 tablespoons salt
3 teaspoons mustard powder
3 teaspoons curry powder
500g sugar
3 cups white or cider vinegar
1 tablespoon cornflour
¼ cup vinegar, extra

Place the tomatoes, zucchini, onions, apple, salt, mustard powder, curry powder, sugar and vinegar into a large saucepan. Bring to the boil, stirring until sugar is dissolved, and continue to boil for 1½ hours.

Mix the cornflour to a paste with the extra vinegar,
add some or all to the boiling mixture and stir until
thickened. Pour into sterilised jars and seal immediately.

Makes about 2kg

January 4

The temperature is supposed to rise to 39 degrees today, with strong winds. This is a somewhat fear-inspiring prospect and already a hint of smoke is in the air from a bushfire burning out of control at Lake Repulse.

On our farm the hoses are keeping things green and last night we were at last able to pick a couple of kilos of raspberries and loganberries. I have some raspberries in the fridge that need to be used, maybe about 300g. We also picked some whitecurrants from a small bush we brought with us from the Neck.

I'm not a big fan of combining different types of berries in general, or mixing them with other fruits. I think it does them an injustice, and they should stand on their own without confusion on the palate. But given the small quantities of both raspberries and currants, maybe I'll give this a try. The currants would add a little texture as well as acidity.

I was just about to add the sugar when I remembered my grandmother's words — 'Don't add the sugar before the currants are really soft. Otherwise they will turn out to be as tough as boot buttons.'

Her advice was always good, so I hold off for a few more minutes to be sure. Texture is one thing, tooth-breaking currants quite another.

I am extremely pleased with result; it has turned out even better than I'd anticipated.

Raspberry and Whitecurrant Jam

You could substitute redcurrants for the white in this recipe.

300g raspberries
180g whitecurrants

¼ cup water
500g sugar

Place the raspberries and currants with the water into
a saucepan and bring slowly to the boil, then simmer
until the currants are just soft.

Stir in the sugar and bring back to the boil,
stirring, then boil over a medium–high heat for
about 10 minutes or until setting point is reached
(see page 393).

Makes about 750g

Today has also been the day to seek out produce for our Sunday class. I
would dearly love to be able to use Tasmanian apricots but the season is
slow starting this year so I compromise and buy some from one of the
large retail outlets.

I bought nectarines as well — maybe to bottle, maybe to jam or
chutney, and stopped at the tomato farm to pick up a couple of boxes of
tomatoes and a large bunch of basil.

By now there is news of fires starting in the south of Tasmania —
one up towards Hamilton, another large one at Forcett, heading rapidly
towards the Tasman Peninsula. Bushfire smoke is thickening in the air
and there seems to be a sense of foreboding. Does this hark back to the
1967 bushfires, the memory of which still remains so strong?

This sense of impending danger and disaster is further reinforced
when our friend Tony arrives. A resident of the Tasman Peninsula, he
was in Hobart for appointments but had been unable to return — the
road had been closed due to the fires. Accommodation around Hobart
was quickly booked out by people in a similar situation and so he had
nowhere to stay. We were delighted to see him, although we wish the
circumstances were different for him.

January 5

On a trip into Hobart this morning we noticed a sign near the river, *Apricots for Sale*. A sign from this particular property means Moor Park apricots, which in my opinion is the best of all varieties. Not wanting them to spoil in the heat of the car, we decide we'll stop in on the way home.

Unfortunately by that time the sign has disappeared. I am so disappointed that Robert suggests I go and ask if I can pick some from the still-laden trees of the orchard. After a less-than-welcoming greeting from the dog, the owner comes out. He'd taken the sign down as he had sold out, except for one bucketful.

I buy it — the bucket is even thrown into the price. The apricots are small due to the dry weather but full of flavour and juice trickles down your chin as you bite into them. I'm not sorry I bought the others, however, as they will provide a contrast that demonstrates to the class of a few days' time the superiority of the Moor Park variety.

January 8

This is turning out to be a busy day. Stephanie decides to come along to assist with the bottling class, which is wonderful. Tony, our 'fire refugee', the term applied to those who cannot return to the Tasman Peninsula, is still with us.

He is worried and anxious to be home. The situation with the Dunalley fires is horrific — over 100 homes, community buildings and agricultural structures have been destroyed in their wake. Media coverage reveals the plight of one family who had to shelter for five hours in the water under a jetty to escape the fires' fury.

Tony is using his super-abundant energy to pass the time by cleaning my windows (a long overdue task), putting out and bringing in the washing and generally cleaning. This is so good, as housework is always such a trial for me.

Not only that, he looks after Jacob and Charly. Every house

should have a Tony come to stay, though not under such unfortunate circumstances for him.

Courtney and her boyfriend Matthew arrive and Courtney helps with the children, pops in and out of the class and fetches things from the house for me. The thing about the classes is that we ad-lib. If something outside what we have planned takes our fancy, we'll give it a try.

Scones are part of the morning tea for each session, made fresh using my super-simple recipe. Lois, one of the participants, asks if I've made lemonade scones. I have, but I don't like the sweetness.

'Could you use soda water instead then?' she logically asks.

Well, I hadn't thought of that, so although the scones have just been set on the tray to cook, we made another batch with soda water for comparison.

The end result? Yes, the soda-water ones are definitely lighter. All credit to Lois.

Soda Water Scones

3 cups self-raising flour
a pinch of salt
1 teaspoon baking powder
1 cup cream
1 cup soda water

Preheat the oven to 180°C. Line or grease a baking sheet.

Mix together the flour, salt and baking powder (no need to sift, just make sure they are combined well). Make a well in the centre and pour in the cream and about three-quarters of the soda water. Mix to a soft dough, adding the last of the soda water if needed.

Turn out onto a lightly floured board and shape into a rectangle approximately 1.5cm thick. Cut into rounds with a cutter (dip into flour before cutting each scone) and place side by side on the baking sheet.

Bake for 15–20 minutes until well risen, cooked through and golden.

Makes 12–16 scones

Over scones our conversation turns to rhubarb. Stephanie tells how she makes and sells rhubarb and raspberry jam. It just so happens that I have a few spare raspberries, picked by Robert just an hour ago. Many of the rhubarb plants under the kitchen window now have very large stalks. Before we know it, we are all chopping away and the jam is in the pot. It takes little time to get to setting point as the produce is so fresh, and is pronounced delicious as it's heaped on scones with whipped cream.

Stephanie's Rhubarb and Raspberry Jam

1kg rhubarb, diced
500g raspberries
¼ cup water
juice of 1 lemon or ½ teaspoon citric acid
1.5kg sugar

Place the rhubarb, raspberries, water and lemon juice or citric acid in a pot and bring to the boil, stirring. Cook for 10–15 minutes over a gentle heat until the rhubarb is soft.

Add the sugar and bring back to the boil, stirring. Boil briskly for 15–20 minutes until setting point is reached (see page 393). Stand for 5 minutes, then pour into warm sterilised jars and seal immediately.

Makes about 2.25kg

There's rhubarb left over so we decide to demonstrate how to make sparkling rhubarb. One problem emerges: I don't have a lemon, but by this stage it's too far along in the making to forget the idea. What to do? Substitute another stick of rhubarb (weighing 140g) and see what happens. (When we drink it a few days later, we find it's equally delicious.)

Sparkling Rhubarb

1kg rhubarb, diced
875g sugar
4.5 litres cold water
220ml cider or white vinegar

Place all the ingredients in a food-safe bucket, mix well, then cover with a tea towel and leave to stand at room temperature for 48 hours.

Strain through a fine nylon kitchen sieve and pour into PET bottles and seal immediately. (Empty soft-drink bottles are ideal, or you can buy new ones from home-brewing suppliers.)

The sparkling rhubarb will be ready in 2 weeks. Open carefully — it's best to refrigerate it before opening.

Makes about 4.5 litres

This group has been a riot — full of fun and great ideas. So far by way of preserves we have made raspberry jam, blackcurrant cordial, lemon cordial, spelt bread, apricot chutney, zucchini pickle and rhubarb and raspberry jam.

Amid the mêlée, Stephanie returned home and came back with her s'mores bars, which are salty, nutty caramel nougat, all coated with chocolate.

During the class we also got a call from Nick from the tomato farm, who said he had five boxes of sauce tomatoes. Did we want them? What a question — of course! So Stephanie went to collect those as well.

January 9

Today is the day of our annual pilgrimage to Chris and Sally's farm (Richmond Cherries) to pick Morello cherries. Nestled at one end of his huge orchards of sweet cherries sit three Morello trees, comparatively untended and growing with wild abandon.

The quality of the cherries is astounding. They've actually been ripe for days and I fear with the heat that they will be little more than squishy blobs, but they are absolutely perfect, the best ever.

I love Morellos for their sharpness, so good for tarts and especially Black Forest cakes. Alistair has said he would like some for his shop — they will turn up in his exquisite cakes, pastries and ice-cream. Sally and I pick for a couple of hours and still we have only touched one tree. I have filled six 5-litre containers, as well as two 10-litre buckets. They look like jewels, so pretty in their varying shades of ripeness.

On the way home I stop in at Alistair's Sweet Envy. He takes the 5-litre containers and I head for home to make plans for the rest.

January 10

There's fruit everywhere here, what an abundance! At least four metres of the bench space in the school is piled high. Time to preserve the produce left over from the classes — the cherries, nectarines and tomatoes. It's going to be a day of it. Excellent!

The Morello cherries, while not so good as an eating cherry, are really nice bottled, and make superb jam.

Bottled Morello Cherries

Use the basic method for preserving by bottling (see page 385). Bring the temperature up to 85°C over 50 minutes, then hold at this temperature for 1¼ hours. If you have a thermostat-controlled preserver, turn on to this temperature and leave for 2 hours.

Freezing Morello Cherries

Simply package in freezer bags or containers and place
in freezer. They can be frozen on trays so that they
are free flowing when you take them out, but as they
separate quite easily anyway, it's not difficult to break
them apart for what you need.

I'd been told about a jam that is a combination of boysenberries and
Kentish cherries, reputedly very nice. I have some Morello cherries
left and, spurred on by the success of the raspberry and whitecurrant
jam, decide to experiment with making another combination jam. The
raspberry canes are producing really well, so I combine these with the
remaining cherries.

I am up to my elbows in tomatoes and juice, Morellos and sugar,
not to mention apricots and nectarines. Tony. Yes, ask him to pip the
Morellos. What a tedious task to inflict on him, but he does it. The result
is even better than the raspberry and currant jam, and certainly worth
making, even if you do have to pip your own cherries.

Morello and Raspberry Jam

This jam is truly wonderful. The cherries add an
indefinable flavour and lovely texture.

500g Morello cherries (pipped weight)
400g raspberries
800g sugar

Place the fruit in a large saucepan or jam pan and
bring to the boil over a medium–low heat, stirring
occasionally. Simmer for 10 minutes, then stir in the
sugar and bring to the boil, stirring.

Boil briskly over a medium–high heat until setting
point is reached (see page 393). Allow to stand

5 minutes, then pour into warm sterilised jars and seal immediately.

Makes about 1.5 litres

January 10

The nectarines I bought at one of the larger fruit markets are a great disappointment. They have obviously been picked green as they didn't ripen and just started going mouldy on the outside while the flesh remains rock hard. So much for preserving them!

I toss any half-decent ones into a pot with some sugar and water and stew them up. They soften a bit but go a nasty shade of grey instead of a lovely scarlet. I tried serving them to Robert for dessert and he politely tried to eat them (as did I) but they were a write-off. Abominable, as I hate waste. No wonder they were going cheap. At least the chickens will probably enjoy them or it's the last step — compost heap.

This is such a disappointment as nectarines are a wonderful fruit when grown and picked correctly. They can be used as you do peaches and make excellent jam and bottled fruit, chutney even.

By the end of the day I have one unholy mess in the cooking school kitchen, but a great deal accomplished. Adding to the general confusion is the sparkling rhubarb still needing to be strained and bottled, as well as the remaining lemon cordial and blackcurrant cordial.

Stephanie, an avid and expert bargain hunter, found Shiploads had very attractive preserving bottles, and cheap at that. Robert stopped off and bought many boxes for me; they will need to be housed somewhere in the kitchen, not an easy task to find the space.

All goes well until I go to bottle the blackcurrant cordial. It has turned to jelly and I know it's my fault. The 8 January class was such fun that I'd paid little heed to how long the blackcurrants and water boiled for, and how hard it boiled. Worse, I'd paid no attention to how long or hard the mixture boiled once the sugar was added. I'd poured a sample for each of the women to take away in lovely little narrow-necked bottles, in which it would now be firmly stuck as a semi-set jelly. How embarrassing.

I always remind people that blackcurrants are high in acid and pectin and so must barely simmer; at most, you don't want the cordial to have this predisposition to gel. What a pity I didn't obey my own rules.

Well, no time to fret, so I boil it for a few minutes more and pour it into jars. It will make lovely blackcurrant firm-set jelly for toast or scones.

If this does happen to you by the way (that the cordial has set in the bottle), just melt it down again by placing the bottles in a jug of hot water or microwave in short bursts of about 20 seconds until the jelly's melted. AND, just in case, whenever you make it, it's a good idea to pour the finished product into wider-necked bottles.

I have found recently that the cordial is less likely to set if you make larger batches, but always keep to the rule of barely simmer rather than boil.

Berry or Blackcurrant Cordial Syrup

3kg berries or blackcurrants
3 litres water
sugar
2 level teaspoons citric or tartaric acid
90ml white or cider vinegar

Place the berries and water in a large saucepan and bring to the boil. Simmer *very* gently for 10 minutes. Strain through a colander, and the resulting liquid through a kitchen sieve lined with a layer of muslin (a clean tea towel will do).

For each cup of liquid add 1 cup sugar. Bring to the boil, then reduce the heat immediately to a bare simmer and cook 2 minutes more. Stir in the citric acid, pour into sterilised bottles and seal immediately.

The cordial will keep at room temperature but in warmer weather or climates it would be best to keep it in the fridge. In either case, refrigerate the bottle once it is opened.

Makes about 5 litres

Blackcurrant Jam

2kg blackcurrants
1 litre water
3kg sugar

Remove stalks from the blackcurrants and place in a large saucepan or jam pan with the water. Bring to the boil, then cook for 10 minutes or until tender.

Add the sugar and bring back to the boil, stirring. Boil hard until setting point is reached, about 15 minutes.

Allow to stand for 5 minutes, then pour into warm sterilised jars and seal immediately.

Makes about 3kg

January 11

I am known for being clumsy and today seems to be one of those days. Early this morning I dropped and broke one of the knobs on the stove in the house. I should have known this would be a downward slide. My Nan used to tell me that trouble goes in threes.

There have been lots of classes now, most of them filled to capacity. We always have such a good time. During today's class, for morning tea, I made an apricot and raspberry cake, a bit of a house speciality. It came time to turn the cake out onto the cooler, then to invert it onto another rack to sprinkle on the topping. It turned out fine, but when I went to turn it over, the cake coolers being pristine and new (and, I forgot, non-stick), it slipped unceremoniously from between them and landed on the bench in a blob. Oh well, at least it wasn't the floor I guess.

It wasn't my finest hour and worse still, the students took a photo of the cake in its compromised state. They said it made them feel better about things that happen to them. I fear they were being much too kind …

The cake was patched back together, duly buttered and cinnamoned and sugared on top, and served in large chunks with cream. The flavour was unaffected, thank goodness.

This is a very easy cake to bake; really it's just a glorified teacake, but becomes a lovely, rich continental cake when fruit is placed on the mixture before baking and the top sprinkled with butter, cinnamon and sugar after the cake comes out of the oven.

Apricot and Berry Cake

You could substitute peaches or nectarines for the apricots in this recipe.

> *1 egg*
> *¾ cup sugar*
> *¾ cup milk*
> *1½ cups self-raising flour*
> *60g butter, melted*
> *grated zest of 1 lemon (optional)*
> *fresh, preserved or tinned apricot halves*
> *½ cup fresh or frozen berries*
> *30g extra melted butter*
> *2 teaspoons extra sugar*
> *½–1 teaspoon ground cinnamon*

Preheat the oven to 160°C. Grease a deep 20cm round tin and line the base with baking paper.

Whisk the egg and sugar, then add the milk, flour and melted butter. Whisk until smooth. Add the grated lemon zest, if using.

Pour the mixture into the tin. Top with the apricot halves, cut side down, and berries, and bake for 30 minutes until a skewer inserted into the centre comes out clean.

Leave the cake to stand in the tin for a few minutes, then turn out onto a cake cooler. Turn the right way up again (carefully), then brush with melted butter. Sprinkle liberally with cinnamon and sugar.

Serve warm with ice-cream and/or custard. The cake is also delicious served cold.

Makes 1 20cm cake

Tom had his part to play on this fateful day. He is such a joy to have around and everyone loves his life story of the wild cat gone tame. Gazing as we were out of the window at the raspberry patch, of which I am very proud I might add, we saw Tom sitting in the grass, then followed his stare of sheer concentration.

'How cute!' was the consensus of all those looking at how still he was. In a split second Tom sprang into the top of the raspberry canes and came out with a mouthful of parrot feathers. He'd seen the offending bird feeding on the fruit. I was so glad he missed his prey — murder in the raspberry patch is not exactly the look I had in mind for the school.

He spent the rest of the day prowling, looking to find the one that got away — through the berry patch and on the roof, wherever he could get to.

Now, at the end of the day, I can look back and think that at least the main goals were reached, despite all the mishaps.

January 12

For many years on the Tasman Peninsula our friend John has provided me with Rocoto chillies. They are also called 'Hot Lips' and for good reason. The fruit matures from green though purple to red, and ranges in heat from medium hot to very hot depending on the weather.

John is deservedly very proud of a recipe he's put together for a hot sauce made from them, a recipe he's passed on to me. His tree is magnificent to say the least — we actually measured it once — 3 metres high and 8 metres around and producing thousands of chillies throughout the year.

When John found out we were moving he made it his mission to get me a Rocoto chilli tree to plant at our new home. He found one in a plant nursery just as we were about to leave — Stephanie picked it up for us and nursed it to health inside the house.

When we moved here it was icy cold outside and not at all suitable for Rocco, as I have come to call him, so he sat on the coffee table by the window in the lounge room. He grew to an immense size, almost reaching to the top of the window frame, and in fact would have reached the very high ceiling if I didn't trim him back.

On warmer days I lugged him outside to sit in the sun, buffeted only by the gentlest of breezes. However, any time I did this he objected violently and sulked for at least a week, dropping leaves all over the lounge-room floor. Is it possible for a plant to throw a tantrum? he makes me wonder.

Finally it was time for him to move out. I prepared a lovely sunny bed for him with nice sandy but well-fed soil and planted him there. Well, after weeks and weeks of considerable misery of countenance, he at last is starting to rally. There are new green leaves and even a flower or two, even if they are a bit pathetic. Nevertheless I feel rewarded for carting bucketfuls of water to him each day and keeping the roots weed-free.

I don't know if he will ever grow into a productive giant of a bush like John's, but I am hopeful that one day he will provide at least some chillies.

Incidentally, I provided a friend at Robert's work with some of the Rocoto chillies. He loves his chillies hot so went home and made a dish akin to stuffed capsicums. I thought the heat would burn his mouth terribly, but he said they were sensational.

For those who love a really hot sweet chilli sauce, this is the way to go.

The chillies can be frozen, as this is what I did with the last of the ones we picked at John's house. I just freeze them whole in a plastic bag.

John's Rocoto Chilli Sauce

150g of long red chillies could be substituted for
the Rocoto chillies here, though you may be able to
purchase Rocotos, under their other name, Hot Lips.

100g Rocoto chillies
2 medium-sized red capsicum
2 teaspoons sesame oil
2 teaspoons salt
2 cups sugar
2 cups white or cider vinegar
2 cloves garlic, crushed
2 teaspoons grated fresh green ginger
3 teaspoons cornflour mixed to a paste with 2 tablespoons
  extra vinegar

Remove the stalks and seeds from the chillies and dice
the flesh. Remove the stalks and membranes from the
capsicum and dice. Cook gently in the sesame oil for 3
minutes, then add the rest of the ingredients except for
the cornflour paste. Bring to the boil, stirring often, then
boil quite briskly for 30 minutes. While still boiling, stir
in the cornflour paste and cook for 5 minutes more.

Pour into warm sterilised jars and seal immediately.

Makes about 1 litre

One of the most popular recipes in *A Year in a Bottle* was the one for
sweet chilli sauce. Since that was written, I've simplified the method so
it's quicker and easier.

Above all other preserves, with the possible exception of raspberry
jam, I'd recommend keeping a supply of this in the cupboard. It is a
wonderful addition to gravies and jus, braises and simply poured over
sour cream or cream cheese as a quick dip.

Sweet Chilli Sauce

250g long red chillies, chopped into 3 pieces
4cm piece ginger, very roughly chopped (no need to peel)
10 cloves garlic, peeled
3 cups sugar
3 cups white or cider vinegar
2 teaspoons salt
3 teaspoons cornflour mixed to a paste with 2 tablespoons
*   extra vinegar*

Place the chillies, ginger and garlic in the bowl of a food processor and process until chopped very finely (but not to a paste). Place in a saucepan with the sugar, vinegar and salt.

Bring to the boil, stirring, then cook over a medium heat for 20 minutes. Add the cornflour and vinegar paste and stir until thickened slightly. Allow to stand in the pot for 10 minutes, then pour into sterilised jars and seal immediately.

Makes about 750ml

January 13

The alpacas Charlotte and Clarence have been very happy here and have kept us endlessly entertained for months. They are obviously uncomfortable with their woolly coats as the summer gets hotter. The bathtubs that contain their drinking water have also served as baths for them. They immerse the entire front half of their body in an effort to cool down. Clarence has so much wool that when he steps out again the bathtub is half empty.

The shearer hasn't had a lot of experience with alpacas, he tells us, he usually shears sheep. But the owner is a friend and has spoken to him, and Stephanie has told him how uncomfortable the alpacas are, so he is coming today.

I suspect this will be a bit of a drama, especially with strong-headed Charlotte. Shearer Kerry brings tranquilliser injections to calm their nerves so that they are manageable. Charlotte takes her injections like a dream, but the usually calm Clarence is quite another thing. He spits in all directions — well that's not strictly true: the person who gets hit the most is ever-helpful son-in-law Nat.

Finally the injections are successfully administered and Clarence calms down while Charlotte is sheared uneventfully.

When it came to Clarence's turn, the injection seemed to wear off immediately. Maybe he hasn't been shorn before; his coat is thick with dirt and sand where he has been rolling in a dust bath to cool down. Comb after comb is blunted on him. He is so terrified, poor thing, that eventually he has to be restrained with ropes around his legs: there is nothing else for it. Even so, in the process he manages to land a fearful kick on the shearer's nose.

Once shorn it could be seen that his toenails badly need trimming, so the secateurs from the shed were called upon.

Finally the task was done. They both look so skinny but seem to hold no grudges. Kerry has taken the blow to his nose in his stride. Clarence goes off to find patches of green grass to feed on now that he can see properly without all that wool around his eyes. Needless to say, Nat has headed to the shower.

We all sit down to afternoon tea afterwards, a mega-feast actually, our promise to Kerry. He tells us he will only shear these two alpacas in the future; alpacas are known for their feistiness. I'm relieved to hear Kerry will return — a brave man indeed, and obviously not holding a grudge against Clarence.

We know that Charlotte and Clarence simply cannot eat all the grass in the paddocks despite their grazing from dawn to dark. Kerry has a very agreeable solution for us. He has sheep he needs to bring from his property around the east coast at Triabunna. They will need a place to stay. And so it is arranged for them to come here in a few weeks' time.

January 15

I've come to realise that if I wait for eight people to sign up for each class the school will never take off — I've only managed that number a few times so far. So, rather than sit idle, I've decided to do classes for parties of two to eight. I'm always cooking, preserving or baking anyway. I'll really enjoy having company to do so. Today is such an example, and the participants want to try their hand at baking their own bread.

This gives me the opportunity to bring out my old wheat grinder. This was given to me by a friend about 35 years ago. It is an American-made electric grinder, given to him by an elderly man who no longer had use for it.

At the time I had no real appreciation for it, I admit. I felt it was too ugly to grace the bench top, but did at least recognise that it had potential, so stored it away in the shed or under the house for about 30 years.

I happened to purchase some organic whole wheat from a supplier and thought I'd try the machine out. It was hauled out from the shed and years of accumulated dust fastidiously removed. I was delighted to find that as it grinds the wheat it sends up a fine haze of flour all around, aura-like, which changed its complexion entirely. Within days I found the flour it grinds is especially good for bread and for starting a sourdough plant.

The following recipe was soon developed. If you don't have access to a wheat grinder, you can use very fresh organic wholemeal flour, which you will most likely need to purchase from a health-food shop.

Sourdough Starter and Loaf

STARTER
½ cup organic stone-ground whole wheat flour
¾ cup warm water
extra flour
extra warm water

BREAD

2 cups organic plain flour
¾ cup organic stone-ground whole wheat flour
½ teaspoon salt
2 teaspoons sugar
2 teaspoons oil
1 cup Sourdough Starter

To make the Starter, combine the flour and water in a glass bowl and mix well. Cover loosely with muslin and put the bowl outside, bringing it in once the cool of the evening sets in.

Each day, feed it with 2 tablespoons more of the flour and 2–3 tablespoons warm water. Continue this process for about 2 weeks. After 10 days it is good to switch to rye flour as the wheat proteins can sometimes be too complex for the plant and it may become sluggish.

To make the Bread, in a large bowl combine all the ingredients with a little extra warm water to make a soft dough, then cover with a tea towel. Leave to rise in the bowl overnight (cover the bowl with a tea towel).

Preheat the oven to 200°C. Grease a deep 20cm round tin, line the base with baking paper and grease again.

Turn out the dough onto a lightly floured bench, sprinkle with flour and knead briefly. Place the dough in the tin.

Cover with a tea towel and allow to rise almost to the top of the tin, then bake at 200°C for 15 minutes, then reduce the temperature to 170°C for a further 40 minutes. Turn out to cool on a wire rack.

Makes 1 loaf, to serve 6

January 16

It's reportedly going to be super hot again tomorrow; no surprise there, so the extreme fire danger is by no means past. In fact dire warnings are given for the Derwent Valley, which is pretty scary.

This weekend my mother comes to visit from Queensland — I would love for the grass to look green and lush when she gets here, to show the property at its best. However, the wind roaring up the valley combined with the heat almost negates any amount of watering with the bore. I fear it is doomed to being dry and brown.

I need produce and will contact Kirkwood Orchards at Campania. They have an incredible number of varieties of stone fruits. I may even need to go out there within the next day or two, even though it's premature for the next class. During the last bout of heat like this 90 per cent of the apricots in one of the close-by orchards were cooked on the trees. Others also lost many of their cherries. I don't want to be left empty-handed.

I have tomatoes galore, access to as many as I need, and have many kilos frozen. I will need to turn the frozen ones into sauce as tomorrow the pork that Jay the butcher promised arrives. I will need the freezer space. Stephanie and I are sharing the pork, so I will make the sauce as we go, with the packing and mincing and even, potentially, sausage-making.

The berry patch is still producing very abundantly. I am not a great fruit picker — I am renowned for missing many — and so usually leave this task to Robert. However, in the relatively cooler evening I decide to help out as the crop today is larger than usual. I thought we had raspberries and loganberries and a smattering of strawberries, but on close inspection I see that there are also youngberries, and another trellis just fruiting turns out to be boysenberries.

Boysenberries have fearful thorns, large and small, but are worth the picking as the fruit is delicious. They can be used in the same way as loganberries, so you could follow the recipes on pages 73–74, simply substituting boysenberries. Their flavour is richer and slightly more tart.

When used in cooking, they hold their shape better. Incidentally, if you want the berries (or any fruit) to hold its shape when stewing, add the sugar sooner rather than later.

January 17

This morning I make a trip into Glenorchy to rendezvous with Robert and to pick up Jay's pork. Jay is very mindful that pork is similar to chicken in that it needs to be frozen or at least refrigerated as soon as possible. He started work at 4 a.m. and left the pork in an esky for Robert to collect.

When I return home I have barely entered the house when our next-door neighbour visits with an apology for not coming sooner. He has brought me two bags of cherries. By cherries I don't mean just any ordinary cherries — these are HUGE, an experiment he has been working on, allowing the cherries to ripen to perfection and to such a size to see if any rot develops and, if so, how to overcome the issue.

Well, there is no rot to be seen in these beauties — dark red of skin and flesh as they are. They explode with juice in your mouth and so are ideal for eating. However, there are more than enough with which to experiment as well. I've not had a great deal of success with cherry jam in the past, and I am out of preserving jars at the moment — over 300 empty ones still sit on the shelves at Eaglehawk Neck. Robert will retrieve them this weekend.

By now our neighbour Rosemary has become our very good friend. I found out recently that it was she who left those much-appreciated donations of eggs, apples, pears and walnuts in our early days here. She has not diminished in her generosity and today she too brings me large, dark, luscious cherries, more magnificent specimens.

All things considered, I think it's an opportune time to try making the jam again. It is notoriously hard to get cherry jam to set, but I have a little trick I've developed for strawberry jam that just might cross over to cherry.

Citric or tartaric acid, natural products, help boost the acid levels which in turn promotes the release of pectin in the fruit. This will be especially important in these varieties of eating cherries.

You will note that there is less sugar than usual. This is because cherries are low in pectin. The rule of thumb is, less pectin, use less sugar — higher pectin levels need more sugar.

Dark Cherry Jam

1kg cherries
1 teaspoon citric or tartaric acid
¾ cup water
850g sugar

Pip the cherries and tie them in a piece of muslin (or any thin cloth) with string.

Place the cherries, bag of pips, citric acid and water in a large saucepan and bring to the boil, stirring often. Simmer for 20 minutes, remove the bag of pips, pressing out all the juice as you go and then add the sugar to the pot.

Bring to the boil, stirring, and boil over medium heat, stirring frequently until setting point is reached, about 20 minutes. Leave to stand for 10 minutes, then pour into warm sterilised jars and seal immediately.

Turn jars upside down for 15 minutes, then invert to right way up — this helps the cherries to stay evenly distributed through the jam, rather than rise to the top.

Makes about 1.75kg

Bottled Sweet Cherries

All varieties of cherries can be bottled in exactly the same way as Morello cherries so you can follow the same recipe (see page 112).

Freezing Cherries

To freeze so that they are free flowing, spread in a single layer on a tray and freeze. Then pack in freezer bags or containers in the freezer.

Alternatively, for solid pack, place in sealed freezer bags or containers in the freezer.

You can pip them if you want, though it's a somewhat tedious process. Sometimes they can be purchased already pipped from farmers' markets.

Our friend Sally had a special large pipping machine made to process cherries from their orchards. During summer Sally has a stall at the Hobart Farmers' Market. When I went to buy a bagful of the cherries from her one Sunday morning, the machine was in full swing, pouring the pipped fruit into bags. Some of the juice escaped into the surrounding air and Sally was covered from top to toe in tiny scarlet dots, a truly pretty sight.

Dehydrating Cherries

I find pipped is best. Place the cherries on racks over a tray if dehydrating in the oven. Dry at 70°C until no liquid is exuded if the flesh is torn. Alternatively use a food dehydrator.

Store in an airtight container in the fridge, or in the freezer.

Bottled Cherries with Brandy

Again, follow the recipe for bottling Morello cherries (see page 112).

To each litre jar, add 2 tablespoons brandy. If you use jars with smaller or greater capacity, adjust the amount of brandy accordingly.

For many years I've wanted to make and have had many requests for Cherry Chutney and so have tried to put together a recipe. For all my best efforts I've not had any success, the end product being ordinary at best and foul at worst.

This year Stephanie came up with a simple, effective and truly delicious solution. She cleverly substituted pipped cherries for the plums used in my plum sauce recipe from *A Year in a Bottle*. Anyone who tastes it becomes an instant fan.

It's especially delicious served with pork or ham.

Stephanie's Cherry Sauce

3kg sweet cherries (pipped weight)
1.5kg sugar
6 cups cider vinegar
500g onion, peeled and chopped
6 cloves garlic, peeled and chopped
3 teaspoons salt
1 tablespoon grated ginger
3 teaspoons ground allspice
2 teaspoons ground cloves
1 teaspoon ground cinnamon
½ teaspoon chilli flakes
1 teaspoon mustard powder
juice of 1 lemon

Place all ingredients in a large saucepan or jam pan and stir over medium heat until the sugar is dissolved and the mixture is boiling. Continue to boil for 2 hours or until the mixture is thick, stirring often.

Strain through a colander, food mill or coarse sieve. Bring back to the boil, then pour into warm sterilised bottles and seal immediately.

You can use the same recipe for **Plum Sauce**, using plums in place of the cherries. Any sort of plum will do, though probably not cherry plums.

Makes about 2.8 litres

Despite all this preserving, yet more cherries remain, with the promise of more on the way. In a few days I will have a preserves class here and so decide to make up a batch of sparkling fruit drink as the weather is bound to be hot.

As there are not enough cherries for a full batch, I head for the rhubarb patch, which is still producing prolifically. The rhubarb will provide the pink colour that the black cherries will enhance. I'm still somewhat short on weight, so I add some frozen Morello cherries, picked the week before at Chris and Sally's orchard. They will provide more colour as well as a delightful acidity. For good measure, and thinking that an extra zesty touch will be lovely on a hot summer's day, I add a tablespoon of freshly grated ginger.

Sparkling Rhubarb with Cherry

Try substituting other fruits for the rhubarb (with the exception of apples and pears) — for instance, quinces, cherries, raspberries, strawberries, plums, crabapples. In the case of cherries, crabapples and plums, prick or slash the skins to release their flavours.

> *500g rhubarb, diced*
> *250g black cherries*
> *150g Morello cherries (or extra black cherries)*
> *1 tablespoon grated ginger (no need to peel)*
> *875g sugar*
> *1 lemon, chopped*
> *4.5 litres cold water*
> *220ml cider or white vinegar*

Place all the ingredients in a food-safe bucket, mix well, then cover with a tea towel and leave to stand at room temperature for 48 hours.

Strain through a fine nylon kitchen sieve and pour into PET bottles and seal immediately. (Empty soft-drink bottles are ideal, or you can buy new ones from home-brewing suppliers.)

It will be ready in 2 weeks. Open carefully — it's best to refrigerate it before opening.

Makes about 4.5 litres

By now I'm really on a roll and wonder how a batch of plain sparkling Morello cherry would taste. Frozen fruit can be used, as I've recently discovered, so before long a bucketful of this is set alongside the other to be left for the requisite two days before bottling.

Earlier in the day, once our generous neighbours left, Stephanie came to help package the pork. Jay said the pig was a little fatter than he had intended, fed as it was on the best pasture and well cared for. Just by handling the meat you can tell it's going to be exceptional — it is nothing like any pork I have ever come across — light in colour (no wonder it's referred to as the other white meat) and soft to the touch. I keep a piece out for roasting for dinner tonight.

Our youngest daughter Courtney arrives and I'm pleased to see she is carrying a large container with dipping forks, candy moulds and various candy-making ingredients.

Courtney invents a recipe suited to making *petits fours* and sets to baking them in the special tins she has brought. They look like little gems once she has dipped them in boysenberry icing. She then forms little jewel shapes with the toffee she has made, sitting them on top of her little cakes, which finishes them to perfection. They look exquisite.

Cake Mix for Petits Fours

The number of *petits fours* this makes depends on the size of your baking tins; if you use quarter-cup capacity tins, you should get about 24 pieces.

2 eggs
1 cup sugar
½ cup milk or buttermilk
1 cup self-raising flour
½ cup plain flour or almond meal
125g butter, melted
½ teaspoon vanilla extract

ICING
180g icing sugar
1½ teaspoons melted butter
½ teaspoon vanilla extract
boiling water

Preheat the oven to 160°C. Grease the baking tins.

Place all the ingredients in the bowl of an electric beater and beat on high for 2 minutes. Spoon into the tins and bake until the cakes spring back when lightly touched in the centre, or when a metal skewer inserted into the centre comes out clean. (Baking times will depend on the size and depth of your tins.)

Allow to stand in the tins for 5 minutes, then turn out onto a wire rack to cool completely before decorating.

To make the Icing, sift the icing sugar, then add the butter, vanilla and boiling water. You can use fruit juice such as the liquid drained from fresh or frozen berries instead of the boiling water.

Makes about 24

She also makes muffins in pretty little pans she found in a cake supplier's shop and these are topped with lovely pink icing. With the leftover bits and pieces of cake, she makes a rum-ball mix of sorts, minus the rum, and using white chocolate instead of dark. She presses the mixture into tiny heart-shaped tins to set. After a short spell in the fridge they are ready to eat — delicious.

By now the jam is done and the drinks made. My attention turns to the bowls of berries in the fridge from last night's picking. I really have enough berry jam for the moment, and decide to make the fruit mixture for a summer pudding to serve for a dinner this weekend. I throw them in a saucepan with a little water, some pipped cherries for good measure and enough sugar just to counter-balance the tartness of the berries and set it over a low temperature to release the juices.

What a mess we've made. The big advantage of the chalet kitchen is that you can walk out and leave the mess until later if you want, but when you have good company the cleaning is a trifling thing.

When we go back into the house, the pork is sizzling in the roasting pan, filling the air with an enticing savoury aroma. Potatoes, pumpkin, sweet potatoes and parsnips are added to the pan to cook in the rendered-down fat. The crackling is shaping up well. Not long ago I was told that vegetables and meat should always be cooked in the fat of the bird or animal you are roasting. It really does make a difference.

The pork is all I expected it would be and more besides. Stephanie and I have put a large leg aside to cook on Sunday when many of the family will arrive to see my mother.

January 25

Finally, finally, it is raining. This dry season has been a real worry, despite the fact that we have bore water. The hills around us have dried out terribly and the local fire chief tells me this is the worst summer since the horrendous fires of 1967. For those of us who remember them this is a scary prospect. I happened to be at high school at the time and can still recall vividly the plumes of smoke, and of waiting at the bus stop for a bus that didn't arrive, and seeing the distant hill behind our house on fire.

Very recently the Dunalley fires have instilled more than the usual fear into us all. We are aware that this could happen anywhere with so much bush around and the undergrowth so tinder dry.

We have cleared what we can, mowing and keeping vegetation down, attempting to keep the grass green, but as we gaze at the surrounding hills, we know there is little point in staying and defending the property. The fire would rush through, devouring everything in its path. This is a no through road so we would need to leave early.

We have bought a generator anyway, not that it's arrived yet, which is a bit worrying. We are told that our bore is one of the best in the valley, but will be useless if the power goes out as it inevitably will in the case of a fire. Not that we'll be here, but maybe the fire service can use it.

January 26

Australia Day sees another preserving class in full swing. One of the participants has been before for the yeast class, and has been looking forward to the preserving one for ages. As is typical of people of the valley and surrounds, she is very generous and brings some magnificent beetroot from her garden and some free-range chicken eggs. She is very apologetic that the yolks are not as yellow as usual — a result of the dry conditions and less greenery for the chooks to feed on as they forage.

The class is great fun as we make apricot chutney, sweet chilli sauce, raspberry and blackcurrant cordial and so much more.

Two journalists from the US have come along as well. I'm a bit worried that they won't like the hands-on nature of food prep for the class, but they soon join in and enter the spirit of things. Robert is outside picking berries and when he brings them in, passes them around for everyone to eat their fill. One of the journalists is staggered at their flavour, sweet yet tangy, totally delicious. It turns out he has a passion for berries in general, so as Stephanie guides the preserves, I quickly throw a batch of berry muffins in the oven — enough for all to share and some to take away.

Others in the class joke that they can say what they like, and I could make it à la minute for them. This is not as silly as it sounds. One of the benefits of living in such a fruitful region is that all sorts of delicious treats can be conjured up at a moment's notice.

Mixed Berry Muffins

1 egg
¾ cup sugar
¾ cup milk
1½ cups self-raising flour
60g melted butter
1 cup berries of your choice, fresh or frozen (strawberries
  should be cut into quarters)

Preheat the oven to 170°C. Grease 12 x ½-cup capacity muffin tins or line with baking cases.

Whisk the egg and sugar together until well combined, then add all at once the milk, flour and butter and whisk until smooth.

Spoon into the muffin tins. Bake for 12–15 minutes until well risen and cooked through.

Makes 12

Mixed Berry Jam

1kg mixed summer berries
1kg sugar

Place the berries in a large saucepan or jam pan and bring slowly to the boil. Simmer for 5 minutes.

Add the sugar and bring to the boil, stirring. Boil briskly over a medium–high heat until setting point is reached (see page 393).

Pour into warm sterilised jars and seal immediately.

Makes 1.5kg

My mother has been visiting from Queensland for several days now. She loves our property and the animals that share it with us, especially Tom, who has taken a great fancy to her and sits on her lap at every opportunity. Today many of the family have come to visit, and we prepare a great feast. Everyone brings a little something to eat — Alistair with a large boxful of beautifully decorated cupcakes.

Charly and Alistair's little Matilda chat away on the front deck, making an afternoon tea of their own with tiny cups and saucers and talking like only young girl cousins can.

January 27

Stephanie's friend Jane has taken on caring for orphaned wildlife. As the animals grow they are going to need more space. She has decided to sacrifice her raised vegetable garden beds so that a suitable enclosure can be built. She has put out a call on Facebook to see if anyone would like the vegetable boxes.

Her husband is all set to go with building an enclosure and has removed the five large vegetable boxes. They are actually old apple crates, 1200cm x 1200cm, very rustic, and I can see just where we could use them. Under the window of the cooking school is an area where the former owners had an above-ground swimming pool for their children. I've tried growing grass on this sandy surface with little success, despite copious amounts of water and tender loving care.

I calculate that at least four boxes would fit into the space quite nicely. It would be handy for growing herbs and other vegetables for use both in everyday cooking and for the school.

So today is the day we go to pick them up. When we arrive, Jane is feeding Jack, the baby wallaby. It is thought that perhaps his mother threw him from the pouch, as they will do if frightened badly. When Jane first took over care of him, he had no fur, but now he is a cute ball of fluffiness wrapped in a purpose-made pouch that Jane has sewn. His bright little eyes are taking in the world and he kicks in his pouch, making ready for the outside enclosure.

Soon his bottle-feed is finished and we meet Molly, a slightly larger orphan, the prettiest little soft bundle of fur you could ever wish to meet. Jane returns them to the playpen that serves as their home while they are so tiny, but Molly is beginning to rebel and will need that enclosure very soon.

We meet the three Corgis and five cats of various breeds, most adopted when former owners could no longer care for them. Then we proceed to load the car with the boxes, ideal for what I have in mind.

The boxes do indeed fit in the space and look even better than I'd expected. A few running repairs, and they will be ready to fill with soil and plants.

January 29

Both Stephanie and Courtney come to visit today. The conversation between the girls, as always, turns to candy-making. The promised candy hook will greatly assist with moulding and shaping the hot toffee — when it reaches a certain stage, barely cool enough to handle and still malleable enough to shape, it can be thrown in a mass over the hook and then stretched and pulled into ropes and twists. Though we don't have marble bench tops, ours are granite and there is certainly plenty of stainless steel. And so the discussion develops a life of its own. Before long candy hooks are being researched on the Internet, and prices (extortionate) found for one that is made in England. Deflated and disappointed, it seems they will have to abandon the idea.

It is then that I remember the metal-makers in Hobart — J. Minty and Sons. I've been told for decades that they are experts, geniuses in fact, with metal, and custom-make purpose-specific cake tins. Would they be worth a try, I wonder. Certainly they can make one when I ask, and give me an estimate.

Their quote comes in at a comparatively low $160 so we order immediately. Personally I can't understand this passion the girls have for toffee. Maybe it's to do with the fact that it pulls fillings from my teeth and I can't stand nuts. Or perhaps it's the fact that I ate so many toffees as a small child — Mum used to make them for fairs — toffee sprinkled with hundreds and thousands set in patty paper cups, and toffee apples by the score.

January 30

I remember being told at the Patchwork book-signing by two kindly ladies that there is a market every day in the Bushy Park hall. I love going to the Big River Market in the Willow Court grounds in New Norfolk, held each Saturday, but most Saturdays are busy with classes and commitments, so I rarely get there.

Today being relatively calm, I decide to venture the 20 kilometres or so to check out Bushy Park. Stephanie and the children come along with me. Walking in, I am absolutely delighted to see artichoke plants for sale. I'd wanted some ever since we moved here, especially as we have plenty of ground. They produce magnificent flowers, which are great, but better than that, the artichokes themselves are delicious and I so badly want to preserve some, antipasto style. I am getting a bit ahead of myself as there are only three plants, but it's a good start and they spread incredibly fast.

Even better, there are five jostaberry plants. Inside the hall are fresh seasonal fruit and vegetables galore — plumcots (a cross between an apricot and a plum), greengages, potatoes, carrots, parsnips, zucchini — all homegrown, all ridiculously cheap.

The rest of the huge hall is devoted to bric-a-brac and a hop museum. Thinking of the alpaca fleece in the shed at home, I am sorely tempted to buy a spinning wheel, complete with its chair and all equipment for $200, but in the end I sadly resist. After all, I don't know how to spin and have no room to store it.

We're delighted with the market and we're sure we will be back here often.

February 1

This is to be a day for gardening, which has been pretty much neglected over the last week or two. Robert has brought home soil to fill the vegetables boxes but they need more so we head for the local timber yard to buy it. Well, that was the plan.

It's a lovely morning to be out and about so I ask Robert if he'd like to take a spin up to Bushy Park to look at the market there. We arrive right on 10, opening time. Already the man who opened the hall has dug pink-eye potatoes from his garden and we are able to purchase several kilos, along with other vegetables. The plants in the entrance have been replenished, so I buy more artichokes and jostaberries.

As we head for home, we notice a roadside stall tucked away by the roadside. We pull over and find Tasmanian leatherwood honey for sale, as well as very healthy blueberry plants.

Please ring the bell, the sign says and I do and eventually an elderly man comes from his garden.

'How much are the blueberry plants?' I ask.

'Ten dollars a plant,' he replies, then goes on to ask me where we plan to grow them. When I reply Molesworth, he says this is OK; he is concerned that people may not be aware that blueberries do not like town water very much as it contains chlorine. Our bore water, though high in iron, will be fine.

'I like my plants to grow well when someone buys them,' he says. Although I'm prepared to buy plants there and then, he advises we wait until March, which is the optimum time for transplanting them. He promises he will have plenty; again he wants us to succeed. He makes sure we know that they won't fruit abundantly for at least two to three years.

For me this is the best of best experiences — meet the grower who takes such pride in what he sells and advises you on how to use what you've purchased, be it plant or produce.

February 2

I am immensely fond of wildlife and don't mind the fact that wallabies frequent the bottom paddocks with the alpacas. Lately, however, there have been huge kangaroos visiting, and worse, they leap over the wallaby-proof fence into the garden area around the house. For days I've chased them off — they glance at me with a couldn't-care attitude before taking the fence in a single easy bound. As soon as I turn my back, they return.

I've decided to tolerate them after many days of this predictable routine, as they are only eating the green grass under the fruit trees. However, it has lessened my affection for them, I have to admit.

I've never been one for eating wildlife, but Stephanie's husband has been given some kangaroo meat and today Stephanie is making kangaroo patties. After much to-ing and fro-ing with recipe ideas, she rings and says they will bring them to cook for dinner here.

As much as I welcome their company, I'm not too sure about these patties — any I've had in the past have been a bit gamey.

As I start to cook them, though, they smell remarkably normal, and as I hesitatingly taste one, they are absolutely delicious. Stephanie has included some pork fat and a little beef mince, along with apples, fresh herbs and breadcrumbs.

We decide to make them as hamburgers, in buns with salad and homemade tomato sauce. The leftover mixture we will use for meatballs tomorrow.

Kangaroo Patties

1kg kangaroo meat
250g pork fat
2 onions, peeled and roughly chopped
3 slices bread
250g beef mince
2 eggs, lightly whisked
1 tablespoon chopped fresh oregano
2 teaspoons chopped fresh thyme

140

2 scant teaspoons salt
2 tablespoons soy sauce
1 tablespoon Worcestershire sauce
1 heaped tablespoon chutney (apricot or tomato)
1 tablespoon tomato sauce

Mince the kangaroo and pork fat, followed by the onions and bread, then run all through the mincer again. Mix with the rest of the ingredients until very well combined. If possible, leave to stand for 2 hours, refrigerated.

Shape into patties and cook for 5 minutes on one side, then turn and cook for 4 minutes on the other side. Alternatively, roll into meatballs that can be cooked in a passata-style sauce to serve with pasta.

Serves 4–6

February 4

Once upon a long time ago I had a passion for op-shopping — for books, cooking bric-a-brac and vintage clothes. Being so far away from town when living at Eaglehawk Neck, this had slipped to the background, but now my love for it has returned.

Perhaps the trigger was the market at Bushy Park, where I bought a very bright hippie top last weekend. It's so cool to wear in the heat but has one downside — the bumble bees find it extremely attractive. Moving the hose turns into a game of dodge the bee.

We are managing to keep the grass green, though it's a bit of a battle. The routine of moving hoses in the early morning until the wind comes up and again in the evening is endless. In the relative cool of the evening I like to water by hand, one of the most therapeutic pastimes in the world. It helps me keep track of how things are growing, and if they need feeding or more water. A couple of days ago I found some photos taken when we first moved here and while it may seem at times that we are standing still, the growth has been nothing short of astounding.

Robert keeps modifying the sprinkler systems that he installed. We bought green soaker hoses that turned out to be a dismal failure — they threw the water high in the air and wherever it touched the house the iron in the water has discoloured the boards. I am hopeful it will wash off with a bit of tank water and elbow grease. Consequently we've now reverted to some different soaker hoses, which give the other trees and plants a good, gentle soak.

The vegetables boxes are now planted out with basil, lettuce and zucchini. They look good already, and in a few weeks will be brimful with edible greenery.

While I do like flowers, they seem like such a waste of space unless they are edible. I've come to an amicable compromise, however. Along the entrance to the school, I've planted foxgloves, lobelia and antirrhinums. They are making a lovely floral show, but in the middle I have some magnificent spinach. I know it's not traditional, but greenery is greenery, and edible plants deserve their place — I consider this companion planting at its best.

Robert has just planted out the original vegetable gardens, that sadly didn't produce so well, planted as they were with cooler micro-climate plants. However Robert's pumpkin patch is like some green monster that creeps up silently in the night. Each morning when I go outside it has stealthily moved further over the fence that was meant to contain it, flowering merrily as it spreads across the grass. This all bodes well for the crop we'll have to harvest. As the day wears on its leaves begin to look sad and limp under the merciless heat of the midday sun, but after an evening's watering it revives and begins the cycle of growth and spread once more.

February 6

The forecast was for blistering hot today and it's certainly living up to expectations. I fear once again for my garden, which no amount of water can save from this baking sun. Remarkably the almost incessant watering has kept the grass greener than most properties in the district.

Even more alarming is the wind, which is stronger than usual. Around lunch time Courtney, who is visiting for the day, and I detect a whiff of smoke in the air. We're not too worried, it doesn't smell like bushfire.

However, soon the radio is announcing that a bushfire has indeed started — at 1.19 p.m. at Molesworth, in Glen Dhu Road, three to four kilometres away. The words of the local firies come back to haunt me — 'driest year since the 1967 fires', 'so much dry undergrowth, a fire would race through here' and so on.

Before long the smoke thickens, and though there is no imminent threat as far as we are aware, it is disconcerting. The power fails now and then, which is a real worry.

Robert is on his way home from work and the smoke now hangs in a heavy pall over our property. Though a bit paralysed by the situation, Courtney and I decide to cook, our family policy being 'Keep calm and carry on cooking'.

The cooking school has gas hotplates and, power blackouts having been common at Eaglehawk Neck, we learned how to use them to good advantage. By the time our chicken schnitzel dinner is ready, the situation is even more worrying. The smoke appears to be creeping down the hill face just behind us. Is there fire under all that haze?

Most concerning of all is that no radios work, nor the TV. The mobile phone will be OK for a while, and the laptop, but it will only be a short time before they too run out of battery power. A great sense of isolation overcomes us. I try not to think of the what–ifs, like what if the fire is heading up this road and we can't get out? What about the animals?

I urge Courtney to leave while she still can, but she steadfastly refuses to do so until at least she knows we have evacuated safely and that the animals are OK. The cats are not a problem, and neither is Della, as they can come with us. The chooks and ducks can surely find a safe spot if we leave the gates open to the green area nearer the house. The alpacas are a bit of a worry — we have no way to transport them. They do have three paddocks in which to shelter, but a grass fire would sweep through those in no time. If we let them into the home paddock around the house, there may be plants that would be harmful for them to eat.

Stephanie also urges us to come to her house in New Norfolk, and Courtney only leaves on the promise that we soon will. Just then, the police come past and strongly advise us to leave. With no electricity to pump water from the bore, it is the best decision. The generator, ordered two weeks ago, is still 'in the mail', and our expertise in fire-fighting could hardly be described as competent.

We eventually decide to open the gate for the alpacas so they can come into the greener area around the house, hopefully maximising their safety and trusting that they will not eat any shrub that may be harmful to them. Their owner could not get in to collect them, even if he wanted to, now that the road is closed.

And so with cats and dog we head for Stephanie's house in New Norfolk. Courtney is waiting there. Ardy is actually her cat, so she takes him home with her — I fear for his reaction as he's been particularly neurotic of late, but he is especially fearful of children and so would be even more traumatised at Stephanie's.

Our situation, though worrying enough, makes me realise just how terrible conditions have been for people in major bushfire disasters. The watching and waiting for news of damage to property, let alone people, is further compounded by an extreme worry over pets and livestock and what has befallen them.

February 7

The fire situation has worsened today and our road is still closed, though rumour has it that residents can get through. We decide to pack up Tom and Della and head for home. We no sooner reach the gate than the police arrive and advise us to leave once more. Though the power is back on it cannot be guaranteed. Furthermore, the winds are high and fickle, swinging from one direction to another.

We are desperate not to lose all the hard work we have put into the garden and so take the risk of spending some time watering the vegetable beds and fruit trees. Tom is extremely disgruntled as he must stay in the pet carrier for the hour or so this takes us. He's had no problem adjusting at Stephanie's house, however — making the most of the situation, sleeping alongside Charly and playing with the children during the day.

Nathaniel has not grown up with pets so finds Tom's presence a little unsettling, especially as Tom has taken a great fancy to him. He targets his toes for biting practice and smooches him at every opportunity, and even, above all other presumptuousness, jumps on their bed at night. It is quite comical, though I'm sure Nat does not think so.

This evening many of Stephanie's friends come around to her house to see how we are. It turns into a party of sorts and to some degree distracts us from the worry of the fire situation. Finally, however, Robert decides to head back home for the night. He will stay awake to ensure that any falling embers are extinguished by the water pump packs he now has at the ready, and will see to it that the alpacas are OK.

February 8

I feel pretty useless with all this sitting about and decide to go home this morning. The fire threat has moved further out and is threatening the township of Collinsvale. It's moving through the hills behind us — up Collins Cap and through Collins Bonnet, and many roads are closed, including ours.

The plumes of smoke have now formed a huge cloud that engulfs not only our region but Hobart and down the Huon Valley.

I feel extremely useless. As usual, all I can think of is to cook. Can I do anything? I ask one of the fire-brigade officers. Sausage rolls would be appreciated, I am told, and so I bake about six dozen or more and take them down to the fire station with six jars of various pickles to match.

I've played about with this recipe for many years now and hope that the fire crew like this version. You can use beef mince in place of the pork and veal, or even all chicken mince, but in my opinion, this combination is best.

Sausage Rolls

250g beef sausage mince
250g pork and veal mince
1 large onion, peeled and grated
1 small carrot, finely grated
½ cup fresh breadcrumbs
3 teaspoons chutney
2 teaspoons soy sauce
2 teaspoons Worcestershire sauce
½ teaspoon salt (or to taste)
2 frozen puff pastry sheets, thawed
1 egg, lightly whisked with 1 tablespoon water

Preheat the oven to 200°C. Line baking trays with baking paper.

Combine all ingredients except the pastry and egg wash, making sure the mixture is very well mixed.

Cut each pastry sheet in half and brush down each long edge with water.

Divide the meat mixture into 4. Form each into a long 'sausage' to fit each piece of pastry, and place one on each.

Roll up and cut into 5–6 pieces. Brush the rolls with the egg wash and prick each twice with a fork. Place seam side down on the prepared trays and bake for 15 minutes or until the pastry is well puffed and golden and the meat cooked through.

Makes 20–24 small rolls

When I take them down in the late afternoon, it seems a paltry effort but all donations are accepted gratefully. The fire station and nearby community hall are a buzz of activity, with helicopters coming and going.

This morning on my way home, as I drove past the Derwent River banks, helicopters were hovering over the water like huge dragonflies. I stopped and watched with many others as they sucked up a load of water, before taking off in a cloud of fine spray, heading back to the fires once more.

The sound of helicopters is ever-present now and, alarmingly, one helicopter has come down among the fires, though thankfully the pilot escaped virtually unharmed.

Even though the fire has moved further away, ash is still falling. Robert has not been able to return to work in case the wind turns once more and our property is endangered.

My mind must, however, return to other things. Tomorrow I am scheduled to go into the ABC for the Jams and Preserves talkback segment and I want to prepare a morning tea for anyone who might be there. I can't prepare as much as I'd like, but am still looking forward to putting a few things together. By late this evening I have little curry pie fillings ready, as well as sausage rolls and the makings for little chocolate and berry tarts that will showcase the very last of our berries.

I froze some of the Morello cherries we picked at Chris's farm a couple of weeks ago so I can make him one of his favourite dishes, Morello Cherry Meringue Pie. It's our annual tradition, and always part of the morning tea on the first 'Jams and Preserves' after the cherries are picked.

Morello Cherry Meringue Pie

PASTRY
125g butter, softened
125g sugar
1 egg
125g plain flour
125g self-raising flour
a little egg white, lightly whisked

FILLING

600g Morello cherries (fresh or frozen), pipped
2 tablespoons water
½ cup sugar, approximately
4 teaspoons cornflour, mixed to a paste with about ¼ cup cold
  water

TOPPING

4 egg whites
¾ cup castor sugar
1 teaspoon boiling water

To make the Pastry, beat the butter and sugar together, then whisk in the egg until well combined. Mix in the combined flours with a metal spoon to make a soft dough. Wrap in cling wrap and place in the fridge for at least 30 minutes before using.

To make the Filling, place the cherries and water in a saucepan and bring to the boil over a gentle heat. Simmer only until the cherries are just cooked. Add sugar to taste and stir to dissolve. Bring back to the boil and thicken with some or all of the cornflour paste, stirring constantly. The mixture should thicken to a custard-like consistency, though not too thick. You *may* need a little more cornflour paste but use with care — too much will make it stodgy and reduce the intensity of flavour. The mixture will by its very nature thicken as it cools.

Preheat the oven to 190°C. Grease a 20cm pie dish.

Cut out a third of the pastry, rewrap in cling film and return to the fridge for another use. Roll the remaining pastry out to fit the pie dish (so that it comes right up the sides of the dish. Trim the edges and prick all over with a fork. Brush with egg white and bake for 12 minutes or until light golden brown. If the pastry shrinks a little, while still hot, press back into shape with your fingers (use a tea towel to protect your fingers).

Remove from the oven and allow to cool. Spoon the filling into the tart case.

To make the Topping, beat the egg whites until stiff peaks, add the sugar and boiling water and beat until stiff peaks form again.

Lower the oven to 140°C.

Spread the meringue mixture evenly over the cherries and onto the crust.

Bake for 15 minutes more or until the topping is set and light golden.

Serves 6

February 9

For several days the alpacas' owner has been in touch, concerned by the fires and for the alpacas' welfare. Though we have been diligent, of which he is very appreciative, he thinks it is time to take them home. NO! We are very fond of them and love to watch their antics — they are our friends and companions.

I can't bear to watch when the deed is done. Jordan is apologetic, but I have always known they would depart one day. Fearful that I'd embarrass everyone and start sobbing, I can't even go out to the car to say goodbye.

'They'll be back,' we're told, but I seriously doubt it. This has an air of finality about it. I guess at least the paddocks are now free for the shearer's sheep, which should be arriving soon. It was going to be a worry because Charlotte chased away anything that dared to enter her domain.

As the day draws to a close we are saddened by the loss, but start to think about other forms of livestock we might introduce here. Our own alpacas maybe? Revisit the idea of goats? Miniature, quiet ones? It serves as a consolation to consider these things at least.

February 10

I am still a bit concerned about the class scheduled for Tuesday — only one person has cancelled due to the fire situation, so it is to go ahead. There seems to be a temporary lull with produce — apricots are now scarce, their season all but over, and this means we can't make apricot chutney.

The chutney can be made with peaches, but they are not plentiful as yet. Plums, maybe. I am still loath to give up on apricots so we wend our way home along the other side of the river in a final attempt to acquire some.

Much to my delight, we find a roadside stall, full to the brim with fruits of the season and among them (hooray) Moor Park apricots. Perfect! It has changed the colour of my day. There are nectarines and peaches as well as early plums.

The elderly man who owns the stall tells me he is always there with his produce and can wax lyrical about everything he has — where it's grown, how it will cook up and so on. I am ecstatic — he is just the person I like to meet, the producer with passion, ever helpful and informative.

He tells me the plums I've purchased are delicious stewed.

'I'll tell you a great recipe,' he says. 'Stew them up with some sugar and then sprinkle cornflakes all over, then smother 'em with cream.' Sounds good to me.

'Yep,' he says, 'I eat it every day this time of year. Doesn't hurt you if you do a bit o' work.'

I'll be returning here often to supplement what I have harvested from the garden, or even just for the cooking tips and conversation.

As we travel home the view of the fires as they spread towards the Lachlan is frightening. The smoke at our house is nothing by comparison to the pall that hangs over the hills, plumes of dense grey rising in several places.

I fear for the people, the places, as well as the livestock and wildlife that may be trapped by those merciless flames.

February 12

There's another preserving class today, only three people, as some more have cancelled due to the fire situation.

First order of the day is always one of the sparkling fruit drinks, which never fails to grab people's attention.

'How does it work?' they ask when I describe the method. I often wonder at this myself, but really don't worry about the science behind it, as it's sufficient for me to know that nature will play its part unfailingly and a delicious drink will be delivered, come what may.

Preserving of many kinds is soon in full swing however, and pots are filled and set on to boil — tomato chilli pickle, zucchini pickle, apricot chutney, tomato relish and sweet chilli sauce. Scones are thrown in the oven — a bit misshapen as I am so busy talking that I forget to add the baking powder until it's almost entirely mixed.

Bread is thrown in next, then the apricot cake and soon it's time for morning tea, after which we'll bottle the apricots.

Preserved (Bottled) Apricots

Use the basic bottling method (see page 385).

I generally preserve apricot halves as these look most attractive layered in their jars. Simply wash the apricots, cut in half and remove the stones. Layer the halves, skin side up, in the jars. When you pour in the chosen preserving liquid, be sure there are no air pockets. A knitting needle or skewer inserted inside the jar is handy to bring any bubbles to the top.

If you have a tremendous excess of apricots you can stew them and then bottle them. They must be spooned or poured into the bottles and preserved while still quite hot (it might pay to warm the bottles first to reduce the chance of breakage). Personally, I have found that preserving stewed fruit is not always successful. Like berry pips, small pieces get caught under the seal or on the rim of the jar during processing. While a good seal might seem to have formed at first, often they spoil quite quickly. I think that stewed apricots are better frozen.

For the halves bring the temperature up to 88°C over 50 minutes, then hold at this temperature for 40 minutes. If you have a thermostat-controlled preserver, set to temperature and then preserve for 1½ hours.

For the stewed apricots, bring the temperature up to 90°C over 50 minutes then hold at this temperature for an hour. If you have a thermostat-controlled preserver, set to temperature and then preserve for 1½ hours.

Freezing Apricots

Apricots do not freeze particularly well and tend to discolour quickly as they thaw. To counteract this to an extent, mix ¼ teaspoon ascorbic acid in ½ cup water per kilogram of apricots before freezing.

Personally, I prefer to stew the apricots before freezing in containers. I freeze them without sugar so that I can make apricot chutney, jam or sauce from them later.

Dehydrating Apricots

You will need to pre-treat apricots before dehydrating. The best method is to make a sugar syrup from equal parts of sugar and water with either the juice of a lemon or ½ teaspoon citric acid per litre. Bring this to the boil, then add the apricot halves or slices and leave for 1 minute in the hot liquid.

Drain well, then dehydrate at 65–70°C for 6–36 hours. Use a food dehydrator or place on a wire rack over a baking tray in the oven. If using the oven, open the door periodically to allow any steam to escape. Dehydrate until no beads of liquid appear when a piece is torn.

Store in airtight containers for 2 weeks in the fridge or 12 months in the freezer.

Personally I prefer to use puréed stewed apricots to make fruit leather. Be sure that the mixture is not too liquid. Don't add sugar, as this will make the leather brittle. A little honey can be added, 2 teaspoons for 500ml at most. Sweetening may not be necessary at all because the natural fruit sugars are concentrated during dehydrating.

One thing I have found extremely successful is dehydrating bottled apricot halves. They need to be the variety that stays firm once bottled, such as Moor Parks. Simply drain off the syrup, pat dry and then dehydrate. No pre-treatment is necessary.

Apricot Jam

Apricot jam is very much inclined to catch and burn. There is a simple trick to reduce the likelihood of this happening — add 4–6 stainless-steel forks to the pot while cooking. It disperses the heat away from the base and through the mixture. The bonus is that it helps the jam set quicker. Be sure to still stir the jam very frequently however.

> 1.5kg apricots, flesh only, chopped
> 2 tablespoons lemon juice
> ½ cup water
> 1.5kg sugar

Place the apricots, lemon juice and water in a large saucepan or jam pan. Bring to the boil, stirring very frequently, and then simmer until the apricots are soft. (You can add the forks at this stage if using.)

Add the sugar and stir to dissolve. Bring back to the boil, stirring constantly, and then boil over a medium–high heat for about 20 minutes or until setting point is reached (see page 393), stirring very frequently.

Remove the forks and pour the jam into warm sterilised jars and seal immediately.

Makes about 1.8kg

Apricot Conserve

The conserve will have more texture than the jam.

> *1.5kg apricots, flesh only, chopped*
> *2 tablespoons lemon juice*
> *1.5kg sugar*

Layer all the ingredients in a large pot or jam pan and leave to stand for several hours or overnight.

Bring the mixture to the boil, stirring constantly (add the forks now as for apricot jam if desired). Cook over medium high heat, stirring very frequently, for 15–20 minutes or until setting point is reached.

Makes about 1.8kg

I don't quite have enough apricots to make a batch of my nan's apricot chutney. However, Courtney has brought me some mangoes she found at a fruit market. They are very ripe and so are not suited to making a jam, but will make up the weight I need for the chutney recipe.

The chutney is a great success and I will certainly be making it again. You could use all apricots, even all mangoes. In the case of the latter I would add some fresh long red chillies, about 125g, chopped finely.

Apricot and Mango Chutney

750g apricots, flesh only, chopped
750g mango flesh, chopped
500g onions, peeled and chopped
500ml vinegar
750g sugar
1 teaspoon salt
1 teaspoon ground nutmeg
1 teaspoon mixed spice
1 teaspoon ground cloves
½ teaspoon cayenne (optional)
1 teaspoon curry powder

Combine all the ingredients in a large pot and bring to the boil, stirring.

Boil for 1 hour, stirring occasionally. Bottle and seal immediately.

Makes about 2kg

February 13

Stephanie drops in this morning for a meeting with the three ladies who are organising the Glenora Preserving (bottling) day Saturday week. The meeting was great fun, and productive on several fronts. Not only are the details sorted for the preserving day, but there is the promise of fruit from their gardens. Tomorrow one of them will deliver nectarines to Stephanie for us to bottle, given the excess she has on her tree.

Stephanie remembers a tree in the yard of one of the New Norfolk offices. The tree is loaded with nectarines that are just dropping on the ground, where they are kicked around like footballs by passing schoolchildren. She doesn't like to ask at the office if she can pick them, but I have no shame in this respect and soon the phone call is made.

They don't mind at all — someone actually stole all the apricots from the tree in the yard, so they are happy for the nectarines to go to a good home, where they will be bottled. There are two peach trees as well and we can also have those. What a luxury — it's years since I've had enough peaches to preserve.

Several boxes later I can imagine what I will be making — bottled halves, chutney, jam.

Bottled Peaches or Nectarines

Use the basic method for bottling fruit (see page 385).

The peaches can be peeled if desired: simply dip each peach for 1 minute in boiling water, then in chilled water, after which the skins will slip off easily. In my opinion it's a painful process so I don't bother. The skins contain valuable nutrients anyway so they are best left on.

To prepare the fruit, cut in half and remove the stones. Fill the jars and cover immediately with syrup to help prevent discolouration on contact with the air.

Once the prepared jars are in the preserver, bring up to 92°C over 40 minutes, and then hold at this temperature for 1 hour 40 minutes. Alternatively, if you have a thermostat-controlled preserver, turn to 92°C and leave to process for 2½ hours.

Freezing Peaches or Nectarines

To help prevent the discolouration that takes place when freezing peaches and nectarines, add ¼ teaspoon ascorbic acid mixed in ½ cup water per kilogram of fruit before freezing.

Personally, I prefer to stew them (as for apricots) before freezing in containers. I freeze them without sugar so that I can make apricot chutney or sauce later.

Dehydrating Peaches or Nectarines

Either fruit will need pre-treatment before dehydrating.

I find the best method for them is to make a sugar syrup of equal parts sugar and water with either the juice of a lemon or ½ teaspoon citric acid per litre. Bring this to the boil, then add the peach or nectarine halves or slices and leave for 1 minute in the hot liquid.

Drain well, then dehydrate at 65°–70°C for 6–36 hours. Use a food dehydrator or place on a wire rack over a baking tray in the oven. If using the oven, open the door periodically to allow any steam to escape. Dehydrate until no beads of liquid appear when a piece is torn.

Store in airtight containers for 2 weeks in the fridge or 12 months in the freezer.

As with apricots I prefer to use puréed stewed peaches or nectarines to make fruit leather. Be sure that the mixture is not too liquid and in the case of these fruits it is best to sieve the stewed fruit to make a purée. Don't add sugar, as this will make the leather brittle. A little honey can be added, 2 teaspoons for 500ml at most. Sweetening may not be necessary at all because the natural fruit sugars are concentrated during dehydrating.

Peach or Nectarine Jam

1.5kg just-ripe peaches or nectarines, flesh only, chopped
2 tablespoons lemon juice
½ cup water
1.25kg sugar

Place the peaches, lemon juice and water in a large saucepan or jam pan. Bring to the boil, stirring very frequently and then simmer until the peaches are soft.

Add the sugar and stir to dissolve. Bring back to the boil, stirring constantly, and then boil over a medium–high heat for about 20 minutes or until setting point is reached (see page 393), stirring very frequently.

Pour the jam into warm sterilised jars and seal immediately.

Makes about 1.5kg

Peach or Nectarine Chutney

You can peel the peaches for this recipe if you like, but I never bother, and certainly not for nectarines. If you choose to do so, dip whole peaches momentarily in boiling water, then plunge into cold. The skins should slip off easily.

1.5kg peaches or nectarines, flesh only, chopped
500g onions, peeled and chopped
500ml vinegar
750g sugar
1 teaspoon salt
1 teaspoon ground nutmeg
1 teaspoon mixed spice
1 teaspoon ground cloves
½ teaspoon cayenne (optional)
1 teaspoon curry powder
1 teaspoon mustard powder

Combine all the ingredients in a large pot and bring to the boil, stirring.

Boil for 1 hour, stirring occasionally, until thickened. Pour into warm sterilised jars and seal immediately.

Makes about 2kg

Stephanie is picking more than a kilo of strawberries from her garden each day and has decided to try a combination fruit jam.

Stephanie's Peach and Strawberry Jam

You could substitute nectarines for the peaches. You will need to stew them a little longer to soften the skins.

1kg peaches, flesh only
500g strawberries, hulled and roughly chopped
½ cup water
1.5kg sugar

Place the peaches, strawberries and water in a large saucepan or jam pan. Bring to the boil, stirring very frequently, and simmer until the peaches are soft.

Add the sugar and stir to dissolve. Bring back to the boil, stirring constantly, and then boil over a medium—high heat for about 20 minutes or until setting point is reached (see page 393), stirring very frequently.

Pour the jam into warm sterilised jars and seal immediately.

Makes about 1.8kg

February 15

It's been quite an adventure today as I've been invited to take part in a tourism advertisement. When I arrive at 8a.m. the scene is set. This is all new to me and it's absolutely intriguing. There are people and costumes and props everywhere. Even an alpaca is to make an appearance. Display tables are piled high with various merchandise for a market scene. There's whisky and pork pies and colourful fresh produce galore. The end result should be stunning.

A bottling class is scheduled for next Tuesday, so I must stop on the way home to purchase jars — each person who attends the class gets to take several filled ones home. Then I must bottle the peaches and nectarines.

I'm bone-tired but it has to be done — no sitting in front of the TV tonight. Robert and I head out to the chalet to fill the jars for bottling. Before long two dozen bottles are in the preserver and I'm so pleased we made the effort. Some of the fruit is still too green but will soon ripen and so can be preserved another day.

There is much to be done as tomorrow I teach Preserving Summer's Bounty at the Agrarian Kitchen, a nearby farm-based cooking school at Lachlan.

We've decided to take my old MG Midget, an indulgence I allowed myself a year or two ago. I bought it from an elderly man who, since he had a stroke, couldn't get in and out of it. I must admit that I am having a few issues there as well, but I adore it.

At Eaglehawk Neck the car didn't get much of a run. I bought it to go collecting fruit — I could just imagine a basket on the back filled with the gleanings and pickings of the fruits of the season. It really is a thing of beauty. Here in the Derwent Valley it should certainly be put to good use.

February 17

Today Robert decided we should go once more to Eaglehawk Neck to do some maintenance and air out the house. When we arrive I cannot believe how quickly it has gone downhill. The house smells musty and the wetland forest is encroaching on the cleared area around the house at an alarming rate. The water bowls we've left out for the wildlife are all but empty, despite the fact that friends occasionally refill them.

The day sees two perplexing dilemmas. First, the power is off, and Robert can't seem to fix it. An Aurora crew is duly summoned from Sorell, some 60 kilometres away.

Robert gets to work trying to get the pantry door off. It has jammed tight and the lock has seized. Finally he manages it and the most disgusting odour assaults our senses. It looks as if mice have had an on-going party. Jars of preserves have been knocked down and broken, and the contents consumed. UHT cartons of milk have been chewed on and spilt, and it smells like a mousy cesspit and looks like one too. Many hours later, with jars thrown out and much sterilising and scrubbing, the situation is still quite dire. I spray everything with the strongest of disinfectants so that in a few days we can come back and scrub some more.

Traps and special bait have done little to lessen the problem, so in a vain attempt to deter them I throw in a flea-bomb. Goodness only knows why, it's not even supposed to deter mice and rats, but feel I have to do something.

In the midst of all this the Aurora crew arrive. It was not a fault on their part — Robert missed a crucial switch that needed to be turned on. Embarrassed, I decide discretion is the better part of valour and hide in the bedroom until they are gone.

By now the day is almost gone, so after a serious disinfecting and showering, we head towards Hobart to stop in to see our eldest son Andrew, partner Emma and baby Hunter. Hunter is the happiest of babies, forever smiling and laughing and the hassles we experienced at the Neck today are soon forgotten.

Andrew is a qualified chef, a passionate cook who has, temporarily at least, returned to the building industry. He's made dahl, cherry jam (that has set better than mine), Worcestershire sauce, apricot chutney (a recipe he's invented), pickled octopus and much more besides. When I see how much he is forever cooking, I know that while you can take the man out of cheffing, you can't take cheffing out of the man.

Stephanie rang earlier in the day to tell me she has picked the nashi fruit from her tree. It's only a young tree, quite small, but has yielded 47.8 kilos of fruit. She is a great gardener, this Stephanie of ours, and her large vegetable patches are highly productive — they make mine seem like I am standing still. I'm sure she takes after my nan, Nanna Little Car, as the children always called her, because in her eighties she owned a bright pink Mini Minor.

Today's dilemma is the temporary lack of tomatoes from the local farm and even our own garden. I did spot, a day or two ago, another roadside stall with tomatoes on offer at nearby Bridgewater. I used to buy from here when the children were small, but it closed down. Today, however, there is a promising sign saying tomatoes are for sale.

As it's quite late, the stall is closed for the day, but I really needed to talk with someone/anyone to find out if I can buy a larger supply for next week's class. I braved it past the No Entry sign — I have no shame when it comes to acquiring fresh produce and so squeeze through the gap behind the gate and sneak down the lane to knock on the door. I'm not particularly scared of dogs; two hounds let me in but are very cantankerous about letting me leave again.

Thankfully a knock on the door finally brings out, not the owner, but his relative, who is caretaking. Could they do tomatoes for us? No doubt, she says, and takes my number for them to call when they come back.

Thankfully the dogs escort me quite amicably to the gate.

February 18

Robert is on holidays so I decide to make the most of it. He's a very good fruit-picker with far more patience and ability than me. I just want to get the produce home to a jam or pickling pot or preserver.

It just so happens that Stephanie received a call from a local grower asking if she needed fruit for jam. She gives me his number, and this is how I came to meet Michael.

I give Michael a call at the first possible moment — something tells me he is going to be a good source of fruit. There has been a bit of a lull in produce-gathering recently; perhaps it's the bushfire smoke still hanging in the air that has dampened people's enthusiasm.

Michael's farm is just a few kilometres past the Salmon Ponds. The Salmon Ponds is the oldest trout hatchery in the southern hemisphere, in operation since 1864. There are six different ponds displaying trout and salmon, including brown, rainbow, brook and tiger trout.

We have instructions on how to get there and a bit of an outline of what he grows. I am in search of plums to bottle for tomorrow's class but he tells me he has mulberries as well.

What a find! It turns out that Michael is a food scientist with an incredible knowledge of fruit and preserving methods, of the science behind the magic. His words are like music to my ears — so that's why this and that works. I have never known why, I just love to make it happen, spoiled as we are here in Tasmania with such exceptional produce.

Soon poor Robert is picking mulberries alone as Michael takes me through the orchard, showing me the varieties of cherries, plums, currants and berries.

He tries to grow a range of varieties of different fruit: five types of Kentish cherries, for instance; and Morellos for the local brewer and for local Polish ladies to make plum dumplings called *povidwa*. He tells me about the treats they make by way of preserves — spoon fruit, for instance — he even has a jar to show me.

Spoon fruit is a preserve served often to guests when they arrive at a person's house in Poland. It is offered in a small bowl, along with a glass of chilled water. What a lovely idea! How is it made? Of course Michael knows — 80 per cent sugar by ratio to the fruit, layered. It is generally made with cherries, but any fruit can serve the purpose. What about mulberries, I think? He speaks of those plum dumplings with a plum paste inside. He describes the method for making the paste and we decide that it must be injected into the dumplings after cooking.

Eventually we return to find Robert spattered with mulberry juice. Sampling them straight from the tree is one of the finest gourmet feasts on the face of the earth.

I recall that my dad, not a gardener by any means, tried to grow mulberries for years with no success. At Eaglehawk Neck our tree just sat and looked sad, and never actually grew, despite all the tender loving care I could possibly give it. We tried moving it here to Molesworth as a last-ditch attempt, but it quietly died.

Here in Michael's orchard they grow prolifically, dropping with their exquisite juices into Robert's new purpose-made picking bucket, a rectangular container suspended on straps that wrap around the shoulders, leaving both hands free.

Michael and I at last have come to help him pick and soon our hands look like we are axe-murderers, stained as they are with the scarlet juices. The way to get rid of the stains is to rub the affected skin with the juice of a green mulberry, but this is too tedious and I really can't be bothered. We give our hands a scrub under a tap and leave the rest for time to eliminate.

While listening to Michael talk, I know we will return throughout autumn.

Home in the afternoon sees the temperature rise alarmingly. The thermometer outside says it's 50°C and it sure feels like it. I loved the Neck for its cool summer breeze off the ocean, but yesterday it was no better than here.

Soon the acrid smell of bushfire smoke fills the air again. Sure enough, Stephanie rings to say a fire has broken out at Gretna, mere kilometres away, and news reports are saying that the Molesworth fire has broken out again. Small wonder, with the strong winds that have sprung up from nowhere. Maybe the bottling class of tomorrow won't go ahead after all.

I curse the fact that the generator hasn't arrived yet. It was ordered weeks ago, but when I made enquiries today, I am told it's not even left their depot, with no apology or by-your-leave. Sometimes shopping online has whiskers on it. It might be here in a week, he grudgingly tells me, maybe 16 days, and my pleas for him to hasten the process, or at least, given the fire situation, to look into it, fall on deaf ears.

Stephanie and I decide to push ahead anyway to do some preserving of one kind or another, primarily of her nashi. Despite giving many away, she still has buckets full.

Nashi Jam with Ginger

1.5kg nashi, peeled and cored
30g ginger, peeled and finely grated
juice of 1 lemon
1 cup water
250g crystallised ginger, diced
1.25kg sugar

Dice the nashi and place in a large saucepan or jam pan with the ginger, lemon juice and water. Bring to the boil, stirring often.

Boil until the nashi are cooked through and just tender, then add the sugar and bring to the boil, stirring constantly. Cook briskly over a medium—high heat until setting point (see page 393). Stir in the crystallised ginger.

Leave to stand for 10 minutes before pouring into warm sterilised jars and seal immediately.

Makes about 1.8kg

Spiced Nashi

SPICED VINEGAR
1 litre cider vinegar
10 whole cloves
2 bay leaves
1 star anise
2 teaspoons ground cinnamon
2 teaspoons ground cardamom
2 teaspoons ground coriander
2 teaspoons ground allspice
1 teaspoon ground ginger

SPICED NASHI
2 cups spiced vinegar
1kg sugar
½ lemon, sliced
2kg nashi, peeled, cored and halved (cleaned weight)

To make the Spiced Vinegar, combine all the ingredients in a large pot. Bring to the boil, then immediately remove from the heat, cover and leave to infuse for 2—3 hours.

Strain the vinegar through 2 layers of muslin. You are now ready to proceed with the rest of the recipe.

To make the Spiced Nashi, combine the spiced vinegar, sugar and lemon in a large saucepan. You may like to divide the mixture between 2 saucepans. Bring to the boil, stirring to ensure that the sugar is dissolved. Add the nashi to the liquid and simmer till barely tender.

Remove the nashi with a slotted spoon and pack the fruit into sterilised jars. Return the vinegar mixture to the heat, bring back to the boil and boil briskly for 10 minutes. Pour the mixture over the pears, then seal.

You should have some of the syrup mixture left over. Bottle this and use as a topping for ice-cream, yoghurt or similar.

Makes about 4kg

Robert goes down to water the artichoke bed this evening and comes across a native hen in distress. Desperate for water, it had tried to get a drink from one of the outdoor bathtubs that we used to keep full for the alpacas. It must have slipped because it was close to drowning from sheer exhaustion.

Robert pulls it out. The poor thing tries to run away, but it is so wet, cold and tired that it can't stand. Tom, forever the hunter, decides this is a great opportunity. Eventually we place the bird in a box and will keep it in the laundry for the night until it regains its strength. Tomorrow morning we will return it to the paddock to be reunited with its folks (it's little more than a baby).

Coincidentally, a mere few minutes before this event, I'd decided to start putting out dishes of water for the wildlife. They must be gasping for a drink given the dry conditions. The bathtubs are fine for the larger wildlife, but it had not occurred to me that the potoroos and other small animals, even birds, cannot access them.

February 19

Today I awake to the best of sounds — RAIN, at last. It is so welcome. I've been very worried about the bore running dry and also the fact that the garden struggles despite our best day-long efforts at watering.

Today is also the first of the bottling classes. Bob has wanted to come for some time and is the only one to sign up, but I'm long past worrying about filling the classes with eight people. He is happy to be the sole participant, so we go ahead anyway.

His lovely wife Jenny was at a class a week or so before. We spoke about Monkey Bun, a totally delicious yeasted bun, from my book *Sweet!* I invite her to come to the bottling class as well — I'll make the bun that day so she can see what I mean.

Stephanie needs to finish preserving the seemingly never-ending nashi. It's much easier doing it here than at her house, so she will bring the haul she has and we'll all preserve together.

By the time I get all the produce on the benches I realise I may have overdone it. There are many varieties of plums piled high, buckets and buckets of nashi, tomatoes galore and a huge tub of fresh basil Stephanie has brought to make pesto. She has so much in her garden and it's threatening to go to seed, so it needs processing.

And mulberries, about 8 kilos, such a luxury! They are there to eat fresh, but I have other plans for them. What if, instead of mixing sultanas through the Monkey Bun dough as in *Sweet!*, I wrapped each little ball of dough around a mulberry or two? I think that would be delicious — a touch of tartness to counteract the intense sweetness of the caramel.

At morning tea-time, when the bun is ready, it turns out to be a great hit — I'll keep the recipe with mulberries. Any fruit could be used, but mulberries for their taste, tang and texture are ideal. Blackberries or boysenberries would be a close second, blueberries even. So that you can enjoy this treat all year round, freeze the mulberries — they will thaw during the baking.

Mulberry Cordial is one of my favourites, vastly preferable to the jam, which can be difficult to set, and so should be combined with apples. Although it's nice as jam goes, the cordial captures the intense flavour of the mulberry far better, and this cordial syrup is exquisite served (neat) over a slice of cheesecake or pavlova.

Mulberry Monkey Bun

You will need an 8–10 cup capacity Gugelhopf tin or a plain ring tin will do.

500g plain flour
5 teaspoons dried yeast
1 teaspoon salt
1 tablespoon sugar
½ teaspoon ground cinnamon
zest of 1 lemon
60g butter, melted
¾ cup warm milk
2 eggs, lightly beaten
mulberries

CARAMEL
250g butter
200g brown sugar
1 tablespoon golden syrup

Mix the flour, yeast, salt, sugar, cinnamon and lemon zest in a bowl. Make a well in the centre and pour in the butter, milk and eggs. Mix well with a metal spoon until well combined. You can mix with a dough hook in an electric mixer if preferred. Cover with a tea towel and leave in a warm place to rise until doubled (about 1 hour).

Grease the tin well.

To make the Caramel, combine all the ingredients in a small saucepan over a low heat until melted, stirring. Cool to warm.

Turn the dough out onto a lightly floured surface and knead until smooth, about 3 minutes. Break off walnut-sized pieces (about 80g each) and roll into balls. Press out flat and place a mulberry or two in the middle. Dampen one edge, then seal the package, bringing the dry edge to the wet edge to ensure a good seal.

Roll in the caramel mixture and drop into the tin. Place the ones on the base so that they are almost touching, then layer the buns progressively up the tin as you go. Pour any leftover caramel mixture over the top. Cover with a tea towel and allow to rise to the top of the tin. Keep an eye on it so that it doesn't stick to the tea towel.

Preheat the oven to 190°C. When the dough is ready, bake for 10 minutes, then reduce the heat to 160°C and bake for 20 minutes more. Leave to stand in the tin for 3 minutes, then turn out onto a wire rack. It's a good idea to place a plate under the wire rack to catch any caramel drips; just spoon back onto the bun.

To serve, each person pulls off a segment of bun with a fork.

Makes 1 large bun

Freezing Mulberries

To freeze so that they are free flowing, spread in a single layer on a tray and freeze, then store in freezer bags or containers in the freezer.

Alternatively, for solid pack, place in sealed freezer bags or containers in the freezer.

Mulberry Cordial

2kg mulberries
2 litres water
sugar
2 level teaspoons tartaric acid

Place the mulberries and water in a large saucepan and bring to the boil. Simmer *very* gently for 15 minutes. Strain through a colander, then through a kitchen sieved lined with a layer of muslin (even a clean tea towel will do).

For each cup of liquid add 1 cup sugar. Bring to the boil, then reduce the heat immediately to a *bare* simmer and cook for 2 minutes more. Stir in the tartaric acid, pour into sterilised bottles and seal immediately.

The cordial will keep at room temperature but in warmer weather or climates it would be best to keep it in the fridge. In either case, refrigerate the bottle once it is opened.

Makes about 4 litres

Bob and Jenny seemed to enjoy the class, despite the mayhem, and sugar, fruit and syrup everywhere. Best of all, they offered to come back in the afternoon to help us bottle the remaining fruit, of which there is still plenty. The afternoon progresses with much industry and fun.

It is during all this activity that the mulberries surface in my mind once more. What am I to serve everyone for afternoon tea?

A friend once told me about a special bun that a bakery in Adelaide made — Elephant's Foot Bun. I found the name of the bakery and rang them in an attempt to duplicate the delicacy he spoke about. Although the bakery no longer produces them they were happy to describe how they were made, and so it was easy to duplicate — a large yeasted Boston Bun-type treat with a filling of stewed apple and iced with pink icing and sprinkled with coconut.

Easy, but today I thought of my mulberries, so luscious and so close at hand. Maybe I'd just use a few more for this afternoon tea. Instead of the apple filling I made mulberry and apple, thickened just a little. Some of the mulberry juice, the dregs in the bowl, I used as the liquid in the icing. And so the bun was made, a hundred times better for the addition of mulberries, nature's little perfect packages of flavour. Any berry could be used in place of the mulberries.

Elephant's Foot Bun

500g plain flour
5 teaspoons dried yeast
1 teaspoon salt
1 tablespoon sugar
60g melted butter
1 cup warm milk
2 eggs, lightly beaten
2 apples, peeled, cored and diced
200g mulberries
sugar
3 teaspoons cornflour mixed with ¼ cup water
1 egg, beaten for egg wash

ICING
2 cups icing sugar
2 teaspoons butter, softened
a few drops cochineal
30g dessicated coconut

Combine the flour, yeast, salt and sugar in a large bowl, then make a well in the centre and pour in the butter and milk. Mix well to form a soft dough, then cover the bowl with a tea towel and leave in a warm place until about doubled in size (about 1 hour).

Meanwhile make the fruit mixture. Place the apple and berries in a saucepan and bring to the boil, stirring. Simmer for 3 minutes then sweeten to taste. Bring back to the boil and stir in cornflour paste to thicken. Cool.

Turn the dough out onto a lightly floured surface and cut off 3 walnut-sized pieces. Roll out the remaining dough to make a dinner-plate-sized circle. Brush around the outer edge with some beaten egg, then spread the fruit mixture in the middle. Gather up the edges and press well together, then turn over with the seam to the bottom, making in effect a small circular parcel. Brush all over with beaten egg. Roll the three small pieces of dough into balls and attach on one edge of the parcel. Brush with egg.

Place the bun on a baking tray that has been greased or covered with baking paper, loosely cover with a tea towel and leave to rise for 25 minutes.

Preheat the oven to 200°C.

Bake the bun for 25 minutes or until golden brown. Cool on a wire rack.

To make the Icing, mix together the icing sugar, butter and enough boiling water or mulberry juice to make a smooth spreading consistency. If you have no mulberry juice, add enough drops of cochineal to turn the icing a nice medium pink. Spread over the cooled bun and sprinkle with coconut.

Serves 6–8

Inspired by Michael of the orchards at Plenty, we decide to make spoon fruit with the last of the mulberries.

Mulberry Spoon Fruit

Spoon fruit should be kept in the fridge. If you would like it to keep longer, preserve with the basic method (page 385). Bring the temperature up to 80°C over 50 minutes, then hold at this temperature for 20 minutes. If you have a thermostat-controlled preserver, set the dial to 80°C and leave for 1 hour.

500g mulberries
400g sugar

Layer the mulberries and sugar in a jar. Leave to stand for several days for the sugar to dissolve, after which the spoon fruit is ready to be served.

Serve in small spoonfuls to guests, or as a topping for ice-cream, pavlova, etc.

I love mulberry jam but it's the very devil to get to set. Often I've added commercial pectin powder, but I prefer not to. There is always the risk that the flavour will be dulled by it. On the other hand, boiling endlessly will mean that the flavour of the fruit is lessened, overtaken by the sugar, which starts to caramelise, and this isn't pleasant either. A good compromise is to incorporate some cooking apples for pectin and some lemon juice or citric acid to help extract all possible pectin from the mulberries.

Mulberry, Lemon and Apple Jam

1kg mulberries
2 tablespoons lemon juice
500g cooking apples, peeled and cored weight
1.25kg sugar

Place the mulberries and lemon juice in a large saucepan or jam pan. Dice the apples finely and add to the pan.

Bring to the boil, stirring often, and simmer gently for 12 minutes. Add the sugar and bring back to the boil, stirring.

Cook over a medium–high heat for about 20 minutes or until setting point is reached.

Allow to stand for 5 minutes, then pour into warm sterilised jars and seal immediately.

Makes about 1.6kg

As the afternoon wears on I confess that I am a little over plums at the moment. Well, I did over-enthusiastically buy! We now have dozens of bottles of preserved plums of all the types we picked at Michael's, including the wonderful greengages. Now it's down to the last of the red plums and I've had enough.

'Leave them,' I say, 'I'll use the rest to make Worcestershire sauce tomorrow.' Good idea, we all agree as we tuck into the Elephant's Foot Bun with great gusto. My word, it's delicious if I do say so myself. All credit to the magnificent mulberry and the helpful advice from the bakery.

During all the peeling and pipping this morning it occurs to me that it would be a good idea to give some of the trimmings to the wildlife over the fence. I really have missed the close contact with the wildlife we had at Eaglehawk Neck. The peelings are soon thrown over and within a very short space of time, maybe 20 minutes, there are several wallabies and a kangaroo feeding. They are startled when I go near, but this is the way it needs to be for them, for their own safety. They need to remain fearful of humans. I plan to put food out at the same time each day just to supplement their diet, lean as it must be or at least devoid of fresh, moist food, given the dry conditions.

Speaking of animals, Tom has turned into a kitchen cat. I know that health regulations dictate that no animal goes in a commercial kitchen, so he sits on a log outside the door looking hopefully and adoringly at us see if he might be let in. He is such a curious cat that if ever he is allowed in, he goes around inspecting proceedings. For the most part, however, he contentedly sits purring as passers-by pat and admire him.

Bob and Jenny admire the rhubarb under the school window and they really like the sparkling Morello cherry drink they had when they arrived.

This set me thinking. How about making some sparkling rhubarb, but use some of the nashi skins and cores to make up some of the weight — a kind of nashi–rhubarb drink? It just might work. Apples and pears haven't been successful on their own, but nashi is a pear–apple cross, and the rhubarb will carry it. Robert brings in some nice thick red rhubarb stalks and soon a batch is on the go. More is picked for Jenny and Bob to take home to make a pie.

Sparkling Rhubarb with Nashi Skins

500g rhubarb, stalks diced
375g nashi peels and cores
875g sugar
1 lemon, chopped
4.5 litres cold water
220ml cider or white vinegar

Place all the ingredients in a food-safe bucket, mix well, then cover with a tea towel and leave to stand at room temperature for 48 hours.

Strain through a fine nylon kitchen sieve and pour into PET bottles and seal immediately. (Empty soft-drink bottles are ideal, or you can buy new ones from home-brewing suppliers.)

The drink will be ready in 2 weeks. Open carefully — it's best to refrigerate it before opening.

Makes about 4.5 litres

February 20

Stephanie arrives to help with the clean-up from all the bottling yesterday. She also wants to make Kirsch from the Morello cherries we picked at Chris's farm. I have frozen a great number of them, which makes them ideal for Kirsch. Freezing breaks down the cell walls so that the juices are released: these Morellos should give a wonderful exchange of flavours.

Kirsch

1kg Morello cherries
375g sugar
3 cups vodka or white spirit

Layer the cherries and sugar in a large jar, then pour over the vodka and screw on the lid. Shake the jar each day until the sugar is dissolved, then store in a cool, dry dark place for 6 months, after which the liquid should be strained off as Kirsch. The cherries can be used in cooking or simply spooned over ice-cream or a slice of cheesecake.

It's just as well my aversion to plums has disappeared because it's time to make Worcestershire sauce.

Nothing makes a house smell quite so pickly and homely as Worcestershire sauce, with its load of vinegar, garlic, ginger, treacle and spices. It's quite a good thing to make outside, or at least shut the rest of the doors in your house if you don't want the smell to permeate all your rooms and clothes.

Plum Worcestershire Sauce

This is wonderful for adding to casseroles and sauces to give extra flavour. You only need to add about 3 teaspoons to your average casserole and a couple of teaspoons to a gravy or jus.

You can use lemons to make this sauce: use 3 lemons instead of plums. I have used apricots or cherries, both of which were really successful.

If you need this sauce to be gluten-free, use cider vinegar instead of the dark malt vinegar.

3kg plums, damsons are best, but I use any sort
3 litres brown malt vinegar
60g garlic
60g salt
2 cups treacle
500g brown sugar
60g ginger, bruised
45g cloves
15g whole allspice
1 teaspoon cayenne pepper

Combine all ingredients in a large saucepan or jam pan.

Boil for 3 hours, strain, pour into warm sterilised bottles and seal immediately. The sauce keeps for years.

Makes 1.5 litres

I am pleased to have such a store of plums for the winter months. Even though we spent a lot of time bottling them, it was well worth it. Plums are delicious for breakfast with yoghurt and/or cereal and I'll use them in pies, tarts, cakes and crumbles. Yum.

Robert has decided to make blackberry nip. He has an especially good eye for blackberry bushes and this morning headed out, new picking bucket in hand, to a well-laden patch not far from the nearby creek.

Rather than using brandy as is usual, he will use vodka this time. It might be quite nice, as the brandy inevitably adds its own flavour, whereas the vodka will champion only the blackberries. He refuses to use a recipe and simply layers blackberries and sugar in a jar, then pours the alcohol over until the berries are completely covered. The bottle will be shaken each day until the sugar dissolves, then it will be stored in a cool, dry, dark place for about 6 months before drinking. It should be jolly good I think.

Blackberry Liqueur

1kg blackberries
350g sugar
750ml vodka

Layer the blackberries and sugar in a large jar and pour over the vodka and screw on the lid.

Shake the jar each day until the sugar dissolves, then store in a cool, dry dark place for 6 months, after which the liquid should be strained off. The blackberries can be used in cooking or simply spooned over ice-cream or cheesecake. Try mixing a spoonful or two into ice-cream.

For **Blackberry Nip**, substitute brandy for the vodka or white spirit.

Makes about 1.8 litres

Preserving together as a family can be a fractious affair with (usually) good-natured debate over preferred methods and recipes and options, and today is no exception.

For instance, I like to use the older bottling method, with lower temperatures and longer times specific to each fruit, temperatures that have worked best for me over the years. Stephanie, on the other hand, favours the newer method of Fowlers' latest instruction book — shorter times, higher temperature.

My reasoning is that the lower temperature retains more vitamins and gives a more pleasing appearance, while Stephanie claims that the advantage of the shorter bottling time is better. It's largely a matter of preference, available time and so long as it all turns out well, it doesn't really matter. However, the debating is always good fun.

Robert was the original preserver of the family. With the tomatoes he shows Bob how to bottle them in carefully cut, neat segments. He pulls out the knitting needle he uses to help with their placement. They do look good in the jars, I admit, but because of the layering extra liquid needs to be added, effectively watering down the tomatoes.

Stephanie and I — in agreement on this score — less than carefully chop the tomatoes, then push them firmly into the bottles, effectively releasing enough juice so that no extra water is needed. We often use the bottled tomatoes to make relish, chutney or sauce later in the year if our supplies run out. Adding extra water will throw out the balance of ingredients and diminish the flavour of the end product.

Poor Bob was probably very confused in the end! We left him to decide what he wants to do at home.

To preserve tomatoes, see page 85.

February 23

Today Stephanie and I are to deliver two workshops at Glenora primary school on bottling fruit, so 8.15 a.m. finds us on the road to Glenora, a small township a few kilometres north of New Norfolk. Already we have met with the Grow, Cook, Eat organisers, who received government funding to establish their extremely innovative and successful program. Participants — the parents of the schoolchildren — are invited to take part in workshops that show how to sow, and how to grow and harvest their produce. Our part is coming in with how to preserve each season's bounty.

The Food For All Tasmanians grant has made it possible that those who took part received a raised gardening bed and soil to fill it, a blueberry bush, basic gardening equipment such as a spade, garden sprayer, fertiliser, seeds, soil conditioners, strawberry and tomato plants, seed raiser, watering can, grafting knife and an apple tree that they grafted themselves. A library of gardening books and cooking books was established and this also includes two Fowler's preserving kits, apple covers and pH testing kits.

It is one of the best programs I've ever come across as it addresses the learning through at least two generations: parents and children literally sow, grow, harvest, cook, preserve and eat together.

The day promises to be stifling hot, but it's all made much easier by the fact that Janene, Bec and Kylie have everything so well organised. The information sheets I have put together have been photocopied and are ready for distribution, and all ingredients are good to go. They assist with the physical running of the class as well — going back and forth with buckets of water for the preserving outfits and doing mountains of washing up.

The class turns out to be great fun. The group learns how to bottle tomatoes, plums and pears, and are very pleased with the results as they are lifted from the preservers. Many questions are answered and soon they are most confident and very enthusiastic about preserving in their own homes.

The groups work so well that we find time to demonstrate how to make a delicious pear slice, topped with sliced fresh or preserved pears.

February 24

Last night a wallaby or possum must have found its way in and has eaten part of the garden at the gate. I am really disappointed to see that my St John's Wort has fallen victim to this grazing. It's a herbal relaxant, so there is one happy wallaby or possum out there today.

The Glenora group yesterday gave us some excellent lettuce plants, grown from seed in the program. They will be ideal for planting out in the garden beds that Jane gave us. I've tried to grow broccoli yet again, but despite dusting with a deterrent, the grubs have attacked them.

I heard a speech not so many months ago by a lady whose family went totally self-sufficient for six months. I remember her saying how people expect to just plant things and see them agreeably flourish, which, she pointed out, ain't necessarily so. I am much mollified by this and don't take it quite so personally when things fail to thrive, but am disappointed in the extreme. I'm very partial to broccoli.

On the other hand, tomatoes are driving us out of house and home — there are now so many. Despite the fact that I have next to no time, I have to find some to prepare a double batch of relish that I'll turn into sauce, otherwise I'll lose most of the fruit.

Two tomatoes along the path to the cooking school are so large that Courtney says she is bringing an old bra to support them. They truly are huge.

The pumpkins are growing well, as is the self-sown corn.

February 25

The fires of recent weeks have driven a lot of wildlife our way. When we drove into Hobart yesterday via the hills of Collinsvale it was clearly evident why: the hills and valleys as far as the eye can see are blackened and barren. The fact that no houses were lost in this area is a testament to the hard work, skill and dedication of the fire-fighters.

There are still a number of wallabies along our fenceline each evening, and sometimes during the day. I have so many peels and cores from the preserving classes that I'm still able to throw them over the fence to supplement what little feed there is.

The situation is even worse at Stephanie's house in New Norfolk. Her front garden, olive trees and cotoneasters are being eaten dreadfully and her front lawn each morning is covered in wallaby droppings. Even so, she feels sorry for them and puts out bowls of drinking water as there is no source anywhere nearby.

I'm told that Bonorong Wildlife Sanctuary is distributing feed pellets for the wildlife and people can apply for some. A phone call to the park soon secures a supply for both Stephanie and me, which is indeed welcome.

Even before we pick up the pellets the wallabies have established a routine. I guess I rather ridiculously stand at the fence calling, 'Wallaby, wallaby, wallaby.' I can feel their eyes on me, even see them on occasion, so I throw fruit peel and cores over and vegetable scraps, and within minutes they creep out from the bush. They are less afraid than they used to be, and one or two let me come near as they feed. I'd love to befriend and tame them, but I would be doing them no favours to take away their instinctive fear of humans.

February 26

The paddocks are to be slashed today. Since the alpacas left a couple of weeks ago, the grass in the paddocks has grown considerably so John is over to slash back the three lower areas. He is unfailingly cheerful, always with a happy story to tell of his encounters with the people he meets as he travels around mowing and slashing.

Today is no exception, and in his usual dynamic manner he is hard at work by 7.15 a.m. The paddocks are transformed as he slashes with his custom-built machine. Although the area is dry, it still looks almost like paradise. The back paddock, which has a lovely aspect and terrain, has not been mown in about ten years in his estimation, and is overgrown with large tufts of sharp grass (called sags apparently). The machine he uses makes short work of them, ripping many out of the ground and so the back paddock is revealed in all its glory. The grass there is interspersed with trees of many kinds — a lovely place for a picnic.

It is here that young Jacob has built his cubby house of straw, where he retreats when life gets too much for a little autistic boy to bear. He keeps company with Tom the cat, Della the dog and any other wildlife that comes very close.

Jacob has a new system for working out what sorts of wildlife are around the property — it's always intrigued him. When I worked as a tour guide at Port Arthur Historic Site a couple of years ago, and wanted to find out what animals roamed on the parade ground at night, I purchased a book called *Tracks, Scats and Other Traces*. In there is a very helpful illustrated page of various animal poos that I've now photocopied for Jacob. Like most young boys, such things fascinate him and he happily wanders off to see if we have wallabies, possums, wombats or even Tasmanian Devils.

March 4

Today a film crew is coming to do a follow-up photo shoot for the new tourism campaign. I love a situation where a number of people arrive as it gives me an excuse to cook up a storm, and today is no exception. We also have a chance to showcase the wonderful summer fruits and preserves we've been working with.

Not long after they leave our friend Lindsay comes to visit. He has excess plums, lovely small specimens. I don't know the name of the variety but they look a lot like the ones my aunt used to bottle when I was a child: small with purple skin and yellow flesh. I am so happy to get them. They are ideal for bottling as so many can be snugly placed in a jar. With larger varieties there is often a lot of wasted space between them, meaning that each jar has less fruit and more preserving liquid.

There will be ample to experiment with, as well as making family favourites.

Lindsay is a beekeeper of some note, with a passion for getting the best possible product through the optimum care of his bees and their hives. He explains rotations, the psychology of bees, and the importance of the strategic placement of his hives. A very informative conversation follows. I now understand why the leatherwood honey he sells is so wonderfully flavoursome and aromatic.

Bottling plums is a simple thing and soon we are hard at it with three preservers full once more.

I was once told that using port as the preserving liquid resulted in a delicious dessert treat. However, when I tried it, the results were less than impressive, the alcohol totally overpowering the delicate flavour of the plums and the jars looked very unattractive on the shelves with the brown preserving liquid.

I think there is potential in the idea, though. Robert had a bottle of good-quality port in the cupboard, so I poured in two tablespoons of port per preserving jar, then topped up the plums with a medium to strong sugar syrup (see page 401). When we taste the fruit two weeks later, it's absolutely delicious.

Plum chutney is a must for the pantry cupboard — I use it to flavour all sorts of savoury dishes. I also want to make a batch of a Chinese-style plum sauce that I've invented during the year. It's extremely good served with or over seafood, chicken or vegetables.

I've also included the recipe for cherry plum jam here, which I really love. You can use any kind of plum, but cherry plums are best as the jam is not too sweet. You could also use damsons.

Bottled Plums

The only plum I would hesitate to bottle this way is cherry plums. Their skins can be very bitter, even more so than in their raw state. It makes no difference how sweet the sugar syrup is, it will always be so.

If you have an abundance, you would be better off making cordial syrup with them (see recipe page 395). Jelly is another option, but it's a bit difficult to get to setting point.

Follow the basic preserving method on page 385. Bring the temperature up to 90°C over 50 minutes, then hold at this temperature for 1 hour 15 minutes. If you have a thermostat-controlled preserver, set the temperature and preserve for 2 hours.

Plum Chutney

3kg dark plums, stones removed
1.5kg sugar
1.5 litre white or cider vinegar
500g onions, peeled and chopped
3 teaspoons salt
3 teaspoons grated ginger
3 teaspoons ground allspice
2 teaspoons ground cloves
1 teaspoon ground cinnamon
1 teaspoon mustard powder
3 teaspoons cornflour mixed to a paste with ¼ cup vinegar

184

Place all the ingredients in a large saucepan and stir over a medium heat until the sugar dissolves and the mixture is boiling. Continue to boil for 2 hours or until the mixture is thick, stirring often.

Strain through a colander, food mill or coarse sieve. Bring back to the boil, then pour into warm sterilised jars and seal immediately.

Makes about 3kg

Chinese Plum Sauce

1kg plums, flesh only, chopped
375g onions, diced
1 knob garlic, peeled and chopped (about 10 cloves)
200g fresh ginger, peeled and chopped
½ cup soy sauce
¼ cup mirin
2 cups white or cider vinegar
1 teaspoon salt
500g brown sugar
3 star anise, ground finely
2 teaspoons beetroot powder or a few drops natural red food colouring (optional)

Place the plums, onions, garlic, ginger, soy sauce, mirin, vinegar and salt in a saucepan. Bring to the boil, stirring, then simmer for 30 minutes. Press the mixture through a sieve or food mill.

To the resulting sauce, add the sugar and star anise. Bring to the boil, stirring, then simmer for 40 minutes.

For better colour, stir in the beetroot powder or red food colouring.

Makes about 2 litres

Cherry Plum Jam

> *1.5kg red or yellow cherry plums (pipped weight)*
> *½ cup water*
> *juice of 1 large lemon or ½ teaspoon citric acid*
> *1.25kg sugar*

Place the plums, water and lemon juice in a saucepan and bring to the boil. Reduce the heat and simmer until the plums are soft.

Return the mixture to the heat, add the sugar and bring to the boil, stirring. Boil briskly for 20 minutes, by which stage it should have reached setting point (see page 393).

Pour the jam into clean sterilised jars (as full as possible) and seal with a lid immediately.

Makes about 2.5kg

March 7

One of the class topics I am most excited about is the one on convict and colonial-era cookery. I've researched the subject for more than fourteen years in my spare time. The recipes and cooking methods fascinate me. As I've said I believe that food and recipes tell a great deal about the broader picture of how people lived at that time. The summer I spent guiding tours at Port Arthur Historic Site provided the perfect opportunity.

The first Australian cookbook was written by a Tasmanian magistrate, Edward Abbott. It contains recipes for all sorts of wildlife along with more traditional fare. It has always intrigued me that the original settlers in Van Diemen's Land (as Tasmania was originally named) led the way in cooking with and consuming these unfamiliar ingredients.

James Boyce in his book *Van Diemen's Land* points out that the island's wildlife was plentiful, a veritable paradise compared to the narrow coastal strip in NSW, where they were scant and hard to catch.

The preserving recipes in Abbott's book remain little changed from those of the colonial era, and each summer saw an orgy of preserving once gardens were established.

While we can no longer eat protected species such as echidna and wombats, other meats such as hare, wallaby and possum are available. I plan to include some of these dishes in the school once I've experimented with them a little more.

In the meantime there are many other dishes to be enjoyed and the Carmichael slow combustion stove in which to cook them, emulating the method of cooking during the colonial era.

Back then, lives centred on working with the seasons — this was by way of necessity. Today a groundswell of people are doing the same, in this instance by choice, appreciating the benefits of living in this treasure trove of fresh, seasonal, unspoiled produce and the benefits to their health and the planet's through doing so.

March 8

The garden is looking picture perfect: the flowering gum is coming into its own in a blaze of orange blossom; the bottle-brush tree is also magnificent, and the black cockatoos visit morning and night, feasting on its flowers.

Robert is under the house hammering as he builds steps and shelves for storing preserves, which are threatening to take over not only the house, but the cooking school as well.

Despite all my years of careful research I'm a little nervous about tomorrow's first colonial cooking class. I hope I can do the subject matter justice.

I decide that I need to get out of the house for a while and so we head to Bushy Park, one of my favourite Tasmanian towns. I am seeking hops for bread yeast. I know hops aren't quite ready to be harvested but you never know, just maybe I will be able to find some.

I also have my sights set on hawthorn berries. The riverbanks on the way to Bushy Park are lined with the trees for many kilometres, so I think it's time for a little foraging.

First, however, to the market.

I ask the lovely ladies serving there about hops. I'm desperate to know if fresh or dried hops were used when yeast was made with hops in colonial times. They don't know either.

I was right, the hops are not ready for harvesting quite yet. Helpfully, they take me to a display in the hall dedicated to the history of hop-growing in the region. There sits a bowlful of pressed hops. Without a second's thought they tip the whole bowlful into a bag for me. No way will they let me pay for them.

They discuss among themselves the unlikely prospect of my obtaining fresh ripe hops. Suddenly they recall that there is a plant in full bloom at the local shop. All I have to do is ask; they are pretty sure that the shop owners won't mind.

I duly present myself to the two young women at the shop. Do they know about hops and how they were used in olden times? One replies that of course they were used dry — otherwise they wouldn't germinate and ferment.

I ask if I can pick a few of the flowers from the magnificent hop plant at the door. They joke that I have to pay $10 per bud. I tell them I'll just fill the hat Robert thrust into my hand.

'No need,' she says. 'Put that hat on your head when you go to pick in the sun, and I'll give you a bag for the hops.'

One huge bagful later, I feel an authentic convict/colonial-style yeast on the horizon. I am so looking forward to showing the people in class tomorrow.

On the way back down towards New Norfolk we spot a place a decent distance back from the roadside, perfect for picking hawthorn berries. It is cool under the shade of the trees and the river bubbling by lessens the oppressive heat of this summer's day.

As is the custom here in the idyllic Derwent Valley, there is much to be gleaned from the local environment. The hawthorn berries grow in abundance, but very soon we notice a rosehip bush close by, then blackberries on the vine, all there for the picking.

Next we head for the refrigeration depot at Brighton where whole milk and buttermilk from Ashgrove Farm await. Then it's home to unload our bounty and to prepare for tomorrow's class.

In colonial times, cooling summer drinks were in great demand and correspondingly many recipes were available — ginger beer, lemonade, fruit syrups and vinegars. I decide a hedgerow cordial syrup is something they would have made, or at least something similar to it, and a nice blend could be made from the produce we've picked.

Hedgerow Cordial Syrup

1kg berries and hedgerow fruits (such as hawthorn berries,
    rosehips, blackberries, raspberries)
1 litre water
sugar
2 level teaspoons tartaric acid or 1 tablespoon vinegar

Place the fruit and water in a large saucepan and bring to the boil. Reduce the heat and simmer very gently for 15 minutes.

Strain through a colander, and then strain the resulting liquid through a kitchen sieve lined with a layer of muslin (or even a clean tea towel will do).

For each cup of liquid add 1 cup sugar. Bring to the boil, then reduce heat immediately to a simmer and cook for 2 minutes more. Stir in tartaric acid or vinegar, pour into sterilised bottles and seal immediately.

To serve, use 1 part syrup to 4–5 parts water or soda water.

For adults, add a splash to a dry sparkling white wine. It can also be served over (or stirred through) ice-cream or poured over panna cotta, yoghurt or a slice of cheesecake.

Makes 2 litres

Hawthorn Berry (Haw) Jelly

1kg hawthorn berries
water
sugar

Wash the berries and place in a large pot with enough water to barely cover. Simmer until the fruit is soft, then strain through a colander, then the resulting liquid through a sieve lined with muslin. To each 500ml of juice, add 500g sugar.

Bring back to the boil, stirring, and cook briskly until setting point is reached.

Pour into warm sterilised jars and seal immediately.

Makes about 1.5 litres

March 9

Today it is the first of the colonial cookery classes. I've planned to make tomato relish, berry jam, the hedgerow cordial, stone-ground wholemeal bread, a fruit shortcake and more besides. I want to show how and why preserving was done in colonial times, and how the cooks from that era — as I do — used their pantries full of preserves to flavour other dishes, sweet or savoury.

By way of a savoury dish, I will cook a leg of lamb in the wood-fired stove. The meat is basted with a redcurrant and thyme sauce. The early colonials loved their meat, referred to as the faith, hope and charity of the Australian diet.

It has been said that the British invented puddings. Europeans generally developed an insatiable appetite for sugar. Desserts included cream puddings, jellies, blancmange, roly-polys, dumplings, shortcakes and flavoured ices — specific examples included Abingdon pudding, half-day pudding and Bakewell pudding. Today, with our current abundance of rhubarb and blackberries, we will make a slice to showcase those.

Confectionery was commonly made, as were cakes such as lipson seed cake (caraway seed), hawthorn cake, German cake and plum cake.

Bread was a staple, and when the Lord's Prayer was recited, it was apparently done so with a great deal of fervour for the provision of their literal daily bread. Last night Robert ground the wheat for the bread and I set it on the rise before I went to bed (the convict-style yeast is slow to work). I am pleased with the fact that the siftings of bran and sugar with water is indeed starting to 'work' and can be used as the raising agent, sourdough style. In the meantime I content myself with my regular sourdough plant (see recipe page 123).

Many back then relied on damper made from flour, the dough made light by including bicarbonate of soda (available earlier than 1840), activated by mixing with an acid such as sour milk or vinegar. In the absence of an oven it was cooked over coals in a large covered saucepan.

The Port Arthur penal colony gave a snapshot of the value of bread. Three men and a boy made 500 to 600 loaves per day. This system was subject to corruption, however, so much so that the bakers had to be locked up at night.

Bread was said to be damp and heavy — extra water was added for weight, flour sold off and substituted in part with pease or bean meal.

When it comes time to light the stove a couple of hours before the class, I am short on sticks and have no time to collect more from the wood heap at the other end of the yard. Robert has vanished and no amount of calling brings him over from the far paddock, so I use what I can find. I set the stove alight and disaster strikes immediately. I've started it before before with no problem at all, but today of all days, smoke is pouring out of every nook and cranny, filling the room with its billowing acrid aroma.

NOOO! This stove is to be the *pièce de résistance* today. Although not identical to a colonial-era oven, its cooking process is exactly the same. How can this be happening?! Robert by now has come running — I guess it's a bit disconcerting seeing smoke billowing from every window in the school. There's nothing for it, no way I can stop it. Robert goes outside and bashes the flue to get some airflow going and finally something works and the smoke goes where it's supposed to, at last. I'd put too big a fire in it, and too few sticks.

Still, my carefully organised day's schedule is now out of sync. I get myself together somehow and we get through the session unscathed with no-one aware of the debacle beforehand.

It never ceases to amaze me that the old colonial methods of preserving and even cookery are very little changed. For instance, a recipe for raspberry jam is still almost exactly the same, the measurements and methods matching to a tee.

Here are some of the recipes we make in class that day (measurements have been converted to metric). The Blackberry and Rhubarb Shortcake is my modern-day equivalent of a colonial-era dessert. In it you'll see the recipe for baking powder. The pastry would have been used to bake fruit mince tarts as well.

Colonial Raspberry Jam

Weigh the fruit and place it in the preserving pan. Simmer for a few minutes to release the juices.

When the fruit is ready, add a pound of sugar for each pound of fruit.

Let it boil 10–12 minutes and then pour into the jars or pots.

Adapted from *The Colonial Cookbook: The recipes of a bygone Australia* by Paul Hamlyn (1970).

Modern-day Raspberry Jam

1.5kg raspberries (or other berries of your choice)
1 lemon, juiced (optional)
1.5kg sugar

Place the raspberries and lemon juice, if using, in a pot and bring to the boil. Cook for 5 minutes over a gentle heat.

Add the sugar and bring back to the boil, stirring.
Boil briskly for about 12 minutes until setting point is
reached (see page 393). Stand for 5 minutes, then pour
into warm sterilised jars and seal.

Makes about 2kg

Colonial Lamb with Redcurrant Sauce

1 leg lamb
1 tablespoon dripping
4 cloves garlic, cut in half
4 sprigs thyme
1 onion, halved
150g redcurrants

Preheat the oven to 450°F (about 210°C).

Place the roasting dish on the stove, add and melt the
dripping and then sear the meat on all sides. Add the
garlic and thyme. Roast in the oven until the lamb is
cooked, about 15 minutes per pound (500g).

Take the dish from the oven, remove the lamb and keep
warm. Drain off the fat, but leave the delicious lamb
juices in there as far as possible.

Add the crushed currants and stir for 1 minute, then
add ½ cup water to the pan, bring to the boil and cook
for 3 minutes. Strain into a small saucepan, bring
to the boil and reduce to a desired consistency. If
necessary, thicken slightly with 1–2 teaspoons cornflour
mixed to a paste with 1 tablespoon cold water.

I found the sauce a little bitter, so added ½ teaspoon
apricot jam, ½ teaspoon sweet chilli sauce (which is
entirely optional) and salt and pepper to taste.

Serves 4–6

Blackberry and Rhubarb Shortcake

BAKING POWDER
125g bicarbonate of soda
45g cream of tartar
125g ground rice

FILLING
300g rhubarb stalks, cut into 1cm slices
¼ cup water
about ½ cup sugar
300g blackberries
1 tablespoon cornflour mixed to a paste with 1 tablespoon cold
*   water*

PASTRY
125g butter, softened
125g sugar
1 egg
250g plain flour
1 teaspoon baking powder (as above)

To make the Baking Powder, combine all the ingredients.

To make the Filling, place the rhubarb, water and sugar in a saucepan and bring to the boil over a low heat. Simmer gently for 5 minutes, taking care that it does not catch, then stir in the blackberries. Bring back to the boil over a medium heat and, when boiling, stir in the cornflour paste until the mixture thickens. Cool.

Preheat the oven to 180°C. Grease a 20cm square ceramic dish or tin.

To make the Pastry, beat the butter and sugar together, then beat in the egg until well combined. Mix in the combined flour and baking powder with a metal spoon to form a soft dough. Wrap in cling film and refrigerate for 30 minutes at least.

On a lightly floured surface, roll out two-thirds of the dough to fit the base of the prepared tin. Spread the cooled fruit mixture over. Roll out the remaining portion of dough to 6mm thickness and cut into strips, then place in a lattice pattern over the fruit.

Bake for 30 minutes until the pastry is golden brown.

Serves 6

The lamb with redcurrant sauce is a huge hit, as is the Hedgerow Cordial Syrup. The blackberry and rhubarb shortcake is also well received. The slow combustion stove works like a trooper after all — anything and everything that comes out of it is cooked to perfection.

The post lady arrives at the gate as I am closing it after the students leave. All have samples of food we've made to take away — buns and preserves.

Before long two journalists arrive: they want to write an article on cooking schools in Tasmania. Could they take a picture? Of course, and please, would they eat while they are here?

They do, and pronounce the lamb delicious. I am so happy that the food won't be finding its way to the chickens, as did three-quarters of a berry cheesecake from a photo shoot here a few days ago. The chickens don't really deserve it — they have stopped laying altogether now. Robert says they are just too old. The practical thing is to dispatch them, but neither of us has the heart for it, and so they spend their days happily foraging in the paddocks, supplementing their already more than ample diets.

At the end of this very busy day, there is plenty of raspberry jam to send to Queensland to our daughter Philippa and her family. Grandchildren Indiana and Hudson love it; they call it Nanny Jam. As often as possible I send a package of this along with other treats for them. Although Philippa can and does make the jam, northern raspberries don't have that wonderful intensity of flavour that is characteristic of the cool-climate ones grown here in Tasmania.

March 10

I've been very much looking forward to having this group from Sustainable Living Tasmania at the school. They call themselves Tassievores, committed as they are to eating as much as is humanly possible that is grown and produced in Tasmania. In the context of the cooking class, this is quite an adventure, and very fitting. There should only be a very few ingredients that cannot be locally sourced.

I've learned a lot about local producers in seeking out seasonal produce for them, taken anything and everything ripe out of Stephanie's garden and picked more hawthorn berries and rosehips and blackberries.

And now the day has arrived. Everyone arrives promptly, as does my dear friend Jenny, who has come to do the washing up. I'm sure she doesn't know what she's in for — I am renowned for being a messy cook! I hate having to stop to clean up — it stifles thought processes and creativity.

The class is soon in full swing, with much enthusiasm from the participants. We make, by way of preserves, plum sauce, raspberry jam, piccalilli and tomato relish, and also some bread and cakes.

We make apricot and raspberry cake, and the overnight wholemeal bread that I mixed and set to rise last evening is now baked in little flower pots. People often find it hard to believe that I use, quite literally, garden-variety clay pots. I first came across the idea when my son Andrew was working at the once-famous Rockerfellers Restaurant in Hobart. One of the signature features of their menu was these little loaves of bread baked in clay pots.

I tried baking them just in a greased pot at first but that didn't work — the bread stuck so badly it was all but impossible to remove. However, when I revisited it a couple of years later, Andrew told me it was necessary to season the pots. To do so, deep-fry the pots (truly) in hot oil (about 140°C) for 30 to 40 minutes, then drain.

You only have to do this once — after this they just need to be greased well before putting the dough in.

Overnight Wholemeal Bread

900g plain flour
375g wholemeal flour
1 tablespoon salt
1 heaped tablespoon brown sugar
1 heaped teaspoon dried yeast
30g butter
1 tablespoon molasses, malt or honey
400ml boiling water
400 ml cold water

In a bowl, mix together the flours, salt, sugar and yeast.

Add the butter and molasses, malt or honey to the boiling water and stir until melted, then mix in the cold water and allow to cool to lukewarm. Combine the wet and dry ingredients.

Leave in a covered bowl overnight or for about 8 hours in a warm place.

Knock down and knead for a couple of minutes. Divide in half and shape each into a loaf. Grease 2 13 x 21 cm loaf tins. Place a piece of dough in each tin, cover with a tea towel and leave to rise almost to the top of the tin.

Preheat the oven to 200°C. Bake for 40 minutes.

Turn out onto a wire rack to cool.

Makes 2 loaves

Our group picks the huge rhubarb from the garden, and consumes litres of the sparkling fruit drink, this week made from Lindsey's plums. Speaking of which, the preserver is now filled with two more batches of them.

Then there was the cordial syrup. We make a most delicious version featuring hawthorn berries following the Hedgerow Cordial Syrup recipe (page 189). Altogether, we used about 500g mulberries, 1.5kg raspberries and 300g hawthorn berries.

I am often asked if the strained fruit can be used for anything else and the simple answer is no. The fruit gives over its goodness and flavour to the cordial syrup and the residual pulp is tasteless and watery. Chooks don't mind it, but it's best for the compost heap.

By now poor Jenny must have realised the enormity of what she'd volunteered for, but she soldiered on valiantly, even finding time and space to fill the preserver with another load of bottles of plums. She truly is a treasure!

As Jenny is leaving Lindsey arrives with more plums. Can I use them? Of course I can. I'll bottle or more likely dehydrate them (see page 397–8).

We have more than two boxes of nashi to deal with as well, since the class opted for the easier option of bottling plums. Maybe I will dehydrate them too. Actually, come to think of it, there is a new product out on the market — dehydrated apple slices dipped in blackcurrant juice … Now, there's a thought. Maybe I could dip them in hawthorn berry juice (there's a box of those left over). Maybe in a day or two!

March 11

Robert and I have decided that today will be a day of relaxation. After all, he's been on holidays for three weeks now and all we've done is pick fruit, preserve and teach classes. We will travel up through the Midlands, visiting the many antique and collectible shops along the way. I always hope for little kitchen treasures. We will seek out any garage sale for the same. And visit any farmgate stalls that are selling fresh produce — today I am after beetroot.

We have only travelled a few kilometres, but no beetroot as yet, when we come to a stall at the small but sprawling township of Bagdad. It brings back memories of a time when we used to visit the town when the children were young — I am sure the same man is at the stall. The produce is exceptional. Chatty as country people are here in Tasmania, we get to talking for a bit about weather and water and stroppy customers he'd come across who had tried to beat his already low prices down even further.

'Where do you get your tomatoes from for making sauce?' he asks. Well, I buy exceptional hothouse ones from either near Granton or sometimes at the Bridgewater farmgate stall. He is scandalised and doesn't hesitate to tell me so.

'Hothouse tomatoes?! They have no flavour and are full of water. They won't make decent sauce. You need field tomatoes, nothing else!'

He tells me I can buy as many as I need from him any time for $1.70 per kilo. It's a bargain, and I certainly will.

His words, however, unmask a debate that goes on here, akin to the Moor Park debate about apricots. This battle is hothouse versus field tomatoes for flavour for eating and performance for bottling. Indeed, the day before at the Bridgewater stall a bowlful of perfect tomato specimens were displayed with a sign that said, *Taste me. See that I taste better than field tomatoes!*

And so the battle rages on. Next week I have another preserving class and I will visit this man for his field tomatoes and buy others from Bridgewater and let the class judge. Field tomatoes have been so difficult to get on the Tasman Peninsula that I've long since stopped expecting to find them.

The scallop pies at the Ross Bakery come highly recommended. I'm told that the baker has been there 25 years; the owners inherited him when they bought the business six years ago. The puff pastry is as light as a feather, and the shortcrust of the base buttery and short. The filling? Well, that is simply sensational, made with the small, flavoursome Tasmanian scallops.

When we arrive home in the late afternoon we are greeted with the sight of a possum sitting on top of a sparsely leaved silverbirch tree. I wonder what drove him up there. Probably he was scared there by Della, though what could be frightened of her, I can't imagine. She is so fat that she just gives a half-hearted bark at best and doesn't even bother to take a step towards any marauding wildlife. A case in point is the fact that my parsley and tomatoes are now being eaten unmercifully. I've had to pick the ones near the school entrance while they are green. Just as well I have a good recipe for green tomato pickle.

I've tried spreading used coffee grounds, which is supposed to deter them, and this seems to work for a bit, but the local café hasn't given me any in ages. I even sacrificed a new packet of ground coffee but that made no difference.

As I look at the possum stuck in the tree I'd like to be cross, but he is kind of cute and looks pretty forlorn. Robert assures me he will be all right — he'll come down when it's dark to do his marauding all over again. Somehow a wallaby has found its way in also, and between the two of them, it's a bit of a battle.

March 13

After a day of tending to the vegetable gardens, and in the comparative cool of the evening, it is time to give the plums and tomatoes some attention. Robert thankfully offers to help and he prepares 12 bottles of plums while I do the same of tomatoes. We could start a third preserver and bottle the nashi, but by this time I've decided they can wait another day or two, which will give me time to work out the best preserving plan for them. They are not the tastiest of fruit, though refreshing and juicy when eaten fresh from the tree. We've found that pickled and spiced is a good option (see recipe page 165).

One of the class members said she uses a benchtop apple peeler and corer to prepare the nashi. The kitchen gadget turns the fruit into a type of 'slinky'. She bottles them this way and they look exceptionally attractive in the bottles. But by now I've had enough, and it will have to be done tomorrow evening.

I've had little time between classes and preserving to stop and take stock of the garden. However, today I stand back and think about it and realise we have quite a bit here.

- apples
- spinach
- silverbeet
- lettuces galore
- spring onions
- a multitude of herbs
- celery
- masses of rhubarb
- an overwhelming quantity of tomatoes of all shapes and sizes
- pumpkin
- corn
- chillies
- beans
- a second crop of raspberries
- boysenberries
- cumquats

That's not too bad for someone who's not a great gardener and considering how little time we've spent tending the vegetable patches and orchard. I'm much encouraged.

We have much more planted out, on their way to being productive — cabbages and cauliflower, zucchini, more potatoes, limes, lemons, horseradish and artichokes. However, the kangaroos that jump the fences at night have attacked them. I expect they might recover as Robert has now fenced around them with loose chicken wire, which wildlife dislikes. I'd hoped to avoid this type of fencing because it could hardly be described as attractive, but it seems a necessity. They are not at all upset by us and certainly not Della. We seem to fascinate them, that's all.

Robert was working in the shed a few nights ago and when he turned to glance over at the door a kangaroo was standing in the doorway, as calm as you please, watching what he was doing.

On the subject of animals, Tom and Della have at last come to an understanding. Tom has disliked Della on principle it seems and bosses her around terribly. In the evenings when Della pokes her nose inside the door, Tom soon sends her away with a scratch on it. The house is his domain, he's obviously decided.

However, they really like the cooking-school arrangement — lots of pats and admiration from the lovely people who arrive. They have joined forces in this regard, Della waddling out to the carpark, tail wagging expectantly for pats or even, she hopes, food. Tom, not to be outdone, walks alongside and rolls on his back, looking extremely adorable and inevitably gets the desired belly rub and matching admiration.

March 15

I have been offered quinces for a mere $1 per kilo — I can pick them up at the local market on Saturday. I can't understand my hesitation and slowly it dawns on me that living in the Derwent Valley, I am becoming more than a little spoilt. Very little of the produce I've been working with I've actually had to pay for as the foraging and gleaning yields in the region are so high.

I also miss the experience of going 'quincing' with Stephanie and I'm glad she and her family will be returning from holidays soon. She has such a good eye for fruit that is unwanted and going to waste, or at best falling on the ground for animals to eat. She found just such a spot down a country lane a few years ago and we've been visiting it each autumn ever since. It falls to Steph's husband Nat to climb the higher branches to pick the best of the fruit, while Stephanie and I pick the middle tier and Charly and Jacob empty the lower branches. In no time at all we gather cases of quinces.

One of the wonderful features of quinces is their aroma. It is truly the smell of autumn, and I keep a basketful on the bench for as long as they will last.

Inevitably there will be trays galore of quince cheese and jelly. The former is wonderful on a cheese platter and the jelly is great for scones and toast. I like adding just a teaspoon or so of jelly to a gravy, sauce or casserole.

Quince Jelly

1.5kg quinces, washed well to remove the furry 'bloom'
juice of 1 lemon (optional)
water
sugar

Chop the quinces, combine with the lemon juice and barely cover with water. Bring to the boil and simmer until tender, about 20 minutes, depending on the quinces.

Strain through a colander, then strain the juice through a sieve lined with double thickness of muslin. For each cup of liquid add 1 cup sugar.

Bring to the boil, stirring occasionally to dissolve the sugar, then continue to boil until setting point (see page 393) is reached.

Pour into warm sterilised jars and seal immediately. The jelly can be eaten at once.

Makes about 1.75 litres

March 16

Last night I heard shooting in the valley. I know that the wildlife is a pest and decimates orchards and vegetable gardens, but still it saddens me. The animals have, after all, been driven this way by the fires that have left the terrain devoid of feed in the valleys over the hill.

Della is very afraid and scuttles around the back of the house, abandoning her basket. I worry for Tom as he is still a wanderer and his eyes glow in the dark in the manner of cats. I console myself with the thought that he is well used to surviving out in the bush and has no doubt dodged a bullet or two in his time.

On a happier note, last evening I was able to do a preserving demonstration at the Habitat store in Hobart. I was surprised when I arrived — our Courtney had come to help. She and I used to do much cooking and catering together when she was still at home. Those were great times. This evening is no exception — she is a whizz in the kitchen and soon we are preparing zucchini pickle, tomato relish, sweet chilli sauce, raspberry and blueberry jam, and raspberry and blueberry cordial. Courtney also demonstrates how to bottle fruit with her precise method of placing apricots in the jars. They really look a treat.

We are a family that hates waste, and there happened to be a few plums and peaches left over, and a punnet of blueberries. Courtney decided to turn them into jam, an on-the-spot invention that she calls Autumn Fruits Jam. It turns out really well and is very well received as a topping for freshly baked scones.

Courtney's Autumn Fruits Jam

Courtney used dark red Japanese plums, which gave a rich purple hue to the jam, and the peaches were yellow-fleshed clingstones, but any variety of either could be substituted, as could nectarines for the peaches.

> 500g peaches, weight with stones removed
> 500g plums, weight with stones removed
> 200g blueberries
> juice of 1 lemon
> ½ cup water
> 1.1 kg sugar

Dice the flesh of the peaches and plums and place in a pot with the blueberries, lemon juice and water. Bring to the boil, stirring, and then reduce the heat and simmer until the fruit is soft, stirring often so it doesn't catch.

Add the sugar and bring to the boil, stirring. Cook over a medium heat, stirring often, until setting point (page 393) is reached. Pour into sterilised bottles and seal immediately.

Makes about 1.8 litres

March 17

The cooking school is overflowing with produce yet again. The last of the nashi will spoil if they are not bottled soon. Would it be easier to consign them to the compost heap? Yes, but how could I even think such a thing, regardless of how tired I am? There are only two large boxes, after all.

Thankfully one thing Robert and I do well together is preserve. We bought the apple peeler/corer that the student recommended — a hand-operated machine that has been around in one form or another since colonial times — that peels as it cores and the flesh is turned into a 'slinky'.

After a few minutes Robert raises the idea of filling the centre of each 'slinky' with rhubarb stalks. Why not? It's a great idea and we try it. It's really only suited to filling the larger jars as the nashi must be returned to their original shape. Still, it looks wonderful, and they keep their form and colour when preserved. The rhubarb should also boost the flavour.

Bottled Nashi

Peel and core the nashi and either halve them or make into 'slinkies' (see introduction).

Fill jars with nashi halves, packed firmly, and cover immediately with the syrup. If you are preparing a large number of nashi, you may like to drop them into half to three-quarters of a bucket of water in which I tablespoon citric acid has been dissolved to help prevent discolouration.

Make a syrup of medium strength (see page 386) and fill the jars to the brim. To each 4 litres syrup add 5g citric acid or 2 tablespoons lemon juice.

Put the lids on jars, then secure with 2 clips. Place in the preserver. Fill the preserver with cold water up to the lid of the bottles. Bring heat up to 90°C (this should take about 45 minutes), and hold at this temperature for 1 hour.

With a thermostat-control unit, turn the preserver to 90°C and leave for 1¾ hours.

⟡

A tragedy has occurred along the way, however. My preserver has started leaking around the base. I am devastated — this preserver holds a special place in my heart. I know exactly how long it is since I bought it.

Twenty-three years ago, when the children of the family numbered four, I was almost nine months pregnant with our fifth child, Elliott. A friend had purchased a thermostat-controlled stainless-steel preserver, a thing I could only dream of at that stage. (I was still using the old stovetop models.)

However, her husband only liked apricots and she was heading back to full-time work and thought she'd no longer have time for preserving. Would I like to buy it from her for a mere $50, including a whole stash of Fowlers jars?

I couldn't believe my luck and was excited beyond belief. It must have had its effect as a few hours later, on 17 July 1988, I went into labour. A quick labour it was too — maybe I just couldn't wait to get home to start using the preserver!

With these memories, it's essential that this preserver is repaired. Robert goes to work with the welder so that it is soon functional once more.

⟡

There is still an abundance of tomatoes and so an all-time favourite is to be made today.

This recipe first appeared in *A Year in a Bottle* as Tomato Chilli Pickle, and has been one of the most popular. I've simplified the recipe to a large extent.

Don't be worried about the oil that may settle on top — it is all part of the preserving process. Once the jar of pickles is eaten, the oil can be used to sauté vegetables or meat, poultry or fish or simply as a dip for fresh, crusty bread.

Kasoundi

2.5cm piece ginger, peeled
20 cloves garlic, peeled
250g long red chillies, roughly chopped
2kg ripe tomatoes
1½ cups cider or white vinegar
1½ tablespoons mustard seeds
1½ cups olive oil
1½ tablespoons turmeric
4 tablespoons ground cumin
1¼ cups sugar
1 tablespoon salt

Place the ginger and garlic in a food processor with the chillies and blitz until a fine paste.

Add to a large saucepan or jam pan with the rest of the ingredients, bring to the boil, stirring, then simmer for 3 hours or until the desired consistency is reached. Pour into sterilised bottles and seal immediately.

Makes about 1.25 litres

Tomato Chutney without Onions

This recipe came about purely through the accidental omission of onions one busy day. It is a good option for people with digestive issues like Irritable Bowel Syndrome for whom the effects of eating onions is a nightmare. Seeds and pips are removed in this recipe for similar reasons. I often have been asked for such a recipe during radio talkback sessions.

To peel the tomatoes, dip for a few seconds in boiling water (it pays to have a pot boiling on the stove), then dip into cold water. The skins will slip off easily. Cut the tomatoes in half, remove the seeds and discard.

2kg tomatoes, flesh only, diced
2 cooking apples, peeled, cored and diced (optional)
2 tablespoons salt
3 teaspoons mustard powder
3 teaspoons curry powder
500g sugar
3 cups vinegar
1 tablespoon cornflour
½ cup vinegar, extra

Place the tomatoes, apples (if using), salt, mustard powder, curry powder, sugar and vinegar into a large saucepan. Bring to the boil, stirring until the sugar is dissolved, and continue to boil for 1½ hours.

Mix the cornflour to a paste with the vinegar, then add some or all to the boiling mixture and stir till thickened.

Pour into sterilised jars and seal immediately. Eat at once or store in a cool, dry and dark place for up to 1 year.

Makes about 2kg

March 18

The hawthorn berries, I am disappointed to see, are past their prime and we will need to gather more.

But there is no time to fret about this. The wildlife is making short work of the tomatoes near the cooking school and it really is time to pick the last of them to make green tomato pickle. This is a great family favourite and is simply wonderful added to stews and minced meat dishes such as meatloaf, meatballs, sausage rolls and patties (rissoles).

Our friend David is coming for dinner. We have known him for decades; in fact he is partly the cause of our avid preserving habits. He used to bring us fruit from his orchard by the boxful, as well as other types he'd acquired from elsewhere — too many for him to use. We set to work to preserve what we had bottles for, and then experimented with other options.

True to form and generous to a fault, David brings with him a huge bagful of quinces, 30 Fowlers jars and a container of rosehips from the bushes that grow wild on his property. It is much appreciated — I really want to experiment with the rosehips to develop an easier recipe for rosehip syrup than the one in *A Year in a Bottle*. Quinces I love — they are second only to mulberries as my favourite fruit. Best of all are the jars — we had only two empty ones left here.

In the late afternoon we go outside to wage war against a horrid flat weed that is threatening to overtake all the grassy areas near the house and beyond. We have sprayed, but still they proliferate, so we are back to digging them out, one at a time. I've decided to return to the hundred-on-average a day, a strategy I used when we first came here. This evening I'm sure I've at least quadrupled it. Still, we seem to have made some progress and I'm sure we will win out.

A passing neighbour some time ago told me that when he moved to his property, he pulled out 40 garbage bags of the things. It became almost recreational, he said, as he and his daughter were the main executioners of the pest. Now when she comes to visit, the two of them go out and try to find more for old time's sake. And this weed-pulling, though a humble and onerous task, is not altogether unpleasant in the cool of the evening as autumn approaches.

March 19

This morning we decide to go to Stephanie's to check her garden as she has asked us to pick the fruit while she is away on holiday. The strawberries will surely need picking, as will the beans and possibly more besides. The rain of last evening has meant the berries need processing immediately.

Stephanie has suggested freezing the beans, but as they sit tantalisingly in the bucket, I think there must be a pickle to invent that would make better use of them. A project for tomorrow, I think.

When we finish the picking it dawns on me that we are now going for the classic old-time Sunday drive. I remember these with my parents. However, we go with a purpose — we simply cannot resist the temptation to do a little foraging. Today we find more quinces, though it seems others have been there before us, as the only ones left are almost out of reach.

We return home and I decide to turn the strawberries into jam and conserve. By the latter method the strawberries can be 'held' by adding sugar and leaving to stand overnight. Next day they are cooked into a conserve. The difference to regular jam is that the strawberries retain their shape and usually the flavour is better.

Strawberry Jam

> *1.5kg strawberries*
> *1 teaspoon citric acid*
> *1.25kg sugar*

Place the strawberries and citric acid in a large saucepan. Bring to the boil, stirring constantly, then reduce the heat and simmer for 15 minutes, stirring often.

Add the sugar and stir until dissolved. Bring back to the boil and cook briskly until setting point is reached (see page 393), stirring often. This should take 20–30 minutes. Pour into warm sterilised jars and seal immediately.

Makes about 1.8kg

Strawberry Conserve

> *1.5kg strawberries*
> *1½ teaspoons citric acid*
> *1.25kg sugar*

Place all the ingredients in a bowl and stir to combine. Leave to stand at room temperature overnight.

The next day, bring to the boil, stirring. Boil briskly over medium heat until setting point is reached (see page 393). This should take 15–20 minutes. Pour into warm sterilised jars and seal immediately.

Makes about 1.8kg

Freezing Strawberries

For free-flowing frozen strawberries, spread on trays and freeze, then place in freezer bags or airtight containers.

Alternatively, place in freezer bags or containers, allowing headspace to allow for expansions and freeze.

Dehydrating Strawberries

Strawberries can be dehydrated on wire racks over a tray in a very slow oven (65–70°C) or in a food dehydrator.

Personally, I like to make pear and strawberry fruit leather. Simply stew peeled, cored and chopped pears with a little water and the same weight of strawberries until a smooth purée forms (ensure it's not too wet).

Spread to 6mm thick on trays lined with baking paper (if dehydrating in the oven), or spread on fruit leather sheets for a dehydrator.

Dehydrate until no liquid is exuded when a sheet of the leather is torn. Cool and store in an airtight container in the fridge (freezer if to be stored for longer than 3 weeks).

March 20

I receive an email this morning asking about my tomato, quince and apple sauce. My goodness, I'd forgotten about that recipe and here I have to hand all the necessary ingredients. Jam jars are scarce though, but I guess I can find something that will suffice.

Tomato Sauce with Apple and Quince

1.5kg tomatoes, chopped
250g apples, peeled and chopped
250g quinces, peeled, cored and chopped
500g onions, peeled and chopped
2 tablespoons salt
3 teaspoons mustard powder
3 teaspoons curry powder
500g sugar
3 cups white or cider vinegar

Place all the ingredients in a large saucepan and bring to the boil over a medium heat, stirring until the sugar is dissolved. Continue to simmer for 1½ hours, stirring occasionally. Purée with a stick blender or in a food processor or push through a food mill or sieve.

Return to the heat and cook until it reaches a sauce-like consistency. Pour into sterilised jars and seal immediately. Store in a cool, dry, dark place.

Makes about 2.5 litres

March 21

There's a photographer coming today, a follow-up to a journalist's visit a couple of weeks ago, so this morning has been a frenzy of baking. I am never sure what will be needed during a shoot, and don't want to keep anyone standing about while I get things together.

I opt to make small steak-and-stout pies. Robert made a stout that was so strong that it was nearly unpalatable if drunk neat. With lemonade, Portagaff-style, it was barely drinkable, also as a Black and Tan with a half-beer. Needless to say, it was less than popular.

I'd seen its potential however, as a gravy in steak-and-stout pies. You could substitute Guinness for a similar result.

Steak-and-Stout Pies

The mince in this recipe adds extra flavour and texture to the gravy.

PASTRY
180g cold butter, cubed
360g plain flour
1½ teaspoons baking powder
¾ teaspoon salt
cold water
1 egg, lightly beaten, for eggwash

FILLING
2 tablespoons oil
500g diced beef
400g good-quality beef mince
1 onion, peeled and chopped
375ml stout
1 teaspoon salt
1 tablespoon Worcestershire sauce
3 teaspoons soy sauce
2 teaspoons sweet chilli sauce
3 teaspoons chutney (any sort)
3 teaspoons tomato sauce
3 teaspoons cornflour mixed to a paste with approximately ¼
     cup cold water

To make the Pastry, rub the butter into the flour, baking powder and salt until the mixture resembles breadcrumbs (or process to this stage in a food processor). Add enough water (about 6 tablespoons) until a soft dough is formed. Wrap in cling wrap and chill while cooking the filling.

To make the Filling, heat the oil and brown the diced steak and mince together, stirring often to make sure the mince is well broken up. Add the onions and cook for 2 minutes more.

Add the stout, salt and sauces. Bring to the boil, then reduce the heat and simmer for 2 hours or until the beef is tender. Thicken with some or all of the cornflour paste if needed. Cool.

Grease 10–12 1-cup pie tins. Preheat the oven to 200°C.

To assemble, roll the dough out thinly on a lightly floured surface. Cut out pastry to fit the bases of the tins and brush all over with the egg. Spoon in the cooled filling.

Cut out pieces of pastry to fit the tops, re-rolling the scraps if needed. Place over the filling and seal the edges well. Prick each pie with a fork. Glaze tops with the remaining egg, then bake for about 15 minutes until the pastry is golden.

Makes 10–12 pies

It's bread-baking day as well and I've made my favourite, spelt bread. Spelt is an ancient grain, a cousin to wheat, and has a lovely nutty flavour. It's very nutritious and is gaining popularity. It can be found in health-food shops and even in supermarkets these days.

This bread is really delicious — you will find that spelt takes up less water than regular wheaten flour. It rises comparatively quickly, so I tend to cut back on the yeast.

Spelt Bread

> 2 cups plain flour
> 2 cups spelt flour
> 3 level teaspoons dried yeast
> 2 teaspoons salt
> 3 teaspoons sugar
> 2 tablespoons oil such as olive or canola
> about 1½ cups warm water

In a large bowl, mix the flours, yeast, salt and sugar. Make a well in the centre and pour in the oil and enough water to make a soft dough, adding a little extra water if needed. Cover with a tea towel and leave to rise for about 1 hour or until approximately doubled in size. At this stage you can take the dough to the following step, or just turn it over with a spoon and let it rise again.

When ready, turn the dough out onto a lightly floured surface and knead until smooth. Shape into 2 equal balls and place side by side in a large loaf tin. Cover with a tea towel and allow to rise almost to the top of the tin.

Preheat the oven to 200°C.

Bake for 10 minutes, then reduce the heat to 170°C and bake for 25–30 minutes more or until well risen and golden, and when the loaf sounds hollow when tapped. Turn out onto a wire rack to cool.

Serves 6

As the photographer is finishing, two tourists arrive. They have come to buy preserves and we spend quite a while chatting over the flour, pastry and pies. They are delighted to taste-test and take a doggy bag away, and will travel on to spend the night at Tara's Richmond Home Stay

B&B. Tara is a dynamo and makes people so welcome. She has extensive gardens and often has baby animals that she is hand-rearing.

About 15 minutes after they leave, the man returns. His wife tasted our flowerpot bread with labna and loved it so much that she simply has to buy one. I won't hear of their buying it — we have extra anyway, and I'm flattered she thought well of the little loaves.

I return inside for a cup of tea when I receive a phone call. Another couple are standing at our gate — could they come in for a chat? Of course! The lovely couple is from a gardening forum and would like to bring a group to visit our garden. Frankly I think 'garden' is a bit of an exaggeration as there is still so much we want to do. But it is green, unlike most places in this drought, courtesy of the bore water, and when you stand back and look at it with a more objective eye than ours, it is very pretty, landscaped as it was by one of the property owners in years gone by.

I am assured that the group would love to come. They are self-sufficient and bring fold-up chairs and a little cooler bag and are content to sit and chat and enjoy the garden.

They come and buy some of my preserves as well. Annette is French and a great cook, though very modest about her obvious talent in this respect. They have seen the recipe for overnight wholemeal bread on my blog and share with me their own recipe, which is similar. As they recite it to me, I can see that it's much, much easier than mine.

This is the sort of day I love, when people just drop in and help to eat whatever has been baked that morning.

Just when I think the excitement is over, the twelve sheep that we are to agist for the indefinite future arrive. I am so happy, as I have been suffering from what can only be described as empty-paddock syndrome. There are not even any wallabies or kangaroos after the shooting of a few evenings ago, just a few stray native hens.

I'd investigated another option of two neutered male goats from Rod at the Agrarian Kitchen and was at the point of arranging this, but the sheep's arrival has turned this on its head. I ask the sheep owner Kerry if he thinks there is enough feed for two goats as well as the sheep and he doubts it, especially as he will bring a ram this weekend. This will soon mean lambs.

I'm happy to see the paddock filled again. The sheep are not so pleased to see me though. When I go down later to meet them they stare at me blankly before scuttling to the other end of the paddock. It's probably just as well that I don't get attached to them — Kerry promised us part of a lamb in return for the agisting.

March 23

Megan and Amanda, teachers, arrive promptly for a class at nine o'clock, greeted as is customary by Della and Tom. We have a great time over the next few hours, baking and preserving. They ask incredibly intelligent questions, breaking down aspects of preserving into component parts and then putting them back together again.

It was then that it was clarified for me that the charts at the end of this book must be included. They will be spending two days in Tasmania, taking in the sights as it's Amanda's first time here, though Megan grew up on the northwest coast.

As they leave with samples aplenty, they are more than mere participants in a class. They have become good friends.

When they leave I decide to finish the trial batch of rosehip syrup. I have long wanted to make it but every batch I've ever trialled has been tasteless. Worse, it needs to be preserved in the Fowlers style. I just don't think this should be necessary, and it tends to turn the syrup into jelly. Also, I want the flavour of the rosehip to be much more pronounced.

I decide to throw out the notion of making the cordial as specified by other recipes, even my own from *A Year in a Bottle*, and start from scratch.

I am very pleased with the result: it is delicious and the flavour of the rosehips has been captured in the cordial. I fairly dance for joy. I've been trying to capture the flavour in just this way for over 30 years. Will it keep well on the shelf? Only time will tell, but I am quietly confident. (Months later it was still perfect, with no sign of spoilage.)

Rosehip Syrup

750g rosehips
3 litres water
sugar
3 teaspoons citric acid

Wash the rosehips and place in the bowl of a food processor with 1 cup of the water and blitz until finely chopped. (If you have a small food processor you may need to do this in 2 batches.)

Place immediately into a saucepan with the rest of the water and bring to the boil. Reduce the heat and simmer for 2 minutes. Leave to stand for 2 hours, then strain through a colander and the resulting liquid through a strainer or colander lined with two thicknesses of muslin.

To each cup of liquid add 1 cup sugar. Return to the heat and bring just to the boil, stirring, then stir in the citric acid until dissolved. Pour into warm sterilised bottles and seal immediately.

Makes about 5 litres

March 24

Today Robert says we simply must to go down to the house at Eaglehawk Neck once more. I admit I always try to weasel my way out of this. It's a bit disconcerting visiting the old house — I still have a fondness for it and miss the sound and sight of the ocean, and feel bad for the wildlife we left behind, even though we never did make them dependent on us.

A few weeks ago when we travelled down, the effects of the fire, while clearly visible, were not quite so bad as I'd imagined. But now, two months or more later, with some of the blackened trees cleared from the verges, the affected countryside is more exposed. Though the grass is green due to recent rains, it only accentuates the forlorn blackened trees and uncovers the remnants of houses that burned to the ground.

At Dunalley gaping holes exist in many places where homes, sometimes decades old and much loved, once existed. The ruins have been cleared in some places so no rubble is to be seen, just stark, bare earth.

I've heard that the community in this region has decided that 'fire' is the new 'f' word, and instead put the focus on regrowth and redevelopment. It looks positively to the future and a new school has risen from the ashes in a matter of weeks.

Even those trees that didn't actually die seem to have adopted this attitude. A brilliant green leafy fuzz trails up the trunks from the ground and out along the outstretched branches. It is a sign of hope and renewal, and a promise that the bush and forest have survived and will soon thrive again.

As is customary, we call in to see son Andrew and Emma and baby Hunter on the way home. I've packed for Andrew, a great cook and enthusiastic preserver, a bag of quinces. I also packed a bag of fresh hops for him to experiment with. However, on the trip down they must have blown out of the back of the ute. I'm sure anyone who finds it will be convinced it's marijuana as (I'm told) they look very similar.

The quinces we've acquired so far this year are a bit disappointing. Could it be the hot weather, so intense and prolonged this summer? A bowlful on the bench will fill a room, if not a whole house, with their wonderful perfume, but this year it is not the case. Even when cooked, the deep scarlet colour does not develop as it should.

Quinces of course, as I have said, herald the onset of autumn and I miss their aroma. Returning to the peninsula as we have and with the thought of picking the fruit in mind, I recall an episode from a few years ago when it turned into quite a stress-ridden adventure.

We knew of a tree with fruit that was dropping on the ground. I found out the name of the person on whose property it grew, rang him and came to a suitable bartering arrangement — a few jars of quince jelly for as much fruit as I wanted, and off we went.

All was fine, and we were picking away merrily, when suddenly a crabby old voice yelled, 'Who said you could 'ave them quinces?'

He hung over the fence wielding a great pumpkin knife in his hand, working as he was in his vegetable garden. I calmly explained to him that we had the owner's permission, to which the man said it was *his* tree and he should have been consulted. He fixed me with an eye reminiscent of that of the Ancient Mariner, then vowed to ask the landowner if I had done such a thing. Even if so, he adamantly maintained I still had no right to touch them!

So off he stomped round the back to consult. We had stashed our harvest into the back of the ute (we'd picked ourselves a generous haul), then awaited his return, as I refused to be labelled a skulking thief. He came out (mega-knife still in hand) and aggressively waved us on.

No way, mate! I asked him what had happened, to which he replied it was OK after all, but I should ask him next time. 'No point me lookin' after 'em if people come 'n' pinch 'em!'

I didn't quite know how to work that one out, and thought I'd probably take him a jar of the jelly to pacify him. Then again, when I thought of that pumpkin knife … I decided against it.

March 26

Before this beetroot I bought from Bagdad a few days ago is beyond using, I simply must set to work to trial the recipes I've been sent by two ABC listeners. Most days, and today is no exception, beetroot holds no appeal whatsoever.

Once I get started it's not so bad. First I trial Betty's recipe, which necessitates peeling and grating a large amount, so half a batch will do. Meg's recipe calls for the beetroot to be parboiled first. I lost concentration and so cook Meg's a bit longer, to the point of very tender, but the end result seems little affected.

When I bring myself to taste the results, ever so tentatively, I am quite surprised — they are not too bad at all, palatable even. I think they are far better than pickled beetroot slices, which always seem to taste a bit too vinegary.

So here are the recipes. The response from various, very honest and forthright tasters is that they are both really nice.

Meg's Beetroot Chutney

1kg beetroot, parboiled then peeled and cut into small cubes
500g onions, peeled and diced
500ml vinegar
250g sugar
2 tablespoons mustard seeds
½ teaspoon ground ginger
¼ teaspoon ground cumin
½ teaspoon ground allspice

Place all the ingredients in a large saucepan and bring to the boil, stirring occasionally, then reduce the heat and simmer for 1½ hours. Pour into warm sterilised jars and seal immediately.

Makes about 1.8 litres

Betty's Beetroot Relish

1kg beetroot
500g onions
¼ cup salt
375g sugar
1 teaspoon ground ginger
1 litre vinegar (I used white vinegar)
1 tablespoon golden syrup

Peel and grate the beetroot and onions and mix through the salt. Leave to stand overnight.

Next day, drain well in a colander, then place in a large saucepan with the rest of the ingredients. Bring to the boil, stirring, then reduce the heat and simmer for 30 minutes. Pour into warm sterilised jars and seal immediately.

Makes about 2 litres

March 28

There is a slow-cooking class in full swing here today when there is a knock at the door. It's Anne, the lady from Australia Post.

Almost from the first day we arrived here, she comes up to the house to deliver our mail. She never utters a word of complaint, though I'm sure she would have good cause, with the steady stream of parcels she has to carry in for us from the front gate.

To get to the door she has to get past Della. Della is not vicious, but is always on the lookout for food, wagging her tail expectantly at anyone who comes through the gate. Anne has turned out to be her adult best friend and even on days when she only has letters for the box out the front, Della is there to greet her.

Anne is kindness itself and carries a pocketful of Goodos. Della is ecstatic to be given one each time they meet.

Sometimes a class is in full swing when Anne comes in with a parcel. Occasionally I can persuade her to take some samples with her — something we've been baking, a jar of pickle or jam for her to enjoy later. Only little things, but today Anne comes with another parcel and has in the crook of her arm a bunch of flowers, which she hands to me.

'For all the lovely samples you've given me,' she says. My goodness, she is so incredibly kind. I'm sure there's not another postie anywhere any better or kinder than Anne.

March 31

A day in the garden makes me realise just how many tomatoes we have remaining, red and green and many shades in between. Looks like there'll be abundant green tomato chutney this year. The following recipe first appeared in *A Year in a Bottle* but I've since simplified it.

Green Tomato Chutney

> *3kg green tomatoes, chopped*
> *1kg onions, peeled and chopped*
> *3 tablespoons cooking salt*
> *½ teaspoon ground pepper*
> *3¾ cups cider vinegar*
> *1kg sugar*
> *3 scant tablespoons curry powder*
> *3 scant tablespoons mustard powder*

Combine tomatoes and onions in a bowl, sprinkle with salt and mix well. Cover and leave to stand overnight.

The next day drain off the liquid and discard.

Place the rest of the ingredients in a large saucepan or
jam pan and bring to the boil, stirring. Cook for 1 hour
or until a chutney-like consistency is reached.

Pour into sterilised jars and seal immediately. Eat
immediately or store in a cool, dark and dry place for
up to 2 years.

Makes about 4 litres

I once made pickled green tomato slices but it was truly horrible.

This year, given the prolific number of tomatoes that surely would
not ripen, I put together this recipe, which is actually very nice and can
be served much like bread-and-butter cucumber slices.

Pickled Green Tomatoes

1.5kg green tomatoes, cut into 1cm slices
375g onions, peeled and thinly sliced
½ cup salt
400g sugar
1.2 litres vinegar
1 bay leaf
2 teaspoons curry powder
1 tablespoon yellow mustard seeds
½ teaspoon dried chilli flakes

Combine the tomatoes, onions and salt and leave to
stand for 24 hours, then drain well in a colander.

Place the sugar, vinegar, bay leaf and curry powder in
a large saucepan. Lightly crush the mustard seeds in
a mortar and pestle and add to the pot with the chilli
flakes. Bring to the boil, stirring, then add the drained
vegetables and bring back to the boil once more.

Spoon the vegetables into jars and then pour over the remaining vinegar. Ensure all the vinegar mixture is used. Seal immediately.

Makes about 3 litres

April 1

Stephanie and the family will be back from their holiday this week. In their absence we have been keeping an eye on the garden and the beans are going crazy. Time we picked some more. Their guinea pigs love them and eat almost all we have picked, but now there are way too many even for them to consume.

I've long wanted to develop a decent recipe for green bean pickle and today's abundant picking certainly gives the opportunity for that. I spend the evening trying to find a recipe — no cookbook, no Internet search reveals anything other than the regular spices that go into such a product.

Back to the drawing board then. One kilo didn't seem an inordinate number to work with in this respect until it came to slicing them. (Belatedly it occurred to me that I had an old bean slicer out in the cooking school.)

A touch of chilli would add a little bit of spice, and just a touch of onion. The mustard and turmeric with sugar and vinegar, maybe a bay leaf.

The chilli is optional of course. I wouldn't use runner beans for which I have a great dislike. Any we've ever grown end up stringy and nasty, even when they are picked in prime condition. Nice young dwarf beans are ideal and rarely need stringing.

This is quite a sweet pickle and nice served with a salty meat such as slow-cooked corned silverside or ham.

Green Bean Pickle with Chilli

1kg green beans, stalk end removed (and strings if there are any)
2 long red chillies (about 50g) (or more to taste)
1 onion, finely chopped

¼ cup salt
2 cups white or cider vinegar
2 cups sugar
2 teaspoons turmeric
2 teaspoons ground mustard
1 small—medium onion, peeled and finely diced
1 bay leaf

Cut the beans into 1cm pieces. Remove the chilli stalks and dice the flesh finely. Place in a large bowl with the onion and salt and mix well. Leave to stand for 3 hours. Drain well in a colander.

Place the vinegar, sugar, turmeric, mustard, onions and bay leaf in a large saucepan and bring to the boil, stirring. Add the vegetables and bring back to the boil, then reduce the heat and cook for 20 minutes until the beans are tender. Remove the bay leaf.

Pour into warm, sterilised jars and seal immediately.

Makes about 1.4 litres

April 2

It's to be a day of comparative inactivity in the kitchen today. To brighten us up neighbour Rosemary comes to visit with a huge bag of Pomme Neige apples. They are very like Lady in the Snow, for which I had such a fondness when I was a child. I remember well travelling to the Huon Valley where apple trees covered the hills, valleys and river flats as far as the eye could see. Ladies in the Snow are very hard to find nowadays, but used to be a child's delight, with their bright red skin and snow-white flesh.

They won't keep well, Rosemary tells me, which won't be an issue. I have great plans for them, plus the grandchildren return from their mainland adventure this weekend and will eat them at a great rate. However, I want to trial a new apple chutney recipe. All I needed was an abundance of delicious apples, so Rosemary's visit is timely indeed.

April 3

The weather is cooling off in the evenings and the early mornings are a delight. Today, for instance, we awoke to a mist covering the surrounding hills, a truly spectacular sight, ethereal even, reminiscent of *Lord of the Rings*. I've not seen such a mist as this in months. At Eaglehawk Neck the sea mists, though spectacular, were seldom experienced.

Here, however, it is shaping up to be a mist lover's paradise and thankfully I am one of those. It waxes and wanes into and around our property — there are truly few more enchanting sights than the ducks foraging among the fruit trees and the sheep with heads bowed to the ground as the gentle mist swirls around their woolly backs.

It is evident that the winter frosts will soon arrive. This means that the pumpkins will need to be picked. Once a frost hits them they are likely to split open and rot.

Time, then, to give some attention to making good use of them. They will keep if they are stored on straw on their sides, but there are one or two on which the stalk has broken already and need immediate attention.

Pumpkin chutney is always popular, especially the recipe that follows.

Pumpkin Chutney

3 tablespoons olive oil
250g onions, finely chopped
1 apple, cored and finely diced
500g pumpkin flesh, diced
4 garlic cloves, crushed
½ cup water
1 tablespoon grated ginger
1 tablespoon salt
350g brown sugar
1 tablespoon golden syrup
2 cups cider vinegar

1 teaspoon ground mustard
1 teaspoon ground allspice
2 teaspoons curry powder
1 teaspoon ground nutmeg
½ teaspoon dried chilli flakes

Heat the oil in a saucepan and sauté the onions, apple, pumpkin and garlic for 5 minutes. Add the water and cook until the pumpkin is just tender. Add the remaining ingredients and bring to the boil, stirring gently until the sugar is dissolved.

Bring to the boil, stirring, then reduce the heat and cook over a medium to medium—low heat for about 40 minutes, stirring often.

Pour into warm, sterilised jars and seal immediately. Leave to stand for 2 weeks before using to allow flavours to develop and mature.

Makes about 1.25kg

I am always horrified at the waste of pumpkin seeds — after all, pepitas, as roasted pumpkin seeds are called, cost a fortune to buy. I'm determined this year, given the good crop of pumpkins, to duplicate (and improve) the product at home.

Roasted Pumpkin Seeds (Pepitas)

Scrape the centre pulp and seeds from the pumpkin. Run cold water through them as you pull away the stringy flesh.

Dry the seeds on a paper towel.

For every 2 cups of seeds, mix with 1½ tablespoons oil (such as olive oil) and sprinkle with salt.

You can cook them in any one of the following ways (in each case make sure the pumpkin seeds are in a single layer only):

Spread out on a tray and bake in an oven preheated to 140°C for about 15 minutes until the seeds start to pop. It's a good idea to shake them about a bit from time to time to make sure they cook evenly.

OR

Place in a microwave-safe dish and cook on High in 1-minute bursts until dry enough. Stir after each minute to make sure that they are evenly cooked.

OR

Roast them in a frying pan, stirring constantly.

Store when completely dry in an airtight container in the fridge.

April 5

I am very proud of my wonderful crop of spinach, which meets and greets the eye of anyone coming to the school. However, there must be a very hungry potoroo who has managed to sneak into the main area near the house, and who each night feasts on my new lettuces, parsley and, worst of all, my magnificent spinach. The patch looks increasingly pitiful each morning. I'm not sure how to go about this — I am, on the one hand feeding the wildlife over the fence, but my affection for this little creature has hit rock bottom and I'm aghast to find myself thinking of dispatching him.

Today Rob from one of the electrical appliance stores is coming to visit. He has been extremely helpful with our selection of electrical appliances for the school, patient as we mulled over options by the hour in the store. He is a keen cook and preserver, so he understands why we are so fixated on choosing exactly the right tools for any given job. He rang a few days ago to tell me that he has a huge number of Beurre Bosc pears from the tree in his garden and he wants to know some ways to preserve them.

Rob arrives in good spirits with his buckets of pears and soon we are bottling away happily. We decide to preserve some in sugar syrup, to which lemon juice or citric acid needs to be added as it helps prevent discolouration.

He particularly wants to make spiced pears so they are next on the menu. This recipe can be used for spiced cherries, plums or quinces as well.

Spiced Pears

SPICED VINEGAR
1 litre white or cider vinegar
8 cloves
2 bay leaves
2 teaspoons ground cinnamon
2 teaspoons ground cardamom
3 teaspoons ground coriander
3 teaspoons ground allspice
1 star anise

SPICED PEARS
2 cups Spiced Vinegar
1kg sugar
2kg pears, peeled, cored and halved

To make the Spiced Vinegar, combine all the ingredients in a large pot. Bring to the boil, then immediately remove from the heat, cover and leave to infuse for 2–3 hours.

Strain the vinegar through 2 layers of muslin. You are now ready to proceed with the rest of the recipe.

Combine the spiced vinegar and sugar in a large saucepan or jam pan. Bring to the boil, stirring to ensure that the sugar is dissolved. Add the pears to the liquid and simmer till barely tender.

Remove the pears with a slotted spoon and pack into sterilised jars. Return the vinegar mixture to the heat, bring back to the boil and boil briskly for 10 minutes. Pour the mixture over the pears, then seal.

You should have some of the syrup mixture left over. Bottle this and use as a topping for ice-cream, yoghurt or similar.

Makes about 4kg

When Rob leaves it occurs to me that quite a lot of the green tomatoes I picked are turning red. Time for me to experiment a little more.

Locally grown capsicum are also readily available, and supplement those from our own garden. The makings for a relish are to hand.

Tomato and Red Pepper Relish

1.5kg firm ripe tomatoes
500g onions
a handful of salt
2½ cups vinegar
500g sugar
1 cucumber, diced
2½ red capsicum, diced
1 level teaspoon mustard powder
1 level teaspoon curry powder
a pinch of cayenne pepper
1 teaspoon turmeric

Chop the tomatoes and onions and place in separate bowls. Sprinkle with salt and leave overnight. The next day, drain off the liquid.

Put the tomatoes, onions, vinegar and sugar in a saucepan, boil for 5 minutes, then add the cucumber and capsicum, along with the spices. Boil for 1 hour until a relish-type consistency is reached.

Pour into sterilised jars and seal immediately.

Makes about 3kg

We've come by some locally grown grapefruit, something I'd not found before. These come from a tree at nearby Lachlan, and I know there's a magnificent specimen at Redlands Estate near Plenty.

They are much sweeter than any others I've tried and we wonder if they will make a decent cordial. I'm not so partial to grapefruit marmalade and you can only eat so many fresh from the tree. The recipe is a great success, very refreshing. I'd serve it with one part syrup to four parts soda water for a really refreshing drink.

Grapefruit Cordial

4 medium-sized grapefruit
2 lemons
1.5kg sugar
1 tablespoon tartaric or citric acid
1 litre boiling water

Finely grate the zest of the grapefruit and lemons. Squeeze the juice from the fruit.

Place the sugar, tartaric or citric acid, grapefruit and lemon zest and juice, and boiling water in a large bowl. Stir until the sugar dissolves.

Leave to stand until cool (overnight for preference), then strain through a sieve and pour into sterilised bottles. Seal immediately.

Refrigerate after opening.

Makes about 2 litres

April 7

This morning we have had an extra hour's sleep — daylight savings has finished at last. I dislike it intensely — why mess with the perfectly good natural phenomena of time? Perhaps I am prejudiced by my grandfather's steadfast resistance to it. He was a very stubborn man and loathed daylight savings when it came into force in his later years. No matter what appointment he had, even an invitation out to dinner, he would arrive at Eastern Standard Time, no matter the inconvenience or confusion to others. My sweet-natured nan tolerated this with good humour, but it must have been a logistical peace-keeping nightmare for her.

His stubbornness extended to other areas as well. He always ate sparingly and Nan told me that if they ever went out to dinner, whether it be to a fancy restaurant or friends' house, if he was served a portion that he considered to be excessive, he refused to eat even a morsel.

Today we hear of a market at the small rural town of Pontville, not too far away — a poultry sale. Birds will be penned and ready for inspection and sale at 9 a.m. and so we plan to see what's on offer. We have no definite plans to buy but it is a possibility, as Robert has now completed the new chook shed, large enough to house six chooks, he estimates.

I expect it will be a low-key affair, but when we arrive it resembles a Boxing Day sale. People are lined up at the roller door of the pavilion and as soon as it's opened, they pour through to inspect the birds on offer.

All manner and varieties of birds are here, from ducks to geese to chooks of every shape, colour and temperament. As we go up and down the aisles of penned birds, they are being bought by their hundreds, it seems, and whisked out of the pens into waiting boxes.

I want not only good layers, but also chooks that don't mind being handled. Some appear quite undaunted by the proceedings and actually enjoy being patted. I jot down the numbers of three pens with seemingly agreeable birds.

'We'll just do one more walk around,' said Robert, ever cautious and never one to impulse-buy.

'There'll be none left by then,' I wail, seeing more and more hens being lifted out and paid for. By now, I am determined to buy.

I actually don't even know how to go about buying, and ask a likely looking browser. He tells me to ask one of the men in orange safety vests. This is how we come to meet Wayne.

A gentle giant of a man, he doesn't seem fazed at all by the pandemonium around us, nor my admission that I really don't have a lot of knowledge about chickens at all. I show him some that I rather like, and he tells us about their laying habits, life expectancy and so on.

He is very likeable and soon I have chosen five young hens. They are quite a placid breed, he tells me, so I am hopeful they will be good pets as well as layers.

By sheer coincidence I have chosen hens that come from his property. He tells me that no animal or bird on his farm is ever killed — they simply are allowed to die of old age after a very agreeable life. Now that is just what I like to hear, as it applies to our place as well, no matter how impractical.

I am very happy as we pay for the birds and head for home to settle them into their new residence. As we leave I look longingly at the baby pet pigs on the back of a trailer — I'd love to buy them but as our son Elliott has borrowed Robert's ute for the weekend, we have no room in my tiny car. It's just as well, really, I have no idea how to look after them. A bit more research needed there, I think.

By now I've determined that these birds will be proper pets in the sense that they will be petted and cuddled. Robert generally feeds any ducks or chickens we've had, but this time I've decided that I will be the one to feed them to encourage their friendliness, and I can't wait to get started.

Any other chickens we've had have been aloof at best. These chickens don't seem to mind at all being picked up and cuddled and I am so, so pleased. This has the makings of a very good relationship. They are even happier once they are fed.

Poultry expert Wayne from the sale has told me to keep them in for a few days until they get used to the property. He has said there will be a definite pecking order and indeed this is so. Top of the brood is a very pretty brown hen — Myrtle, I decide to name her (she reminds me of a lady I once worked with in a hospital kitchen). She is the first to eat and the others must wait or she delivers a sharp peck to the top of their head.

The one black hen among them seems to be the kindly teacher. She is quite smart and though they are used to having grain thrown on the ground for them, she soon works out the feed and water dispensers and demonstrates to the others how to use them.

We are told that we need to feed them bread and fat in the afternoons to help them through the chilly nights.

April 8

Stephanie and Nat's return from their holiday this evening means they will be coming for dinner. This is really exciting after five weeks of not seeing the grandchildren. They arrive mid-afternoon for a planned feast to be cooked in Carmichael, the wood-fired, slow-combustion stove.

I light it with a little trepidation after the last smoke-out, but all goes well and soon roast lamb is sizzling away, along with a potato bake and many other vegetable dishes on the hotplates. There is nothing like the aroma of the wood stove in action, and the food is likewise incomparably better than any cooked by other means.

Nat, always on the go, has taken to pruning many of the bushes around the cooking school and beyond, a task that sorely needed doing. Soon the wheelbarrow is full to overflowing with rosemary and other herbs. Even the lemon tree gets a therapeutic trimming.

Elliott and partner Cassie arrive and soon Elliott and Nat embark on one of the philosophical debates they enjoy so much. Grandchildren Jacob and Charly curl up on my lap for a cuddle and a story and really, I think to myself, life is supposed to be like this.

April 10

More pears have come my way today. Rob has picked two boxes more. Alistair is keen to share in the spoils of this beautiful crop. He has a cake in mind, he tells me.

We've also picked him a boxful of our rhubarb, which will become part of his repertoire of exquisite pastries. He gives me one of his rhubarb tarts, no simple rhubarb tart at that, but one he calls Dexter, which has several layers of flavour, truly sensational.

When I asked if he wanted some of the hops I'd picked by the roadside at Bushy Park, his response was, 'Yes, of course, though I don't know what I'll do with them yet.' Something incredibly delicious, no doubt.

Apparently, according to all the experts I've consulted, there is really nothing that carries a guarantee that wildlife won't eat it. Aromatic herbs are usually the last thing they'll go for, but even my prostrate rosemary is now being munched away at.

I decide to try for a native pepperberry. I love the berries and have used them to flavour gin and vinegar; the former to drink neat or as part of a cocktail, the latter for salad dressings, aioli and mayonnaise. I also make a tomato and peperberry relish. So precious are the leaves that I dehydrate them, then crush them to a powder which I sprinkle over breads before baking.

Right, so pepperberries it is. I buy eight plants and will put them in the ground this weekend. I already have a male plant slowly growing, but these are all females so hopefully the mix will be productive.

My theory is that the potoroo or wallaby will suck or chew on a leaf and dislike the heat and subsequently leave them alone. We shall see.

Tomato and Pepperberry Relish

1kg tomatoes, diced
2 tablespoons pepperberries
375ml cider vinegar
2 teaspoons salt
250g sugar

2 onions, diced
2 teaspoons powdered pepperberry leaves
1 teaspoon mustard powder

Place all the ingredients in a large saucepan and bring to the boil, stirring. Boil for 30 minutes or until a chutney-like consistency is reached.

Pour into warm sterilised jars and seal immediately.

Makes about 1.5 litres

April 12

I have been watching some grapevines behind a shuttered-up shop at the edge of a carpark in the township of New Norfolk. Stephanie told me about these before she left on holidays. Despite the dry conditions, clusters of small green grapes have been slowly ripening on the vines that stretch for several metres along a wire fence.

I want desperately to make verjuice, to see what all the fuss is about. It comes highly recommended. I've read that it is simply the juice of unripe wine grapes. Are these wine grapes, I wonder? Possibly not, but they are unripe and they are free, so will provide the opportunity to experiment at least. Sour in the extreme they surely are, as I find out when I taste one, enough to turn your face inside out.

I pull out my ancient electric juicer. I see no need to buy another. I bought this one at the Showgrounds Market one Sunday for a mere $8. It goes like a dream, albeit a bit noisily.

Today it churns through the grapes with a spitting of pips and a roar of its engine. I am very pleased with the bright green juice. Is this verjuice? I suspect it might be, and imagine the vines behind the shop may have been planted to that end.

A couple of nights ago I threw a handful of the grapes into a chicken casserole, recalling an old recipe called Chicken Veronique, though this particular casserole bears no real resemblance to it. The end result is quite stunning. The grapes have added a certain pleasant piquancy.

I am hopeful that the grape juice, hopefully verjuice, will do the same. I am left with the dilemma of how to preserve it, as obviously it will soon spoil or ferment.

My philosophy is that when in doubt, bottle it. There's bound to be a use for it before next season comes around.

Preserved Juices

Heatproof bottles are ideal for this purpose. There is no need to sterilise them first as this takes place as part of the waterbath method.

Follow the basic preserving method (page 385). Rings and clips are not usual for bottles used for cordials.

Place the bottles in the preserver and fill to the lids with cold water. Bring slowly up to 82°C over 50 minutes, then hold at this temperature for 40 minutes.

Alternatively, if using a thermostat-controlled preserver, turn on to the required temperature and leave for 1½ hours.

On the subject of grapes, here are some successful ways to preserve them.

Bottled Grapes

I like to bottle these whole, though you can halve them, especially with the larger varieties.

Follow the basic preserving method (page 385). Bring the temperature up slowly over 50 minutes to 88°C, then hold at this temperature for 1 hour.

If you have a thermostat-controlled preserver, set the temperature to 88°C and process for 1 hour and 45 minutes.

Freezing Grapes

To freeze so that they are free flowing, spread in a single layer on a tray and freeze, then store in freezer bags or containers in the freezer.

Alternatively, for solid pack, place in sealed freezer bags or containers in the freezer.

Dehydrating Grapes

These are absolutely delicious but take an age to dehydrate, up to about 36 hours for whole grapes. You can halve them, which will reduce the time significantly.

Place the grapes on racks over a tray if dehydrating in the oven. Dry at 70°C until no liquid is exuded if the flesh is torn. Alternatively use a food dehydrator.

Store in an airtight container in the fridge (in the freezer after 3 weeks).

Grape Jelly

I like this recipe made with sour green grapes, but the darker, sweeter varieties develop excellent colour and flavour, though it is more difficult to achieve a good set with the jelly. A mixture of sour and sweet grapes will help overcome this.

1kg grapes
1 litre water
sugar

Place the grapes and water in the saucepan and bring to the boil, then reduce the heat to a simmer. Cook until the fruit is soft. Strain through a sieve, then through a sieve lined with muslin.

For each cup of juice add 1 cup sugar. Bring to the boil, stirring, then cook briskly until setting point is reached.

Leave to stand for 5 minutes, then pour into warm sterilised jars and seal immediately.

Makes about 1 litre

April 13

Today is the ABC radio segment and I feel like death — well, that's a bit of an exaggeration, probably 'half-past dead' as the song says is more like it. Just a cold, but it's a pest and I will sound dreadful on radio.

There is one serious downside to the cold, far worse than the symptoms themselves. I have no sense of smell, let alone taste, and this is a serious problem. Robert can take on the role, but he is beastly careless about food and will say it tastes 'fine' unless there is something abominably wrong with it.

Thankfully a neighbour comes to visit and he is immediately conscripted to the role as well. He, too, says everything tastes 'fine' and so I take their word for it. Interestingly a day or two later, his wife calls in and I tell her that he's been a great help. She tells me that she doesn't quite know how that would go as he thinks a good tasty lunch is a chilli sauce or honey sandwich!

I'm up early and into the baking, an antidote to all ills. I'm still hooked on mulberries and so make mulberry-and-apple-filled buns, along with jaffa buns and the usual savouries — steak-and-stout pies, steak-and-kidney pies and sausage rolls, and quince and apple tarts.

In the midst of making the quince and apple tarts I decided to use the cores and peels of the fruit to try to make a quince and apple jelly. It develops the characteristic deep amber hue of quince jelly and is as clear as crystal. That goes into the basket as well, a gift for today's presenter, Jane Londhurst.

The questions have come in thick and fast, including one about pickling peppers, which I fear I answered less than adequately. Time for experimentation in earnest when I get home. Capsicum, garlic and chillies are notoriously hard to preserve without spoilage.

Quince and Apple Jelly

This jelly can be made from the whole fruit, chopped, instead of the trimmings, but if like me, you were making pies and had the peels and cores a-wasting, this is worth a try.

> *1.5kg quinces and apple peels and cores, roughly chopped*
> *or*
> *1kg quinces and 500g cooking apples, chopped (no need to peel)*
> *juice of 1 lemon*
> *water*
> *sugar*

Place the peels and cores or chopped whole quinces and apples in a large saucepan with the lemon juice and enough water to cover. Bring to the boil and simmer until the quinces are very tender. Strain through a colander, then the resulting juice through a sieve or colander lined with a double thickness of muslin. (If you don't have muslin, you can just use an old pillowcase, single layer.)

For each cup of liquid add 1 cup sugar. Bring to the boil and boil briskly for 20–30 minutes or until setting point is reached. To check for set, place 2 teaspoons of the mixture on a chilled saucer and place in the fridge for a few minutes. If the mixture sets, then your jelly is ready.

If scum forms on the top of the jelly as it's cooking, simply remove with a slotted spoon.

Makes about 1.4 litres

It seems that every farmers' market is now overflowing with capsicum, red, green and yellow. I purchased some a few days ago from the Hobart Farmers' Market. One year I tried preserving them in oil, following a likely looking recipe fastidiously, but still they soon spoiled.

They can be frozen, even dehydrated, but I decide to have a go at pickling them in vinegar. This will create an acid environment in which bugs will find it difficult to survive. Oil is merely a way to keep the air out, which is most often not an effective enough method on its own.

Pickled Peppers

10 red or green capsicum
2 cloves garlic, crushed
1 litre vinegar
1 tablespoon salt
1 tablespoon sugar

Cut the capsicum in half and remove the seeds and membranes. Flatten out with the palm of your hand and place the capsicum under the grill and cook until the skin is blackened. Wrap in cling film and leave for a few minutes, then the skin will easily peel off. Cut into 8mm strips.

Bring the garlic, vinegar, salt and sugar to the boil in a saucepan, add the capsicum and cook for 2 minutes.

Spoon the capsicum into sterilised jars and pour over the hot vinegar mixture. Seal immediately.

Makes about 1.8kg

April 14

As Stephanie is having a stall with her products at the Derwent Valley Autumn Festival today, I am looking after Jacob and Charly.

Charly always wants to cook here and today is no exception. I have planned to make pies for dinner, to serve with a large range of fresh vegetables from the garden. Stephanie is also coming down with this cold and the cool morning and evening at the festival is guaranteed to make her feel worse, let alone having to cook a meal when she gets home.

Soon Charly and I are on a roll — I am impressed with her innovation with flavours for one so young. We make steak-and-kidney and steak-and-stout pies with the remaining mixtures from the ABC offerings yesterday. There is a large bowl of stewed quinces and apple and as we fill yet more pies, she suggests we add a little cheese to the filling. Why not? After all, I often make cheese pastry for an apple pie.

Several dozen pies later, we are very satisfied with the results of our hard work and just in time, too, for Stephanie and Nat's arrival.

Charly and I also invented a jam — banana. I bought too many bananas at the market because they were of good quality and inexpensive, but with trolley loaded I did a final round of the vegetable stalls to seek out any bargain I might have missed. Forgetful as always, I thought I hadn't yet added bananas, so added another two-kilo bag. How ever on earth were two people supposed to eat that many?

Bananas freeze well and are ideal for cakes or even frozen icy-poles for the children (especially if one end is dipped in chocolate). However, freezer space is in short supply, full as they are of fruit and vegetables and loaves of bread and much more besides.

Many years ago I'd made banana jam from a recipe in an old Esk Valley cookbook. However, when I went to find the recipe, it was nowhere to be found. So it was back to the drawing board to invent another. I was so pleased with the result and it was an instant hit too.

I was very happy with that, but even more so to cook alongside Charly. They've been away for five weeks and how she's grown in body, mind and opinion since then — she's become a real wildlife warrior.

When we made the pies, the conversation went something like this: 'What is this meat, Nan Nan?'

'It's steak and kidney, Charly. It's really nice, you'll like it,' says I, who loathes kidney.

Charly was scandalised. 'But Nan Nan, you CAN'T eat echidna! They are protected and really cute!'

I protested my innocence and explained it was kidney, part of a lamb/sheep, all to no avail. By this time Jacob had entered the fray and I was doomed, and finally just left the subject alone, thankful that something else had taken their attention.

Charly took me to task for the pace at which I worked. She was fitting pastry into the tins and then putting tops on the pies.

'You are working too fast, Nan Nan. Just settle!'

What can you say? She has such good intentions.

Jacob, back inside after another wildlife-seeking expedition, pronounced the rosehip syrup I made while they were away really, really yummy and drinks four glassfuls in a very short space of time.

After dinner, tired and snugly, they pack up their pillow pets and head for home, Jacob with a jar of banana jam under one arm for his breakfast toast tomorrow, and a bottle of rosehip syrup for later.

It's been a wonderful day spending those hours with them. They are the greatest yet kindest of critics — always open and honest without any hidden agendas. Charly loathed the potato cakes for which Jacob invented the recipe at lunch, but everything else was a hit. These young tastebuds gives me hope for a future where people will again, as indeed today's trends indicate, appreciate food that is fresh, seasonal and free of additives.

Banana Jam

> *1.2kg medium—ripe bananas*
> *juice of 2 lemons*
> *finely grated zest of 1 lemon*
> *juice of 2 oranges*
> *finely grated zest of 1 orange*
> *3¾ cups sugar*

Peel and mash the bananas and place in a large pot with the rest of the ingredients. Bring to the boil, stirring often, making sure the sugar is fully dissolved.

Boil over a medium heat for 20 minutes, stirring often, after which you may need to reduce the heat a little as it

246

may be inclined to catch. The mixture by now should have a jam-like consistency. If not, cook for 5 minutes more.

Pour into warm, sterilised jars and seal immediately.

Makes about 1.8kg

April 16

Today has been set aside for fruit-picking, to see what is available through the Derwent Valley. A man went into The Cake Lady Shop in New Norfolk and, noting Stephanie's product on the shelf there, gave owner Jean a bag of quinces along with his contact details. Did Stephanie want to purchase more? Stephanie is always looking for quinces, from which she extracts the juice to freeze and subsequently make into quince jelly.

These factors alone make this fruit-gathering trip well worth the effort. Rob, the owner of the tree, is duly contacted and after dropping the children at school we are on our way.

The autumn mornings are sublime. New Norfolk is often blanketed by fog, though in this early autumn it's mostly just a fine, swirling mist. In the coming weeks we will experience dense morning fogs.

The quince tree is the best I've ever seen. It must be decades old and, courtesy of a leaking tap underneath it, is able to bear incredibly well. There must be over 100 kilos of quinces on the tree, despite the fact that another person has been before us and picked the lower branches.

As I've noted, the quinces I've had thus far this autumn have been less than aromatic and certainly less flavoursome than is usual, but the scent of the fruit from this tree is immediately apparent on the gentle morning breeze.

How many did we want, Rob asks?

'About 30 kilos in all,' we reply.

He supplies us with a purpose-built hook that makes plucking the fruit from higher branches a very simple task and soon all our containers are full. Such a pity we have no more to fill, as the fruit is so good. However, I suddenly remember that I have shopping bags in the car and before long we have over 75 kilos. There were more to pick but we leave those for another day or even another person.

The adventure did not finish there, though. Rob wants to learn about preserving. He is busy with shearing now, but will join our Friday group at the cooking school. He invites us to walk over and watch the shearing — just a small operation he tells us, a couple of hundred sheep and 300 lambs. The sheep look fat and contented, despite the shearing, which doesn't seem to faze them at all. They placidly observe us as they wait to be let out of the holding pen to feed on the small marrows that have been thrown over the fence to them and then amble on to the grassy paddocks that are their home.

The property stretches out for 70 hectares or more and Rob takes us to survey the scenery just over the rise, which is absolutely breathtaking. Seed cabbages are planted in tidy rows on some of the land, so fertile that this can be seen by the casual, even uninformed, eye.

'Volcanic soil,' Rob explains and points to a mountain in the distance. When it erupted in the past, the soil was enriched as the ash blew this way.

However, the greatest sights were still to come. We drove down to the banks of the river. Rob would like to share this space with others, not in any grand commercial sense, but as a boutique tourism experience, where small groups could come and share a meal of local Tasmanian produce. By local he refers to meat from his lambs, quinces from his trees and vegetables from his garden. He also keeps bees and would like to start packaging and selling his honey.

The setting is idyllic; we watch a platypus play in the quiet backwater pool, surfacing for air now and then. Fish jump out of the water to catch passing insects and at a bend in the river an eagle's nest can be seen perched halfway up an ancient tree.

The reflections on the water add another dimension — the still and the quiet, the almost unimaginable beauty of this spot is breathtaking. It is what so many strive to find and even duplicate, but this was put in place by nature, its simple exquisite beauty crafted over time.

Already a pile of boulders form part of this shady riverside retreat, perfect for a campfire catering for a select few — they would even provide seating. Stephanie, just back from her camping holiday, can immediately see its possibilities for campfire cookery. While the cooking was quietly underway, naturally formed pathways would entice the visitors to explore further along the riverbank.

Across the river is a brick building, not large, but an unusual shape, very tall, and apparently windowless. Its reflection on the water cannot help but draw attention. Rob tells us it was used as a tobacco-drying kiln, or so the anecdotal history goes.

Rob takes us to another spot further along the river, a grassy expanse with the occasional tree to provide shade. This would be an area exceptionally suitable for larger picnics, where facilities could be set up for cooking with very little effort.

Rob's thought to make this available to others encapsulates the pride in Tasmania's hidden places that exist outside or even concealed within the regular tourism routes.

The shearing finished and the shearer needed paying, so we take our leave with the happy prospect of seeing Rob again on Friday.

From here we travel to Bushy Park to visit the daily market. Today the blackboard outside announces that there are late peaches for the purchasing, tomatoes, parsnips and more. Best of all, there are apples galore so I can make the cider I have in mind. Stephanie has offered the fruit from her trees, which is wonderful, and added to these are the several kilos I am able to buy. I can set to work as soon as I get home.

There is a good knife set to buy as well, and a lovely pottery jug that will fit well in the school.

On the way back to Molesworth I am able to purchase a box of very good sauce tomatoes and two very inviting herb plants at the same roadside stall. Into the final miniscule spaces still left in the car I squeeze three more herb plants, purchased at another roadside stall at Granton for a mere $1 per pot, actually 50 cents for some.

Unloading the car takes ages and soon the school kitchen's benches are full of jars and produce, a welcome sight and holding the promise of really good days to come.

April 17

Stephanie has buckets of olives from her own trees and so she picks the remaining crop from our tree here to add to the abundance and will preserve the whole lot together.

She doesn't like to use the slightly loose cultural recipe that I favour, but a more modern version. I like it — it demonstrates that there is a whole new generation of preservers who are intensely interested in making the most of seasonal produce, using it in ever expanding, ever improved, ways.

Stephanie's Preserved Olives

Place the olives in a food-safe bucket and cover with fresh water. Change the water each day for 4 days.

To make the brine, for each kilo of olives, use 100g salt dissolved in 1 litre water. Bring to the boil and cool for 10 minutes.

Place the olives in heatproof sterilised jars, then pour the brine over.

The olives will be ready to eat in 5–6 months.

April 19

It has turned out to be a wonderful quince season after all — we are still finding trees in fields along the country lanes and can't help but pick them, otherwise they may go to waste and that would be a huge tragedy.

In my theory of capturing everything possible in a bottle, I decide to preserve the quinces in segments. They will be used, mixed with apple, later on to make pies and crumbles.

If you choose to do this, substitute half of the apple in your regular apple pie recipe for diced quince. If you use drained bottled quince, the cooking time will be the same. If using fresh, allow a little longer.

Bottled Quince

There are more than enough quinces to preserve as well, though this is not for the faint-hearted. Quinces are difficult to peel and core, and discolour quickly, and so have to be packed in the jars and covered with syrup immediately.

However, should you choose to do so, they are a great staple for the pantry shelves. Quinces can be added to sweet or savoury dishes. My favourite is quince and apple strudel.

To preserve quinces, peel, core and place in jars (best to do so one at a time), and cover immediately with the syrup of your choice and then put the lids on. In the case of Fowlers jars, put on rubber rings, lids and clips. (Actually, it's better to put the rings on before the jar is filled.) Using this basic preserving method on page 385, bring the temperature up to 95°C over 55 minutes, then hold at this temperature for 1 hour. Alternatively, if using a thermostat-controlled preserver, set to temperature and process for 2 hours.

Freezing Quinces

Put the whole unpeeled quinces in freezer bags and place in the freezer, where they will keep for 12 months. When you take them out, you will find that they are almost exactly the same in texture and flavour as when they went in. They are decidedly easier to peel once partially thawed.

I still have a box of tomatoes that will hold until next week, and so many more quinces, pears even. Pear will not be so good for jam as they have been off the tree a while now, which means their already low pectin

251

levels will have dropped significantly, as happens with all fruit. I could make the old-time favourite, pear ginger, but this has limited appeal in our house. However, their flesh is still quite firm and so can be bottled or even spiced (see recipes on pages 24 and 232).

The new chooks have gone missing, Robert tells me (in a state). How could this happen? Well, they must have decided to go AWOL for the night and have stayed down among the trees at the bottom of the house paddock. He fears for their safety as the owl calls can be heard in the still of the cold evening. I suspect they are too smart to be caught — they are real characters — and will turn up at the thought of food tomorrow morning. Part of the issue is Lucy, the fractious duck, who dominates the poultry yard. She guards the gate with a fervour that borders on fanaticism, and only under protest lets the chooks who have been free-ranging for the day back through to their coop.

There is not much time to dwell on this, though, as baby grandson Hunter has arrived and is bellowing with gusto, infuriated at being left with us for an hour or two. Amid the din, farmer Kerry arrives with a ram and another ewe to go into our bottom paddock.

April 20

Today is our second session for teaching the group of parents from Glenora and the surrounding schools.

Back in March we bottled seasonal fruits. We hope today will be even more fun, as it's jams, pickles and cordials. On the menu are piccalilli, tomato chilli pickle, sweet chilli sauce, blackcurrant cordial, tomato chutney and raspberry jam.

After a slight hiccup, Stephanie and I arrive a few minutes late to find the women all hard at work preparing their piccalilli for salting down. Jars are in the oven being sterilised.

Stephanie and I love coming here to teach — they are such a jolly lot of people. Many are farmers' wives, with several children, or grandmothers or even young single women. Pots and pans are going in all directions for the many products being prepared.

Stephanie has mixed up a batch of bread dough, which is soon baking in the oven, ready to accompany the samples of the pickles and jams that are being made. The tomato chilli pickle and piccalilli will be mixed with cream cheese to make delicious dips to serve with sticks of fresh homegrown carrots and celery or homemade bread.

During the session one of the girls tells me about her experience in making the sparkling rhubarb. She made the recipe but only had empty fruit-juice bottles in which to store it. When it came time for bottling it off, she noted that the seal was not all it could be. However, she had no other option, so went ahead anyway. Soon the brew was fermenting as it should, but with an ominous fizz leaking from under the lids.

Her husband was away at the time, making her a mite nervous and all the more so when she heard a disturbing thump in the night. She crept out to the kitchen, fearful for the safety of herself and her children, only to find with relief that one of the bottles of liquid had fermented to the point where it swelled at the bottom and keeled over with a tremendous thud.

One of the nicest things with the morning group is that another of the mums has made sparkling fruit drinks that we spoke about in the last session. She's held onto it for weeks now to share with the entire group.

She has prepared two batches — blackberry, and the other made with strawberries. The fruit is from her own garden and so the drinks are really good. Many pronounce their preference for strawberry, but I really love the blackberry. I've not tried using blackberries myself, and it is a shock to me just how flavoursome it is. It doesn't always work this way — for instance, I was a little disappointed when I made mine from blackcurrants, which you would think would be more flavoursome, but quite the contrary. It's very nice but not nearly so tasty as I'd expected.

The blackberry to me tastes of fruit picked fresh from the brambles and reminiscent of the autumn chill on grassy hillsides. It may sound strange, but all of this seemed encapsulated in the tingle on the tongue of this sparkling delight, prepared with the simplest and best of Tasmanian fruit, picked by this lady's own hand. What could possibly be better?

Sparkling Blackberry

900g blackberries
900g sugar
1 lemon, chopped
4.75 litres cold water
180ml cider vinegar or white vinegar

Place all ingredients in a food-safe bucket, mix well, then cover with a tea towel and leave to stand at room temperature for 48 hours.

Strain through a fine nylon kitchen sieve and pour into PET bottles and seal immediately. (Clean, empty soft-drink bottles are ideal, or you can buy new ones from home-brewing suppliers.)

The sparkling blackberry will be ready in about 10 days to 2 weeks, maybe sooner. Check by carefully opening the lid a fraction; if it's fizzy, it's ready.

When serving, open carefully — it's best to refrigerate it first.

Makes about 4.5 litres

One of the other ladies has made blackberry jam and scones from the recipes in my books. I am incredibly impressed at the generosity among these women as they work alongside each other, laughing as they go, happy to share the results of their labour.

The raspberries purchased for the class are maiden fruit, the autumn crop, and what fruit it is! A mere few minutes of boiling brings the jam to setting point, so its flavour is the best I have ever known in such a jam. I'd love to purchase the half-bucket that is left over, but it is earmarked for a further stage of their programme. The berries have come from Westerway, a few kilometres up the road, and so it's a tempting thought to travel that way before we go home to see if any more are available.

The day ends on time, with the afternoon group as hard-working as the morning group. They were so industrious that more jars were needed and so Stephanie and I return to her house in New Norfolk for extra jars from her store during the lunch break.

When we are done, I swing the car around towards Westerway — I can't bear the thought of missing out on those raspberries, no matter how small the chance that some are available.

We are delighted to see the OPEN sign still out — we've arrived in the nick of time, as the owner's wife is about to head off to the local shop. In the fridge are several one-kilo packs of jam raspberries in excellent condition.

You have to be very careful when buying 'jam' raspberries, which are not always all they could be. Sometimes when desperate for supplies, Stephanie has been known to go to one of the fruit and vegetable markets. The raspberries, stored in buckets out the back, were covered in mould, which the retailer simply scooped off the top before offering to sell her the liquid mass below.

In such a case, beware! Not only will the pectin level of the fruit be abominably low, almost guaranteeing a poor quality jam that will not set, but it is dangerous. Mould sends out spores and tendrils unseen by the naked eye, and is very dangerous to health, and almost certainly will lead to spoilage of the jam.

You are far, far better off buying frozen raspberries than to use 'jam' raspberries in such poor condition. It is false economy to buy raspberries long picked from their canes.

At Westerway, however, the jam raspberries are exquisite, better by far than many labelled for eating in miniscule punnets at supermarkets. There is a nice mix of dark red ripe and very light, so desirable as the ripe give exceptional flavour and the less ripe have more pectin, ensuring a jam with a good set.

The owners find us 15 kilos, ten of which Stephanie generously allows me to take for the upcoming classes and orders. Interestingly we are told that the last of the raspberry harvest is picked by machine; the

255

fruit of this picking is to be sent to the cordial factory to make their raspberry syrup.

Apparently an unexpected phenomenon occurred this season: the raspberry canes fruited again, providing a wonderful crop of maiden fruit. For the next two weeks more will be available, and after that, it's season's end.

In the meantime the challenge is to capture their vitality in a bottle in every possible way. If all cannot be processed straight away, freezing is a good option, to be made into jam later as needed.

You can make all your jam now, but I'd recommend placing the jars in the freezer once this is done. A strange suggestion, you may think, but raspberry jam, like apricot, tends to discolour on the shelf. Placing the jars in the freezer keeps the colour and flavour fresh. It never actually freezes due to the sugar content — it's just very cold when you take it out, but after standing at room temperature for a few minutes it will taste as if it was made yesterday.

It's been a wonderful day, made even better when I arrive home to find that the new chooks have come to no harm and are very keen to go back to their own bed. The nights are very chilly now so I'm sure they worked out that it was the better option.

Tom, too, has developed a routine of arriving inside for a warm night's sleep on a comfortable bed with an electric blanket. Della is still a worry as she is getting too old to sleep outdoors, so we are determined to coax her into the cubbyhouse at the very least.

April 22

An uneventful day, other than shopping for the group coming in a few days' time. They are not so keen on doing preserves and would like to work with eggs, oats, cheese, spinach and nuts. What a motley crew of ingredients, but I'm sure we can put something together. Various ideas float around in my head — sticky date and walnut puddings with caramel sauce, choc-a-berry muffins, honey oat bread, spinach gratin, pesto. A breeze.

Tom has taken up residence indoors most days and today is no exception. He follows me into the bedroom, hoping for a hug, and there at the door sits a little grey-and-white cat. She looks forlornly through the window with her big green eyes and my heart goes out to her. Tom looks none too impressed. Though I've seen him playing with her outside, he gives the appearance of being ever fearful of losing his pride of place in our household and is quite aggressive.

After a time she vanishes and I am ashamed that I've not offered her food. If the two cats could peacefully co-exist, I see no reason not to adopt her. Ardy, after all, has remained at the Courtney's house. I'm assuming it's a female, by the way.

Robert is not at all impressed, well used as he is to my taking in strays. He claims she is quite fat, so therefore has a home, but I beg to differ. She is simply fluffy so it's difficult to ascertain if she is thin or fat and I fear she might be pitifully thin.

As I look in the fridge today I see that there are bits and pieces that need using up. You can never have too much chutney and with the last of Stephanie's strawberries, it should be a simple thing to make a chutney that can incorporate these scraps. Of course you could vary it according to what you have on hand. Just make sure that the total weight of fruit remains the same.

Mixed Fruit Chutney

1 large tomato, diced
500g green apples, peeled, cored and diced
250g strawberries, halved or quartered,
depending on size
1 onion, diced
1 red capsicum, diced
1 cup cider vinegar
⅔ cup sugar
2 teaspoons salt
1 teaspoon ground allspice
½ teaspoon curry powder

Place all the ingredients in a large saucepan or jam pan and bring to the boil, stirring. Simmer over a medium—low heat for about 25 minutes or until setting point is reached (see page 393).

Pour into warm sterilised bottles and seal immediately.

Makes about 1kg

April 23

Ann is coming today. She is a writer for one of the large newspapers. As usual, I'm not quite sure what to expect, wondering if our humble little school will be taken as it stands. For us, it's all about the produce and the cooking.

Ann turns out to be a wonderful person and we are immediately chatting about cooking, families and more. She loves the property — the lush green, and the fact that the trees do not encroach but rather skirt the border of the property in a very fetching way. I'd not thought of this before, but she is right. I always imagined it was for fire safety purposes and this is surely the case, but aesthetically it is very pleasing.

We make a range of preserves and breads — always preserves at this time of the year, and Ann is stunned at how easy it is. I have a pot of toffee quinces on the stove, the remains from a boiling up of a day or so ago.

Toffee Quinces

1.5kg quinces
1kg sugar
juice of 1 lemon
a small strip of lemon zest
1.75 litres water

Wash the quinces, making sure that the 'bloom' is removed.

Place the whole quinces in a large pot with the sugar, lemon juice, zest and water. Bring to the boil, stirring often. Reduce the heat to very low and barely simmer for 2–3 hours.

Lift out the quinces and serve as a dessert with cream, ice-cream, yoghurt or mascarpone.

Pour any remaining liquid into warm sterilised bottles and seal immediately — this will set into an exquisite, intensely flavoured quince jelly with small pieces of quince skin and flesh suspended in it. Serve as a delightful topping for fresh bread, scones or toast.

Makes about 2.5kg

Ann could not believe that quinces could taste so incredibly delicious. We spend what I consider to be a delightful afternoon for she is such a willing participant, and very capable. She leaves laden with tiny jewel-like jars, and I wouldn't be one bit surprised if she starts making preserves herself, as well as bread, now that she knows it's so easy.

April 24

Today's class requested an 'As You Like It' session, and we are working with those simple ingredients — oats, spinach, cheese and eggs. The fact that it's Anzac Day tomorrow brings Anzac biscuits to mind, and I invent a recipe for choc-a-berry muffins. Honey Oat Bread, pesto and vegetarian quiches are duly prepared. Pizza, made from spelt dough.

When the girls arrive the atmosphere is electric — some of these ladies I know already and they are great fun. They express their preference for savoury over sweet products, and once again, the menu is tweaked on the spot. I really like to be adaptable and flexible enough to make immediate adjustments if participants want a special item prepared or, from my perspective, if new and exciting produce comes through the door.

As the days are getting cooler I decide to light the slow-combustion stove, still with trepidation after my episodes of smoking out the house. However, all is well: I now have it all under control and not so much as a puff of smoke escapes its doors and crevices. That is, with the exception of a few startling moments when I turn on the extractor fan above the electric/gas stove and the draught pulls smoke out in a great cloud. However, it is only momentary and with that final trick sorted, I know the stove and we will now be good friends forever.

Its great advantage is that the flue goes out through the back of the wall, ensuring that much of the convective heat is not permeating the room itself. In summer this would make the heat insufferable; even in this cool autumn it would be excessive. As it is, the heat is comfortable and companionable. People always back up to it for warmth, as is customary with any wood-fired stove.

The class passes in no time at all and we decide to make the quiches as originally planned. I make the pastry in the food processor. I made pesto in there a little earlier and I don't bother to wash the processor — the residual pesto will add flavour to the pastry. A few scraps of grated parmesan were thrown in for good measure and soon a pastry is ready.

Many and varied ingredients find their way into the tart cases and then I make the filling — eggs, a little mayonnaise, sweet chilli sauce and salt. Well, at least I thought it was salt, but then I see that I've instead grabbed the jar of citric acid. Disaster — the mixture tastes odd, to say the least.

The mixture can't be used, but loathing waste, I decide I'll convert it into something else tomorrow — maybe a chilli chocolate mousse cake, something I saw on *My Kitchen Rules* a night or two ago.

So it was back to the start to make the tart filling all over again.

Sweet Potato or Pumpkin Quiche

PASTRY
250g plain flour
¼ teaspoon baking powder
½ teaspoon salt

125g butter

1 tablespoon grated parmesan (optional)

2 teaspoons lemon juice

about 3 tablespoons cold water

FILLING

1 tablespoon olive oil

375g sweet potato or pumpkin, peeled and chopped into small pieces

1 small onion, peeled and finely chopped

1 red capsicum, seeded and chopped

1 clove garlic, crushed

1 cup grated cheese

1 cup milk

4 eggs, lightly whisked

salt and pepper to taste

2 teaspoons mayonnaise

1 tablespoon basil pesto

1 tablespoon sweet chilli sauce

Preheat the oven to 200°C. Grease a 20 cm deep pie dish.

To make the Pastry place the flour, baking powder, salt and butter (and parmesan if using) in a food processor and process until it resembles breadcrumbs. Turn out into a bowl and mix with the lemon juice and enough water to bring together into a soft dough. Wrap in cling film and place in the fridge for 30 minutes if possible. (This pastry can be rolled out immediately if needed, but it's easier if it spends a little time in the fridge.)

Meanwhile, make the Filling by heating the oil in a saucepan and gently cooking the sweet potato or pumpkin, onion, capsicum and garlic together, placing the lid on after a few minutes to allow the vegetables to caramelise slightly and become tender. Cool.

Whisk together the remaining ingredients in a jug or pouring bowl.

On a lightly floured surface roll out the pastry to fit the base and sides of the dish, and trim the edges (any leftover pastry can be frozen for another use).

Sprinkle the vegetables over the base of the dish, then pour over the egg mixture.

Bake for 5 minutes at 200°C, then reduce the heat to 150°C and bake for 30–40 minutes more or until the filling is just set.

Serves 6

With boxes laden with goodies to take home, the girls depart.

Suddenly, as if from nowhere, the little grey-and-white cat arrives once more. Tom seems none too impressed as usual, but I'm happy as I feel I've neglected her badly. She mews at me pitifully, then rolls over for a tummy rub and I find she's not so thin after all — quite plump in fact. Maybe she does have an owner or maybe she is a stray and is pregnant. I offer her food, which she rejects outright, despite the fact it's the best of the best. This reinforces the notion that she has an owner, or maybe she's a bit fearful. Either way, she soon vanishes again. Maybe she won't be part of our household after all.

Della has become resentful that Tom gets so much attention that she has commandeered Tom's basket at the front door as her own. She has a large basket filled with warm rugs and lambswool coats, but she stubbornly sits in Tom's, her ample proportions oozing over every edge. She's a stubborn dog at the best of times and will not be dissuaded, so we leave her to it. If she wants to be so uncomfortable, that's her prerogative.

April 25

The girls yesterday were cleaning whizzes. It's certainly not an obligation for class participants to help clean up, but my goodness, it's a help when they do. Still, there are residual things I need to do and so much in the way of preserving.

Family and more are coming to visit — Stephanie has a slow cooker on the go with delicious pulled pork almost ready to eat. She's baked fresh bread rolls as well and made taffy for us to try.

I have a mountain of mince to make into meatballs and a pot roast to cook gently in the slow-combustion stove. An order of raspberry jam needs to be made for my publisher's Sydney office, and there's more of the Tasmanian grapefruit to make into cordial, not to mention tubs of quinces, a box of tomatoes, apples to make into herb jelly, and a box of pears.

Stephanie lends a hand and soon pots and pans are bubbling away on the stove.

Then I remember that I've wanted to try pickling chillies forever. Today seems like a good opportunity as I have about a kilo on hand. The Rocoto chilli bush is now producing quite well, so a batch of pickled mixed chillies could be salted down.

Soon the benches are piled with experiments on the go, as well as the time-honoured favourites. The quiche mixture, the disaster of yesterday, looks up at me forlornly. I'd planned to make that chocolate mousse cake, but I'd forgotten that I'd added pesto — the mayonnaise, the chilli — well that could have worked, but the pesto is a step too far.

Furious with myself for my stupidity, I recall that in the freezer is a packet of ready-rolled shortcrust pastry sheets I'd accidentally bought instead of puff pastry. I really should wear my glasses to the supermarket these days. It would be no loss to match the products to see what comes out of it. Quiches galore are soon made and in the oven.

Once cooked, to my utter amazement, they are pronounced very good indeed. The pastry is not so great but the filling is really delicious. How can this be? I am still a bit puzzled but then I guess it's not that much different from adding some lemon juice or sour cream to the mixture.

Maybe there's even a recipe in there somewhere — add a pinch of citric acid for extra flavour? For those who are brave enough to try it anyway!

Stephanie and Nat have been quince-picking again this morning at Rob and Jacqui's house. They've scored some figs as well and Stephanie is keen to try out a recipe for figs stuffed with feta and wrapped in prosciutto that Jacqui has told her about. Soon they are baking in the oven and the results are sensational. Jacob and I especially love them, partial as we are to all things salty.

Two girls arrive from the *Mercury* — each Saturday there is a segment on Tasmanian towns and soon Molesworth is to be featured. It's really good as we can share with them all that we've been making and baking, and send them away with some for later.

The jam order is done, the chillies are salting down. I didn't get to the herb jelly I'd planned, nor the pears or most of the quinces. However, recipes have been discussed for some — we'll try making peri from the pears with the sparkling fruit drink recipe, and more cider with the apples.

After they leave the day winds down as only these wonderful autumn days can. We take the food back down to the house, too much as always, but leftovers can be saved until the weekend when there will be more visitors and family. The children curl up sleepily, Jacob in an armchair, Charly on my bed watching TV with a cup of chocolate milk.

Nat kindly offers to feed the new chickens and I am stunned that they run away from him, regardless of the fact that he has their afternoon potful of bread and fat. I'd thought that chooks have little care for people as individuals, and they always come running for Robert or me when we call. Maybe I need to reassess their intelligence and loyalty levels.

The chillies are ready for the final stage of pickling.

Pickled Chillies

125g salt
500ml hot water
1 litre cold water
1kg long red or green chillies
1.5 litres cider vinegar

40g salt (extra)
20g sugar

Mix the salt with the hot water and stir until dissolved. Pour in the cold water and leave until cool.

Remove ends from the chillies and place in the salt solution, weighting them down with a plate or just press a piece of cling wrap onto and just under the surface.

Leave for 12 hours, then drain well and rinse.

Place the vinegar, salt and sugar in a large saucepan and bring to the boil, stirring occasionally, and cook for 2 minutes.

Pour over the chillies and then seal the jars immediately. Make sure that all the vinegar is used and if the chillies float, press some crumpled baking paper into the top of the jar, ensuring there are no air pockets underneath.

The chillies are ready to eat in 6 weeks.

Makes about 1.8kg

April 27

Today I have to deal with the last of Rob's pears and to make apple cider. While I am at it, I am going to put the slow-combustion stove through its paces more thoroughly with a whole range of dishes, now that I've mastered the art of lighting it without filling the room with smoke. I've made a roast, somewhat overcooked, but still tasting delicious, but I want to try out other things like bread and cake and biscuits. It would be a lonely-ish kitchen day as Robert needs to tend to outdoor things.

However, just as I was about to head out to the cooking school, Stephanie and Nat arrive with the children. Nat has made me a wrapped toffee-shaped plaque for the wall and on it the bracket for the taffy hook that we picked up a few days ago. It is amazing — a total work of art — and soon it is placed on the wall. Stephanie has brought glucose and various other ingredients and before long the toffee is being boiled and cooled and then pulled over the hook to form long silken chocolate toffee ropes. Once the toffee reaches the desired consistency and thickness, the children snip it into lengths and wrap them in cute little toffee papers. It's incredible how much it makes and how tasty it is.

As Stephanie works I trial bread dough in the oven — pizza, actually, to go with the pumpkin soup I've made. The crust is far, far superior to that cooked in my (very expensive) electric oven — crisp on the outside and moist and light on the inside and cooked in a trice.

Date and walnut muffins soon follow — light and moist as well. Jacob and Charly exhaust my supply of store-bought dry biscuits and so we invent a recipe on the spot and they are baked in moments to perfection, courtesy of the stove. (These biscuits are really just savoury pastry such as in the recipe for the Sweet Potato or Pumpkin Quiche, page 260, but with the definite inclusion of the parmesan that appears only as an optional extra there).

To be quite frank, I wasn't quite sure if my recollection of the quality of baking in an old slow-combustion oven was a bit exaggerated. After all, it had been years since I used one. But my goodness, I wasn't looking through rose-coloured glasses after all — if anything, it is better than I remember and I am even more enamored of my old Carmichael.

With lunch over, we turn our attention to the produce I originally was going to address — all those apples and pears and the peaches lurking in the crisper drawer.

Stephanie deals with the apples, chopping them for herb jelly tomorrow.

April 30

The time has come well and truly to attempt to make this jelly, a skill that's eluded me for years. There's a very good one in *A Year in a Bottle* but technically it's not a traditional jelly as it contains sieved apple pulp, and I've always wanted to make one based on strained apple juice. You can use other herbs — rosemary, parsley, sage, thyme. The jelly could be served with meats, or used as a glaze when roasting them.

The apple and vinegar juice is already strained off, the first part of the process. The next step is the trickiest. I've estimated with great care the amount of sugar to maximise setting, and estimated the amount of herbs needed for flavour. Some recipes recommend boiling up the stalks with the apples, but to me this seems to leave a hint of its being overcooked. I want to add the herbs at the end so their fresh flavour is captured in the mixture.

As I make the mixture and attempt to bring it to a soft set, I am pleased with how promising it looks and tastes, just the right amount of acidity. At what I estimate to be the right time, I scoop off any scum, which is minimal anyway, and quickly stir in the chopped mint.

Then comes the waiting game — will it set? I really want the herbs to be evenly distributed throughout the jelly and so watch it like a hawk for the next couple of hours. Inevitably they will rise at first in the still hot liquid, but as the jelly cools and solidifies, if I turn the jars over every half an hour or so, it should be able to be accomplished.

Two hours later I am ecstatic — it's worked! The jelly tastes amazing and the herbs are evenly spread through the jar. It is even acceptably set — not too firm, which would make it difficult for spreading as a glaze, but still holding its shape. After years of trial and much error, here is the recipe for a really good herb jelly.

Herb Jelly

> *1kg cooking apples (such as Granny Smith)*
> *5½ cups water*
> *sugar*
> *325ml white vinegar*
> *1 cup finely chopped mint or other herb*

Cut the apples (no need to core or peel) into 1cm pieces and place in a large saucepan with the water. Bring to the boil, then reduce the heat and simmer until the apples are soft. Strain through a fine sieve.

For every 600ml of the resulting liquid, add 500g sugar. Bring to the boil, stirring, and then boil briskly until setting point is reached, about 30 minutes.

Remove from heat and skim off any scum from the surface with a slotted spoon. Stir in the mint and pour into small warm sterilised jars and seal immediately with a screwtop lid.

Every 15–30 minutes, turn the jar upside-down so that the mint is evenly distributed as the jelly sets.

Makes about 1.25 litres

May 1

The last of the apples beckon enticingly from their bowl and I think of the alcoholic apple cider I've been planning to make. I have the hops, after all, and a recipe that looks half-promising — that is until I come to make it and major modifications are needed. However, the smell of the rehydrated hops is amazing, redolent of summers decades ago when we visited the hop sheds at Scottsdale. This year I've been able to pick them growing wild and so have far more than I need. I'm amazed at how such an intense aroma (and hopefully action) can result from so few hops — a mere 8g for this recipe.

Stephanie rings to tell me that she has found chillies at an incredibly cheap price — do I want some? I do — I can add those to the ones that our Rocoto chilli bush is bearing. This will enable me to make one of the house's signature sauces, excellent served with lamb, but other meats almost equally well.

Tomato Chilli Sauce

You can halve the recipe if you like but the sauce is
guaranteed to be popular so I find it best to make this
quantity. The chillies can be left out if preferred.

6kg tomatoes, chopped
1.5kg onions, peeled and chopped
1.5kg cooking apples, such as Granny Smiths, cored and
* chopped*
60g garlic, chopped
250g–400g long red chillies, chopped
120g cooking salt
1½ teaspoons ground cloves
1½ teaspoons ground allspice
2 cups cider vinegar

Place all the ingredients in a very large saucepan or
jam pan and bring to the boil, stirring. Cook over
a medium–low heat for 2½ to 3 hours, then strain
through a colander or food mil. Bring back to the
boil, then pour into warm sterilised bottles and seal
immediately.

Makes about 6.5 litres

May 3

There is a book-signing today at the ABC shop in Hobart. I always
worry that no-one will come, but all is well today and I leave the shop
without the humiliation of sitting there, pen in hand, with no-one
giving me so much as a passing glance.

After a coffee with my friend Helen, I head for home, but I thought
I'd just check out the supermarket for bargains. I have plenty of chillies,
but today the supermarket has reduced their price to a mere $2.98 a kilo.
How could I resist? I left a few for anyone who might come after me
and need them, but I have visions of a superb chilli paste and magnificent
curries to follow.

The evening is spent bottling off the alcoholic apple cider. It smells incredibly good, but the recipe I started out with was a bit loose. The yield wasn't particularly good either: a mere 1.8 litres from 3kg apples. Still, you never know — it has potential and is supposed to be ready within a week.

With Robert away at the large agricultural show Agfest, I have been feeding the chickens their breakfast. The two we brought from the Neck are still pretty silly, ever fearful and run away, but the new ones are more agreeable. The sheep have been coming over to the fence to see what I'm doing.

I'm not much of a one for sheep, knowing little about them, and don't want to get too fond of them after the alpaca episode.

However, the sheep seem to ask for affection and occasionally allow me to pat them. I offer them some of the mash on the tips of my fingers today and ever so gently they lick it off and win my heart in a moment. They are so gentle and sweet. I'm sure I'll never again be able to look at a leg of lamb with good conscience.

When I went to the fridge this morning I realised that I'd forgotten, or at least not been able to get to, the buttermilk. I'd ordered quite a bit as I'd found a recipe for buttermilk cheese. Sounded good, but do you think I could find the recipe again? Of course not, no matter how hard I scoured the cookbooks here.

Buttermilk, I figured, will add extra nutrients to bread, a nice cheesy flavour and also a finer-textured dough. I'd read a recipe somewhere for potato bread with buttermilk and so try to resurrect that from the corners of my mind, with little success, so need to invent my own.

Potato adds nutrients to the bread and if actual potato works anything like potato water, it will keep the bread fresher longer.

First to go in the oven is the spelt bread with buttermilk. If it tastes as good as its aroma suggests, it will be stunning. All I have done is substitute buttermilk for the water in the recipe on page 215.

The buttermilk bread with potato is slower to rise but still looks promising.

Although these recipes are not preserves, they are delicious served with them — try with pesto, labna and various pickles, fruit pastes and jams.

Potato and Buttermilk Bread

4 cups plain flour
2 teaspoons salt
1½ teaspoons sugar
5 teaspoons dried yeast
2 tablespoons oil
1½ cups buttermilk (lukewarm)
150g potato (peeled weight), finely grated

In a large bowl, mix together the flour, salt, sugar and yeast and make a well in the centre. In a jug, mix together the oil, buttermilk and finely grated potato. Pour the liquid mixture into the well and mix until well combined. Sprinkle just a little flour over the top and then cover with a tea towel.

Preheat the oven to 200°C.

When ready, turn dough out onto a lightly floured surface and knead until smooth. Shape into 2 equal sized balls and place side by side in a large (13 x 21 cm) loaf tin. Cover with a tea towel and allow to rise almost to the top of the tin.

Bake for 10 minutes, then reduce the heat to 170°C and bake for 25–30 minutes more or until well risen and golden. The loaf should sound hollow when tapped. Turn out onto a wire rack to cool.

As a variation, make a 6-cup flour dough and use two-thirds for the loaf as above, and the rest to make bread rolls or scrolls with various fillings.

To make **Spelt or Wholemeal Loaf**, use 2 cups spelt or wholemeal flour instead of 4 cups plain.

Serves 6

It's one of those times of the year when there are bits and pieces coming in from the garden, and many times on the radio I've had requests for a pickle that is akin to the all-time favourite Branston Pickle. I made it especially for a gentleman on his request and he pronounced it to be very good indeed and said I should sell it. I call it British Brown Pickle as it seems to appeal to the British palate and is certainly worth trying.

You could vary the vegetables according to what you have on hand.

British Brown Pickle

150g diced carrot
200g cauliflower florets
300g diced zucchini or marrow
300g diced onions
3 cloves garlic, peeled and chopped
1 large stick celery, finely diced
6 pickled gherkins, finely diced
125g dates, chopped
juice of 1 lemon
400g diced tomatoes (or use fresh or bottled)
2 teaspoons salt
½ cup brown sugar, firmly packed
1.25 litres dark malt vinegar

Placed all the ingredients in a large saucepan and bring to the boil, stirring. Cook for 1½–2 hours or until the pickle has thickened. If it is still a bit runny after this time, thicken with a paste made from 2 teaspoons cornflour mixed to a paste with an extra 2 tablespoons brown vinegar. If you prefer a sweeter pickle, just add extra brown sugar (little by little) to taste.

Pour into warm sterilised jars and seal immediately.

Makes about 3kg

May 4

Today is scheduled for another book-signing, this one at the ABC Shop in Rosny. Over the years, I've met some incredible people with such a passion for food and today was no exception. A young man held back from coming up to the table until all others had left. He told me he loved my books, had all of them and cooked from them all the time. I was tremendously pleased; he is so young to be cooking so regularly for his family.

He told me about a project he was initiating at his high school, exploring the link between food, cooking and poverty, and their cultural aspects. The project is multi-faceted and he hopes to bring it to the attention of the wider community and take steps to improve people's life through food and cooking. By this he means good, everyday recipes that are sustainable, so that people find them easy, tasty and affordable, and the routine of preparing good food becomes a way of life.

I am astounded at his perception and his passion, not only for food and for the poorer in our own community, but by extension, other cultures as well. I am immensely flattered that he chose my books as a catalyst for this.

After he left a gentleman called Andrew came up. He brought me jam melons. They can be found at this time of year at farmgate stalls, farmers' markets and even large fruit and vegetable markets.

Decades ago they were very popular, when people used to make melon and lemon jam, even melon and ginger. Andrew called me a few weeks earlier during the ABC radio talkback segment, and promised these melons. I am touched he has taken the trouble to bring them.

A few years ago, when I last had some to experiment with, our Courtney invented a melon cheese, after the style of quince cheese. The end result was exquisite. The melon flesh became translucent and the cheese a shimmering jelly of lime green. Served with soft cheeses, it was incredibly good. The melons were enormous, so I'll certainly be making that again. What luxury. I read a recipe somewhere for candied melon but I think I'll make a cordial syrup. If it's anything like the cheese, it will be very refreshing.

This recipe cannot be used with watermelon, rockmelon or honeydew melon. Andrew is hoping to grow a large crop of jam melons, along with other more unusual old-fashioned fruits.

I've read that melon chutney used to be a staple in pantry cupboards in the 1930s and 1940s, so I'll try making a batch of that as well.

Melon and Lemon Jam

A few years ago an elderly lady gave me this recipe, one she had perfected over many years. I trialled it on the only other occasion that I'd had a melon to play with, and found it worked really well.

1.75kg melon flesh, diced
1.5kg sugar
½ cup finely shredded lemon zest

Place the melon in a bowl with half the sugar, stir and leave to stand overnight.

Place the lemon zest in 200 ml cold water and leave to stand overnight.

Next day, place the lemon zest and water in a pot with the melon mixture and bring to the boil, stirring. Add the rest of the sugar and bring back to the boil, stirring.

Boil briskly until setting point is reached. Pour into warm sterilised jars and seal immediately.

For **Melon, Lemon and Ginger Jam**, add about 250g glacé ginger, diced, 5 minutes before the end of cooking time.

Makes about 2.8kg

Courtney's Melon Cheese

1kg diced melon flesh
½ cup water
sugar

Place the melon and water in a saucepan and bring to the boil, stirring, then reduce the heat and simmer until the melon is tender. Pass through a sieve or food mill.

For each cup of the resulting purée add 1 cup sugar. Bring to the boil, stirring, then cook over a very low heat for about 2 hours, stirring often, and cook until a paste-like consistency is reached.

Pour into a dish that has been sprayed with cooking oil spray and leave to set at room temperature. Turn out and cut into squares. Store between layers of silicone paper in an airtight container.

Makes about 520g

Melon Chutney

This chutney is very nice served with ham or pork.

1.1kg diced melon flesh
1 onion, diced
1 long red chilli, seeded and diced
1 red capsicum, diced
120g tomato, diced
1 small stick celery, diced
1½ tablespoons salt
1¾ cups sugar
2 cups white or cider vinegar
2 teaspoons mustard powder
1½ teaspoons ground turmeric
3 teaspoons cornflour mixed with 1 tablespoon vinegar

Place the melon, onion, chilli, capsicum, tomato and celery in a bowl and mix with the salt. Leave to stand for 1 hour, then drain in a colander.

Place the vegetable and melon mix in a saucepan with the sugar, vinegar, mustard and turmeric. Bring to the boil, stirring, then reduce the heat and cook for 20 minutes. Thicken with the cornflour paste if needed.

Pour into warm sterilised jars and seal immediately.

Makes about 1.6kg

Melon Syrup

A syrup with a lovely subtle flavour, it's quite refreshing. It is a popular Lebanese drink. Serve with lemonade, soda water or just plain iced water. If using lemonade or soda water, a splash of gin or vodka and a slice of lemon is also delicious.

> *2kg melon flesh, diced*
> *2 litres water*
> *juice of 1 large lemon*
> *sugar*
> *2 tablespoons lemon juice (extra)*

Place the melon, water and lemon juice in a saucepan and bring to the boil. Simmer for 20 minutes. Strain through a colander then through a fine strainer (lined with muslin for a clearer cordial).

For each 3 cups of the resulting liquid add 3 cups sugar and the extra lemon juice or ½ teaspoon citric acid. Bring to the boil, stirring, then simmer for 3 minutes.

Pour into warm sterilised bottles and seal immediately.

Makes about 2 litres

Another lady calls past, not to get a book signed, but to tell me that she just made my recipe for scallop pies from *Out of the Bottle*. She used to love the ones from the Ross Bakery, the one closest to the bridge, but wanted to make some herself so she is hopeful (as am I!) that my recipe will serve her well in this respect.

But where did she get the scallops? I ask, as she has told me that they are Tasmanian, the tastiest of all. I am not a great one for seafood, growing up in a household where its very presence was rare. Dad loathed the smell and taste of fish.

Occasionally when he went away on business trips, in scallop season Mum would take a billycan down to the wharf and bring home enough to make one of her favourite dishes, curried scallops. Unfamiliar as they were to my palate as a child, it wasn't really a favourite.

However, some years later I tasted some battered Tasmanian scallops and fell in love with their flavour and texture at once. Smaller than their counterparts from other places, they are sweet and succulent, little bursts of flavour. Their season is all too short, the demand for them so great that they are hard to come by.

She tells me her source; they'll be frozen but that's OK by me. As she leaves she says he sells wild rabbits as well. Music to my ears and I'm determined to visit on the way home. As soon as the signings are over, I head that way.

The source of all these goodies must remain one of Tasmania's secrets as he doesn't want me to write about it. Suffice to say that it's a little tavern just out of town. When I call in the scallops were available, and when I ask about the rabbits he tells me they had been frozen for a few weeks, but I could have them for $7 each. We get talking about meat and recipes and he pulls from the freezer a haunch of wallaby that he gives me free of charge.

As we talk of mince and fat, he pulls out a pack of his homemade beef mince, as lean as could possibly be. He describes its virtues for such dishes as Bolognese sauce. Do I want the offcuts for my cat? Of course, Tom will be pleased. All of this for such little cost.

For a tavern owner, he is a wealth of information and has an astounding passion for food. The chef was cooking up hare mince for their lunch. Hare? Amazing — I will ask him about getting some in future — I don't like to be so presumptuous to ask about this now, given his generosity with all he has given me.

What a great day. I head home well satisfied and anxious to work with the ingredients. Robert's due back from Agfest tonight and had asked for soup and some decent bread for dinner. Little does he know it will be kangaroo tail soup, which I know he will love.

Kangaroo (or Wallaby) Tail Soup

This soup dates back to colonial times. You could add a tablespoonful of barley to give extra body to the soup. Some older recipes advised adding a little Worcestershire sauce at serving time — if you choose to do so, a good option would be one made from the recipe on page 338, or even just a dash of the commercial variety.

1 tablespoon oil
2 teaspoons butter
1 kangaroo or wallaby tail, cut into segments
300g lean diced beef
1 large onion, diced
2 carrots, diced
1.5 litres water
3 teaspoons chopped fresh thyme leaves
1 teaspoon salt
3 teaspoons cornflour mixed to a paste with 1½ tablespoons
    water

Heat the oil and butter together over a medium–high heat and brown the tail pieces. Add the beef and cook until it changes colour also. Add the rest of the ingredients except the cornflour paste and bring to the boil.

Reduce the heat and simmer for 3 hours or until the meat is tender. Remove the tail pieces, then thicken the soup with the cornflour paste. Add salt and pepper to taste.

Serves 4

I will use the mince to make Chilli Con Carne, which I have always disliked if the mince was fatty. I'll enrich the sauce with dark chocolate, as is often done in Mexican dishes. Only a small amount is needed — about 15g to a four-serve batch, but it makes all the difference to the flavour.

I haven't cooked with rabbit for such a long time. I remember my mother buying them from a boy who sold them door to door. She used to make a tasty stuffing for them, then roast them covered in bacon, as they tend to dry out otherwise.

May 5

This morning we awake to a major frost. Wisps of mist hang on the hillsides, suspended between the valley floor and the hilltops. It is a spectacular sight.

Further down the valley the yellow blaze of the autumn poplars has been blown away by the fierce winds of Saturday and now sit barren, waiting for the intense winter cold to overtake them. Today was going to be a quiet one, other than bottling off the apple and pear ciders. However, Elliott has rung and is coming to advise us on some electrical work. He and partner Cassie live in a rented house and the oven is giving them grief. Cassie is an enthusiastic budding cook and she is getting discouraged as her cakes come out overcooked on the edges and way undercooked in the middle, no matter how she sets the temperature. She is becoming disheartened, and would love to come and cook with me.

What wonderful news — I would love to. When they arrive we set to work. She fancies making choc-a-bloc cookies from *Sweet!* I help get the recipe underway, but mess up a step right at the start. Time for recipe first-aid and hope that all will be well. The recipe is forgiving and the biscuits turn out really well, except for the half-cooked batch I drop upside-down on the floor. My clumsiness will be the death of me. Cassie is unperturbed and is even quite pleased that she's seen me make a mistake — makes her feel better, she says. I fear she is much too kind.

We cook a roast lamb dinner, for the first time accompanied by my new herb jelly made with mint — it is received with enthusiasm.

Stephanie and Nat and the children call in around midday. Nat has heard about the rabbits and has announced that he will cook them for me. Excellent. He has an old recipe given to him by a mutual friend who recently passed away. Mary was a really special lady and an excellent cook. Nat has said this recipe of hers is amazing and he has cooked it many times.

This morning Robert has asked for eggs and bacon for breakfast. I was ashamed to serve him the watery thin strips that I had bought on special at the supermarket a day or two ago. This week, for sure, I am determined to make good by the simple (as Stephanie tells me) process of curing. First, buy your pork belly, which I will now be able to do through a Tasmanian supplier I'd heard about.

Robert and Nat spend the afternoon doing sundry chores here. The loquat trees have been removed. Although they have been in leaf since we arrived, never a flower or fruit has been seen, so their removal will make way for apple, mulberry or Kentish cherry trees. It's a big sacrifice in some ways, but they simply show no sign of fruiting. I have in the past made the following recipes successfully and if you have loquats you may like to try them.

Loquat Jam

> 1kg loquats, pips removed
> ⅓ cup water
> juice of 1 large lemon
> 850g sugar

Place the pips in a piece of muslin and tie with string to form a bag.

Dice the loquats quite finely, then place in a saucepan or jam pan with the water, lemon juice and bag of pips.

Bring to the boil, stirring, then simmer until the loquats have softened.

Remove the bag of pips. Add the sugar and stir until dissolved. Bring to the boil and then cook over a medium heat until setting point is reached (see page 393).

Pour into warm sterilised jars and seal immediately.

Makes about 1.5kg

Loquat Jelly

1.5kg loquats, chopped
1.75 litres water
juice of 1 large lemon
sugar

Place the loquats, water and lemon juice into a large saucepan or jam pan. Bring to the boil, reduce the heat, and simmer for 20 minutes or until the loquats are soft. Pour the mixture into a colander that has been lined with muslin and leave to stand for several hours, collecting the juice underneath.

For each cup of the resulting liquid, add 1 cup sugar.

Bring to the boil, stirring, and then boil briskly over a medium–high heat until setting point is reached. Pour into warm sterilised jars and seal immediately.

Makes about 1.25kg

May 8

We are coming to the 'shoulder' of the preserving season. Produce is starting to thin out and all that remains are apples, pears and quinces. However, many berries have been frozen, capturing their flavour so that they are ideal for later use.

There is a preserving class here today. Stephanie is coming later in the morning as between us we have bought two boxes of tomatoes, which she needs to preserve for making chutney later in the year. They can be frozen, but freezer space is at a premium and the jars of preserves will last several years, just quietly sitting on the shelf, waiting till their time of usefulness.

By the time everyone arrives the room is toasty warm from the slow-combustion stove. It is such a great invention, the old wood-fired stove. As it burns it not only heats the oven but can also heat the hot-water cylinder. The top of the stove has a large hotplate that can hold up to six or even seven pots at a time, as well as a smaller hotplate to the side and a heated area to the front. All it takes is a few pieces of wood, strategically placed, to get the whole thing in motion, working on several cooking fronts. It is saving so much by way of gas and electricity and will just keep on keeping on, regardless of power failures. It even has a warming oven.

Monkey buns and spelt bread and various pickles and jams are on the go. Stephanie can't resist making her raspberry toffee that tastes very much better than the commercial variety. It never ceases to amaze me just how few ingredients can make such a huge number of toffees.

The new chickens have turned out to be quite the characters and are now very comfortably settled. As I sit in my study in the late afternoon, they gather under the window to remind me that it's bread and fat time. They have become keepers of the yard and at last have formed a friendship with one of the other two chickens that were here before they came. The other remains steadfastly hostile or at best in a sulk with them and now wanders alone or keeps company with the ducks.

I heard the chicken and small holdings expert on ABC radio in Hobart say that letting chickens run under the fruit trees will help eradicate the common pest coddling moth. So ours now roam freely in the orchard all day. They are more than welcome to eat any of the larvae or moths that they can find. They resent the presence of the currawongs in their space and chase them off at every opportunity.

May 10

I discover today that the freezer must have been turned off accidentally last weekend and though most of the contents are fine, there is some fruit that will need to be used, as well as several roasts. The cat and dog should do well from some of the minced meat that has thawed.

It was only by chance that I came across this inadvertent slip-up. I'd been asked to make some raspberry jam for a fundraiser function for Willow Court historic site.

Once this is done I can survey the damage to the contents, which is in fact quite little. However, some of the raspberries near the top would be best to be used. I also found some redcurrants partially thawed, so raspberry and redcurrant jam it will be. It turns out to be an exquisite colour, with a refreshing tart aftertaste, so good that the recipe is included here.

Decades ago when country cooks bottled raspberries, a redcurrant was placed in the centre for the sake of appearance when entering their products in shows.

Raspberry and Redcurrant Jam

1kg raspberries
600g redcurrants
½ cup water
1.6kg sugar

Place the raspberries, redcurrants and water in a large saucepan and bring to the boil, stirring occasionally. Simmer for 5 minutes.

Add the sugar and brig to the boil, stirring. Boil briskly for 12–15 minutes or until setting point (see page 393) is reached. Pour into warm sterilised jars and seal immediately.

Makes about 2.8kg

The roasts, only partially thawed, will provide a feast for the weekend on Mother's Day so there is little actual loss. The power point to the freezer, however, is now securely taped into the 'On' position to avoid further similar mishaps.

The rest of the redcurrants can be made into jelly, which I use all year round to enhance gravies and casserole-style dishes, as well as their more customary use on scones and toast. Any type of currants can be used — red, white or black; all are very intense in flavour, totally delicious.

Redcurrant Jelly

2kg redcurrants
1 litre water
sugar

Place the currants and water in a large saucepan or jam pan and bring to the boil. Simmer until the fruit is soft. Mash well with a potato masher, then pour into a colander that has been lined with muslin. Leave to drip for several hours, catching the liquid underneath.

For each cup of liquid add 1 cup sugar and bring back to the boil, stirring. Boil until setting point is reached (see page 393).

Pour into warm sterilised jars and seal immediately.

For **Blackcurrant or Whitecurrant Jelly**, simply substitute blackcurrants or whitecurrants for the redcurrants. Whitecurrant jelly is good for glazing fruit tarts.

Makes about 1.5 litres

May 11

We will go to Eaglehawk Neck today. The house still hasn't sold, and we need to tend to the gardens once more as the property is to be featured in a local newspaper next week. While the greater area looks after itself, or the wildlife sees to it, the vegetable gardens are overgrown with weeds of every description. Forget-me-nots, though attractive, threaten to overtake the grassy areas.

I'm taking vegetables seedlings to plant out in the vegetable beds there. They will look tidier, and we can harvest the produce later in the year.

The car trip down once again emphasises the extent of the devastation from the January bushfires. Stark gaps remain where people once lived. In the Dunalley, Boomer Bay and Murdunna areas some are still living in caravans, tents even. Once the cameras have gone, it is all too easy to forget the legacy of deprivation that people endure until houses and lives are rebuilt. I've heard that the fires have even left some firefighters traumatised, such was the magnitude of the inferno and its aftermath.

There have been great efforts to restore fences, with volunteers travelling from around the state and even interstate, and only a few unfenced stretches remain, with signs warning that livestock could be roaming on the road. Although power was incredibly quickly restored, more permanent power poles are now being put into place.

Our part of the peninsula was really fortunate to have escaped the inferno, sheltered as it is on the ocean side of Pirates Bay Drive. As we pull into the driveway I am again quite reluctant to sell. I know we must, but who could not fall and remain in love with the idyllic setting? I miss the contact with wildlife more than anything: possums and wallabies were friends we fed each day.

I really want to go to the market that's being held today at the hall on the Neck, to see how it's changed and to sniff out a bargain if I can. There are more vegetables for sale there now, very good quality, and free-range sausages and hamburgers, which conjure up interesting mind pictures, but they smell jolly good. Inside is the type of stall I like best — one selling off unwanted kitchen gear. There is a huge Arco steel pot with a lid in immaculate condition and a small electric dehydrator.

Friends are contemplating purchasing that but decide against it and I snap it up. A mere $15 for each item, and I am deliriously happy. My old dehydrator, while still perfectly functional, is hardly a thing of beauty and is a bit decrepit to bring out as an example for the cooking class after 20 years' overwork. This small dehydrator is in pristine condition and is perfect for demonstrating in the school.

We head for our house and set to work in the garden. Well, actually, I check the letterbox first and a voice in the distance takes me to task over emptying the letterbox.

'Get out of that!' comes a call from a campfire a couple of hundred metres away.

'But we live here,' I reply, somewhat affronted.

'No, you don't,' he says, and then I realise it's our neighbour from up the road, having a joke at my expense. I am so embarrassed not to have recognised him. Mind you, my eyes have been bad of late: I must get them seen to. I first realised this when I mistook the red on guideposts for possible pickable fruit by the roadside.

He comes over for a chat and asks me if I would like some apples (he has a box in his truck, just picked from his trees this morning). The aroma is astounding; Golden Delicious. He talks of other varieties he has in the orchard — would I like some of those too?

Of course, of course! Soon we are picking several varieties on his property. He cuts one of the apples into pieces and though I am not usually a raw apple eater, this one is magnificent. Before long I have another huge boxful to go. Was I interested in any kitchen gear, he asks?

Recently a relative has died after a prolonged illness and he has boxes full of various bric-a-brac. My goodness, I would love to take a look. Soon I am loaded up with all sorts of kitchen equipment, from casserole dishes to serving spoons and plates. All these things have been a bit lacking in the school, set up on the smell of an oily rag as it was. He is delighted that I will have a use for it.

An old Kenwood Chef sits discarded to the side and this comes my way as well. It even has a glass bowl, which is a huge treasure as far as I'm concerned. I once had to buy a bowl for mine when the original broke, and even though it was only plastic, it cost me over $50. A glass one would cost far more. I love Kenwood Chefs, the old originals. I know they are noisy but they have a right to be. They have so much power and my modern equivalent (different brand that I expect should remain nameless) is a real under-performer by comparison.

By the time I leave I am also loaded up with vegetables from his garden, and finally a handful of figs from his tree, the last of the crop.

May 12

I've decided that today is the day to test the cider I've made. The bottle is a bit of a challenge to open — I should have tested it sooner. It is incredibly delicious though, and certainly has been worth the wait.

Apple Cider (Alcoholic)

3kg apples (e.g. Granny Smiths)
2 litres cold water
8g hops
1¼ cups sugar
1.25 litres boiling water, approximately
a few sultanas

Chop the apples into 8mm pieces, then place in a large saucepan with 6 cups of the cold water. Bring to boiling point, then remove from the heat and pour into a food-safe bucket.

Meanwhile, place the remaining 2 cups cold water, hops and sugar in another pot and heat to boiling point, stirring. Add to the bucket with the apples.

Pour the boiling water over and stir to combine. The apples should be fully covered. I place a plate on top for a couple of hours to ensure this happens. If there is not enough liquid to cover, pour in more boiling water.

Stand for 24 hours, then strain through a fine sieve (or a colander lined with a single thickness of muslin) and pour into plastic bottles, filling only to the neck. Place a sultana in each bottle.

Leave to stand at a warmish room temperature for 1 week, by which time it should be fizzy. Refrigerate after opening and, even then, open with care.

Makes about 3 litres

May 14

This afternoon I meet with Jenny at a local café. She has finished making me some customised aprons for the school. She's gone to such trouble and the aprons are beyond fantastic. She has ordered special kitchen prints from the US, then gone to the trouble of having special pockets embroidered for them. We were going to sell them to participants at the school, but Stephanie and I decide we cannot part with them and will use them ourselves in the school and at future events.

The afternoon feeding of the chickens is quiet today. Robert and Nat have enclosed the sheep in the bottom paddock and they are not at all pleased as they see me dole out the afternoon mash to the ducks and chooks. They have taken to thundering up the paddock as soon as they see me in the chook pen, sending the startled chickens in all directions. I only feed each of them the proverbial hollow tooth full but they seem to think it a great treat. Deprived as they are today, they stand and bellow at the bottom gate. Tomorrow I'd better let them into the other paddock. It's looking like I'll have to make a separate bowl of mash for them.

May 15

Today, aside from the inevitable paperwork, I have seedlings to plant out. Things have been so busy that I've neglected the garden beds. Jenny of the aprons has kindly kept for us some broccoli and cauliflower plants and a whole punnet of beetroot. The beetroot are the sort that grows into long carrot-like shapes, which makes them easier for bottling.

As I've said, I don't particularly like pickled beetroot, but others do. They can be used in salads and sandwiches and wraps even, provided they are drained and patted dry first.

They can be later drained and puréed and mixed with sour cream and a little grated horseradish to make a very nice dip.

Pickled Beetroot Slices

1kg beetroot
½–1 cup sugar
1 litre white or cider vinegar
1 teaspoon ground cinnamon
1 teaspoon ground allspice
8 cloves
10 peppercorns
1 teaspoon salt

Cook the beetroot in boiling water, then peel and slice or dice. Leave whole if using baby beetroot. Pack into sterilised jars.

Combine all the other ingredients in a large saucepan. Bring to the boil, then remove from the heat.

Allow to stand (covered) for 20 minutes if possible to allow the vinegar to cool a little and the flavours to infuse.

Strain the vinegar, then pour over the beetroot slices in the jar, making sure they are well covered with the liquid. Seal immediately.

Makes about 1kg

May 16

For days, even weeks, now we have been thinking about organising a sausage-making day, just for the fun of it, and to see if we can actually do so. We like to, wherever possible, eliminate artificial additives in our food. By making our own sausages, we will have control over the fat content, which can be as high as 50 per cent in commercially available products.

In an attempt to find a regular top-quality reliable meat we have stumbled across a discount meat supplier. I've rejected this in the past as I thought 'discount' equals lesser quality, but nothing could be further from the truth. Son Elliott alerted me to this butcher. Elliott likes to experiment with recipes for meats. A great conversationalist, he spoke with the owner, who told him that all the meat comes from local farms, either the Derwent Valley or around Sorell.

Sceptical at first, I tried some of the meat and was pleasantly surprised. I then got to talk to Todd, a young man who is part of this family business, and was very impressed indeed. He is happy to deliver to me at Molesworth any time I need.

Included in my order today is pork belly of exquisite quality. Last week's episode of the breakfast bacon has inspired me to try curing my own. The pork is so good that Stephanie and I share it, each of us to make different cures by way of comparison. Stephanie has made her own bacon many times before and this morning we purchase the necessary ingredients and begin the curing process in the afternoon.

Last night the mystery of the little grey-and-white cat was solved. I rang a neighbour to ask for the local residents' phone numbers so I could ring around and see if she had a home. He knows of the cat and yes, she has an owner, so it looks like she is very smart — gets a cuddle and a feed here, then heads home for the same. I'm really happy about this as integration into our household with Tom's antipathy would have been challenging to say the least.

This morning the tree in front of the kitchen window lost almost all its leaves. It has served us well over summer, its abundant foliage shading us from the worst of the summer sun. Now it's letting in the softer winter warmth.

Today Robert's made a fence of sorts around the orchard and now the sheep can graze in there. The worrying words are 'of sorts' and I wonder if it will hold them in. After all, they are a pretty formidable force when they push up to the fence for their little bit of mash in the afternoons. One can but hope.

May 20

This morning is the whitest frost I have ever, ever seen, and I've seen plenty by now. The frost is like a sheet of ice across the home paddock and beyond. As the sheep bend over grazing and the sun tentatively breaks through the mist, steam rises off their backs.

I soon find my qualms about the effectiveness of the temporary fence Robert's rigged up to keep them in the orchard were well founded. The sheep have pushed over the gate and escaped into the main area around the house and are eating everything they fancy — in fact, they have now vanished and could be anywhere.

Robert is hastily called and heads for home immediately, though I doubt he'll make it before dark. Rounding up sheep is not in my job description; I am certainly no sheep dog and neither is Robert, but there's nothing else for it. That ram is a determined fellow so it's going to be a battle and a half.

We could ring their owner but that would be a mite embarrassing and so we will try to sort it ourselves. As it turns out, it's not quite as difficult as we'd imagined. We round them up with little trouble.

May 22

Today is to be the first of the making and baking yeast products class. Many people, including some who are coming to the class, think it's difficult to bake with yeast, but in actuality it is one of the simplest and most rewarding of all types of cooking. For this reason I am really looking forward to changing their view.

I'm a little uncertain how to manage this as yeast, especially with the current chill in the air, can take its time to work. However, I get up early and mix several batches of sweet and savoury dough. I have in mind to make a variety of sweet baked products: jaffa buns, fruit buns, cream buns and cinnamon scrolls. By way of savoury fare there will be pizza, spelt bread and focaccia.

Robert gets the wood heater in the house going and soon the doughs are rising, to be ready in good time.

As an accompaniment to the more savoury of the breads a huge pot of pea and ham soup simmers away on the slow-combustion stove. In the oven the pork belly that we've cured to bacon is roasting away contentedly. The plan is to slice and dice this to serve as crisp lardons to garnish the soup. A slight touch of apple mint jelly should add the finishing touch to bring together and enhance all the flavours.

By now the breads are cooked and ready to serve, and all the buns are decorated as planned.

After lunch, when everyone is winding down from the morning of intense baking, we sit and chat and I show the group how I made the dough in the first place in the early hours of the morning.

I am very pleased that the flow of the class has worked out well. It is necessary to do things kind of backwards; if the doughs were mixed early in the class we would just be standing around twiddling our thumbs, waiting for it to rise to the shaping stage.

Rob of the quince tree arrives to talk some more about the sausage-making day. He will provide the lamb component and will also access the pork fat for us. Maybe they will come for dinner on Sunday night? Stephanie and Nat will come, as is becoming wonderfully customary.

He too partakes of the soup and then a bacon and tomato fry-up. This bacon is addictive: in fact it's pronounced by all to be very good indeed — this is obviously a recipe with merit. Never again will I buy factory-prepared bacon. There simply is no comparison.

Now that I know it works it's safe to pass on the recipe. We actually trialled two methods, one using less salt than the other. The lower salt version almost lost me one batch of pork belly — another day, and I would have had to throw it out.

If you choose not to use the sodium nitrite your bacon will be brown instead of pink, but it's purely an aesthetic issue, so leave it out if you wish.

It is best to get pork belly without the eye fillet. As this is thicker it takes longer to cure and the whole piece may cure unevenly.

Home-cured Bacon

There will be more cure than you need for the 2kg pork belly in this recipe. Leftover curing mix can be stored in an airtight jar for later use. Keep far out of the reach of children.

CURE
500g kosher salt
250g sugar
60g curing salt number 1/pink salt (6.25% nitrite)

about 2kg pork belly
2 tablespoons maple syrup

To make the Cure, mix together the salt, sugar and curing salt. Sprinkle some of this mix liberally into a large shallow dish and add your prepared pork belly, then turn over to coat the other side. Spray lightly with liquid smoke if desired (I don't but Stephanie does).

Place the pork in a zip-lock bag and pour in the maple syrup. Seal the top and place the bag in a container in the fridge. Turn each day for a week until the meat becomes firm.

Remove the meat from the bag, rinse well and pat dry with paper towels. Sit on the benchtop for an hour or so (in the fridge in hot climate) until the surface is dry.

Preheat the oven to 90°–95°C and bake for 2 hours or until the internal temperature of the pork reaches 65°C.

Cool and slice thinly into rashers, at which stage it can be frozen for later use or cooked immediately. Alternatively the bacon can be smoked before slicing.

As a variation, try substituting 2 tablespoons quince jelly from Toffee Quinces (see recipe page 258) for the maple syrup.

Makes about 2kg

In the relative calm of the evening I receive a phone call. This is often the time for telemarketers and I admit to being a bit curt when answering the phone at this hour.

I hear dulcet tones whisper, 'They've dropped!'

What? Maybe it's a highly suspect call … and then it registers. It is our friend Kaye ringing about the medlars. They were once quite commonly grown, especially in English-style gardens. Medlars are a tan colour when on the tree, but at this time of the year they drop to the ground, where a clever person will have covered the surface with straw to prevent any soil sticking to them. The fruit is then generally left on straw or in cardboard boxes to ripen to dark brown and soften, a process called 'bletting', which is the stage at which they can be made into jelly or steeped in vodka to make liqueur.

For about a decade now we have had the yearly ritual of the old medlar tree that grows in Kaye's garden. Usually there's an email saying they've dropped — in fact often we wax lyrical by nonsense poems on the subject of medlars. This year, in all the hustle and bustle of setting up the school, it's passed me by.

It will be so good to see Kaye again. She is a lithographer, an artist of considerable note and a singer with the Hobart Chorale. One Christmas recently I heard through the open doors of the State Library the most hauntingly beautiful singing of carols. So enchanting was the sound that I was transported back to my childhood — it was like the voices of angels. My feet carried me inside, and it was only then that I realised that Kaye was part of the group.

We make arrangements to pick up the medlars very soon and I will pass over a bottle of last year's medlar liqueur, also customary each late autumn or winter.

The fact that Kaye has rung on this of all nights is creepily coincidental. Just yesterday I made a recipe of her mum's. Tilly, Kaye's mum, lived with her for several years before she died and each year when we went to get the medlars it was lovely to chat with her. She was always full of stories and recipes to share.

After she passed away, Kaye photocopied Tilly's ancient handwritten recipe book for each of the family, to be passed down from generation to generation.

I was enormously pleased and privileged when Kaye gave me a copy as well. Tilly's Sweet Indian Beef Curry was adapted and included in *Slow Cooker* and just yesterday I made her bean pickle.

Tonight Kaye tells me that Tilly used to serve it with brawn, that good old-fashioned favourite. My nan used to make it too and it was one of those inimitable recipes, made by instinct rather than prescribed ingredients. It was incredibly delicious, but I was never able to duplicate it properly. It was a primary craving for me with one of my pregnancies and Nan got more than the usual number of visits when the cravings were too much to bear. She used to make it in an old green enamel bowl with a somewhat chipped grey rim. It's one of those memories that stay with you forever.

The pickle is also lovely served with corned silverside and very probably other hot or cold meats, though I admit it's a poor second to the brawn.

Tilly's Bean Pickle

The only modification I have made to Tilly's recipe is the use of cornflour instead of flour to thicken.

> *3 cups vinegar*
> *2 cups sugar*
> *1 tablespoon salt*
> *½ teaspoon pepper*
> *4 large onions, diced*
> *2lb (1kg) beans, ends removed and sliced*
> *2 teaspoons ground mustard*
> *2 teaspoons ground turmeric*
> *3 teaspoons cornflour mixed to a paste with 2 tablespoons*
>   *vinegar*

Place all the ingredients except the cornflour paste into a saucepan and bring to the boil, stirring. Boil for 20 minutes, then thicken with some or all of the cornflour paste.

Makes about 2.2kg

May 23

Today our Courtney is coming to visit to help me bake 60 or more little lemon meringue tarts. Daughter-in-law Emma would like them to serve at grandson Hunter's first birthday party on Saturday.

First, however, clean your chalet. This is no small undertaking as the benefit of the school is that I can just shut the door on the untidiness and go back to it tomorrow. Now my sins have found me out and so I have to pay the price and clean up first. Still, it's great to chat as we work and soon Courtney has the pastry underway. A leg of lamb roasts gently in the oven.

I've discovered a fact about this slow-combustion stove, which may cause you to think I'm quite mad. The last few times I've lit it, the stove has rewarded me with billowing smoke. Yesterday morning before the yeast class, I decided to call the stove by name, hoping to coax it into cooperation. Carmichael is its brand and hence his name. Whatever the reason, he immediately stopped smoking and performed beautifully all day. It's all mindset and madness, I know, but if it works, why not?

One of the group even comments on Carmichael's efficiency, which is very valid. Quite aside from the huge stovetop, there's a warming drawer that I've not yet used. At the same time he keeps the room warm and cosy on these cold autumn days. I guess it's not so different from my dad's saying that if you want something to work properly, you have to hold your mouth right.

By the time Courtney leaves, the tart cases are made, as is the lemon filling, ready to be put together early Saturday morning.

This recipe was a good opportunity to use the lemon curd I'd made recently. You can use any citrus fruit — orange, lime, mandarin, tangelo and so on. You can also make passionfruit curd by using a half-cup of passionfruit pulp in place of the citrus juice.

Instead of individual tartlets, you could make a whole citrus meringue pie, using a 20–23cm tart plate.

Citrus Curd

>3 teaspoons cornflour
>1 cup castor sugar
>½ cup citrus juice
>2 teaspoons grated citrus zest
>3 egg yolks
>125g unsalted butter, softened

Combine cornflour and sugar in a saucepan, gradually stir in the juice and water with the zest, egg yolks and butter. Whisk until smooth.

Pour into warm sterilised jars and seal immediately. Store in the fridge for up to 2 months.

Makes about 375ml

Citrus Meringue Tartlets

PASTRY
125g butter
125g sugar
1 egg, separated
250g plain flour

FILLING
1 recipe Citrus Curd (see page 297)

MERINGUE
4 eggwhites
1½ cups caster sugar
1 teaspoon white vinegar
1 teaspoon cornflour
2 teaspoons boiling water

Grease 24 x ¼-cup patty tins.

To make the Pastry, cream the butter and sugar. Whisk in the egg yolk, then fold in the flour with a metal spoon until well combined. Wrap in cling film and place in the fridge for 30 minutes at least.

Roll out the pastry thinly on a lightly floured surface. Cut 24 rounds to fit the patty-tin bases and sides. Brush with a little beaten egg white and prick each base twice with a fork. Place in the fridge for 30 minutes before baking.

During this time preheat the oven to 190°C. Bake the tart cases for 8 minutes. If the tart cases have tended to shrink down a bit, press back into shape with your fingertips while still warm. (Protect your fingers by using the corner of a tea towel.)

Pour the cooled curd into the cooked pastry cases.

To make the Meringue, place all the ingredients in a bowl and beat until thick peaks form. Pipe or spoon the meringue over the lemon filling.

Reduce the oven temperature to 120°C and bake for 12–15 minutes or until the meringue topping is crisp and lightly coloured.

Makes 2 dozen

May 24

Today will be my first opportunity to make sauerkraut, and I'm determined to get to it. Ideally I would have made it earlier in the week, but things have been way too busy for that. Still, the recipes I've read have said that it doesn't really matter but today is the day.

I also want to experiment with making an old recipe, common in the early nineteenth century, Colonial Goose. I am thinking Sunday night would be good. I ring Todd at Tassie Discount Meats, my new best friends, and ask for two legs of lamb. I told him how the shank had to be cut, according to a recipe I'd researched, and he promised to bring them to me later in the day.

A short time later he rang back. Now this is a butcher with passion for his trade. He has taken the time and trouble to research the recipe himself. He searched the Internet, rang an elderly butcher friend up the north of the state, as well as his ex-teacher at TAFE. As a result of all this investigation, it has been confirmed that a forequarter of lamb was used rather than the leg. This makes sense, as marinating the meat would tenderise this normally tougher cut. He describes in great detail how this cut was prepared.

I am delighted he has taken such an interest and wait with even more anticipation for the lamb to arrive. I will marinate it for several hours, after which it will be placed in the slow-combustion stove to bake.

Colonial Goose

This dish is best started off early in the morning.

MARINADE
250g sliced carrots
2 large onions, sliced
1 bay leaf

3–4 crushed parsley sprigs
1 sprig thyme
1 cup red wine

STUFFING
1 medium-sized onion, finely diced
1 cup fresh breadcrumbs
¼ teaspoon salt
¼ teaspoon dried thyme or 2 teaspoons fresh, finely chopped
¼ teaspoon dried sage or 2 teaspoons fresh, chopped
1 egg, lightly beaten

1 leg or forequarter of lamb, boned (ask your butcher to do this
    for you)

To make the Marinade, mix all the ingredients together in a large dish.

To make the Stuffing, mix all the ingredients together until well combined, then press into the cavity of the leg of lamb, tying with butcher's string if necessary to keep the leg intact.

Place the leg in a baking dish large enough for the lamb, and then add the marinade mixture. For the next 8 hours or more, turn the lamb over regularly in the marinade. For this reason it's best to start the dish in the morning.

Preheat the oven to 180°C and bake the lamb for 20 minutes, then reduce the heat and cook for a further 1½ hours or until the meat is tender.

Strain off the marinade and use about ¼ cup to make the following **Gravy**.

1½ cups chicken stock
¼ cup marinade
1 teaspoons quince or redcurrant jelly
2 teaspoons cornflour mixed to a paste with 1 tablespoon cold
    water
salt and pepper

To make the Gravy, whisk together all the ingredients
in a small saucepan and bring to the boil, stirring until
slightly thickened. Add salt and pepper to taste.

Serves 4–6

⁂

I still have a box of apples to preserve. I could cook them up to a
lovely purée and freeze it for apple crumble or pies, or to serve as an
accompaniment to pork. But I rather have a fancy for slicing or dicing
them and preserving in a light sugar syrup. They would be more versatile;
in a pie or crumble there would still be texture, and the slices or dice
could be drained and used in an apple strudel or in apple muffins, a
Dutch Apple Cake and so on.

Bottled Apples

Peel, slice, quarter or dice the apples. You will need to
work quickly as they will discolour within minutes. There
are a couple of ways that you can slow this down, however.

Half-fill a bucket with water and for each litre of water,
add 2 tablespoons salt or 1 tablespoon citric acid.

It's good to have your preserving syrup of choice at
the ready (see page 386). When you estimate you have
enough prepared apples to fill 2–3 jars, fill them at
once and pour the liquid to the rim and place on the
lids and clips or screw-on lids.

Apples Stewed or Puréed

The apples should be bottled while still hot. I have
done them when lukewarm but have added an extra 15
minutes to the preserving time. The preserver should
be filled with warm water rather than the usual cold
water in this case.

If you are using jars other than Fowlers style, seal them as is appropriate according to the manufacturer's directions.

Use the following chart as a guide to preserving apples.

Apple Preparation	Temperature	Time
Purée or pulp	85°C	2 hours
Apple quarters	80°C	2 hours
Sliced or diced	80°C	2 hours

For many years I've wanted to make sauerkraut, whose sour savoury taste I love. Its natural fermenting process makes it very good for digestion. For years now, no trip to Hobart's famous Salamanca Market is complete without indulging in a bratwurst sausage with hot sauerkraut.

I'd been told it was not possible (by a *self-appointed* expert, I later found) to make sauerkraut in Tasmania. In a discussion one day with my friend Rosa, she adamantly assured me this was not the case and volunteered to show me how to make sauerkraut by her traditional Croatian family method. We lived at Eaglehawk Neck at the time but I figured it was worth the effort to go to Hobart to buy all the necessary gear. I purchased a large plastic barrel for the purpose, rather too large, as it turned out (it holds about eighteen cabbages) and Rosa ordered the produce from her favourite supplier.

I had visions of shredding the cabbages by the bucketful and salting it down. However, Rosa's method was quite different; she leaves the cabbages whole, hollowing out the core of each cabbage with a large knife, then packing the empty space with cooking salt. They are then packed tightly into the barrel. Rosa adds a handful of peppercorns, bay leaves and pours a brine mixture over to cover. The cabbages are then weighted down and left for several weeks. Another date was arranged for me to go back for the tasting, and for Rosa to show me how to make cabbage rolls.

Now, I really thought I knew how to make cabbage rolls, pretty much a staple when our children were growing up, but I was soon to learn a serious lesson. When Rosa lifted the cabbages from the barrel, they looked sensational. The flavour was wonderful, not too salty, not too sour.

It was then I finally realised why the cabbages were preserved whole. Rosa took the outer leaves, rinsed and dried them, then wrapped them around a tasty mixture of pork and beef mince, onions and spices. The inner leaves were shredded and a layer placed in the base of a heavy pot, the rolls placed on top, more shredded sauerkraut to cover, along with a flavoursome homemade tomato sauce. The lid was placed on the pot and the dish was left to simmer for an hour or so. Any pride I'd had in my paltry offerings of cabbage rolls was instantly dispelled once I tasted Rosa's — they were simply delicious. Rosa told me she used to make them for a shop they'd had before coming to Tasmania, and she could barely keep up supply. Small wonder, I thought.

I started a batch of sauerkraut at home, in a much smaller barrel that held only six cabbages. After a couple of months I lifted the lid, at which time the aroma that filled the kitchen, indeed the whole top floor of the house, was so overpowering that young Courtney and her boyfriend Matthew ran from the house gagging, vowing they would never, ever eat such a concoction.

I placed the lid back on and it still sits there to this day while the house is waiting to be sold. Rosa kindly kept me supplied until we moved away — I never did tell her about my efforts. There was actually probably nothing at all wrong with the sauerkraut I'd made, but the reaction of the kids left me too hesitant to ever eat it.

I've heard of others who have tipped their sauerkraut out because of that incredible aroma. One man told me he tipped his onto the compost heap where in the open air it didn't smell so bad. He tentatively tasted the top of the pile and realised he'd just thrown away one of the most delicious things he'd ever eaten.

Well, today I decided to try again. I've researched a great deal and bought a book that expounds the virtues of preserving by fermentation. Other books concur with the ratio of salt to cabbage that are recommended, and my four cabbages are good to go.

It will be a while before I know if the recipe has worked. It seems to be one of those intangibles — mostly a matter of knowledge passed on from generation to generation, but I am hopeful that this time I will be successful.

I've read that the time it will take varies according to temperature: from 22–24°C will take about three weeks, 18–21°C about 5 weeks, and 15–17°C, approximately 6 weeks. Temperatures over 25°C are likely to lead to spoilage.

May 26

I have a pile of cabbage leaves left over from making the sauerkraut. They can be included, but I wanted a fine shred. Robert tells me he will feed them to the sheep.

Now I am a bit worried about this. As a child I used to read the James Herriott books and recall sheep that blew up with bloat and had to have their sides pierced to give them relief. Cabbages to my mind seemed to be a prime candidate to bring on this problem — not that I know much about sheep.

I surreptitiously try to ring their owner, but couldn't reach him and worry about this as I see Robert head for the paddock with a bin full of the leaves.

No harm has come to the sheep, so all is good. Tonight the owner finally rings. I tell him of my concerns and all is OK. He said they'll be fine so long as we don't overdo it.

I tell him how I've become quite attached to these sheep of his, given the fact that they suck the chook's mash off my fingers every afternoon. He was astounded. 'But they are wild sheep,' he said, 'no-one can handle them.'

I feel secretly but quietly proud that they've taken to me. I know it's just for the food, but it's rewarding anyway. Besides, I really like their company when I'm outside — they obligingly and, to my immense satisfaction, enthusiastically feed on the cape weed I hurl over the fence to them as I wrench it from the garden. Weed murder at its best.

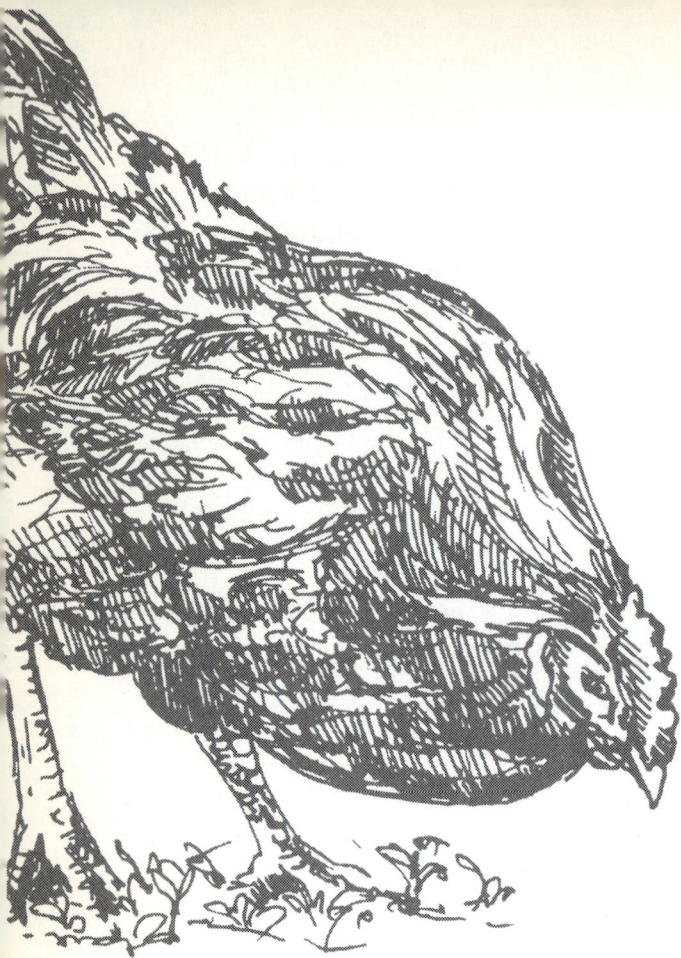

June 2

We had a wonderful day yesterday, with neighbours and family calling in, all of us chatting comfortably by the warmth of the wood heater with innumerable cups of tea and various edibles. Terry brought two huge bagfuls of walnuts from a tree on a nearby property. For anyone who buys just the pre-shelled supermarket variety, it's worth trying them cracked straight from the shell.

Today, though, is a day for work in the garden. We want and need to extend the garden beds so that almost all the produce used in the cooking classes can be picked fresh from there.

Robert has rotary-hoed another plot at the bottom of the house paddock. It needs fencing. Try as we may, potoroos are finding their way in and the chicken-wire enclosures I'd hoped to have left behind at the Neck are now smattered across, around all the beds and orchard.

It's unexpectedly pleasing work, this kneeling on the earth, warmed by the winter sun, pulling weeds and picking out stones. Soon there are rows of cavolo nero, baby bunching broccoli, spinach and kale plants, and abundant parsnip and swede seeds set out. Despite the fact that the chill has meant less evaporation, the ground is very dry due to the shortage of rainfall and so everything needs to be watered. Thank goodness for the bore water.

Meanwhile Robert is re-establishing the sprinkler system in the orchard. It has been a bit haphazard until now, providing water to some trees and not to others and in varying amounts. Now finally new piping is laid and new sprinkler heads installed so that everything has a good supply. We've purchased many new fruit trees — Mulberry, Moor Park apricot, Kentish Cherry and more besides and so should get a good yield next summer.

Mowing has always been a rather large task, time-consuming, though not really onerous from any other perspective. It's a good, contemplative time now that I've mastered the driving, and the scenery is stunning. I particularly enjoy one stretch of grass where, as you ride down the slope, the hills opposite change in colour. They almost seem to be alive as they are seen from each perspective — the trees' foliage changes from green to purple hues as the light strikes them from different angles. It is mesmerising.

These days, however, we have new mowers on the block. The sheep have been looking longingly at the lush green of the house paddock for some time now. It's not that they haven't enough to eat in the other paddocks, but nevertheless, this area has to look pretty appealing to them. Robert has let them into the orchard to feed as there are no leaves on the trees for them to graze on. It's always a pain to mow that area and they prove very much up to the task of keeping the grass down. They now know the routine of going back to their home paddocks at dusk so there is no more trying to round them up.

I've found that they are not as dumb as I'd imagined. Perhaps it's their eyes that give that impression; they are a bit blank. The sheep are at the very least good time-tellers. They know the time that I feed the chickens their bread and fat each afternoon, and now there is no stopping them. They want part of the action.

In fact there has come to be quite the afternoon ritual. As I take the saucepan full of food over, now morning and night in the chill of winter, there is the baaing of the sheep and their thundering hooves as they pound up the paddock. The chooks race to get through the gate so as not to be chased by the sheep. I've also spied magpies and currawongs, hopeful for their share of the booty. A small flame robin perches on the orchard fence post, expectant of a morsel or two, and green rosellas scrabble among the clumps of grass for any stray seeds or wheat. Tom follows to watch the sport and Della lumbers over, hopeful that I'll leave the gate open far enough open for her to squeeze through so she can gobble down anything in sight. Woe betide anything that gets between Della and food.

It must seem a queer procession to any casual onlooker but I'm happy with the menagerie in tow. Tom comes back inside as I return, to settle on his blanket on the couch, protected this year from the winter nights he endured cold and hungry for so many years.

June 3

In a quest to work with some of the produce that the early colonials would have used, I've been researching access to native wildlife as food. Wildlife is now being farmed or humanely culled. The meat is tender and tasty, lean and healthier than many alternatives.

It is by chance that I make a phone call to a supplier on Bruny Island. I'd actually hung up before he answered, as I still feel a bit uncomfortable about eating wildlife. However, my call is returned, having been picked up as a missed one on their phone, and so a fascinating discussion ensues.

Knowledgeable in the extreme and passionate about the advantages of eating such healthful meat, acquired locally and humanely, we are soon talking recipes and various uses for wallaby and possum. Already I have tasted meat cooked by one of his friends when he was doing a segment on ABC radio. The rabbit stroganoff and wallaby stew were exceptional.

The discussion finished with the promise that Richard will provide me with some of the meat so I can experiment with different recipes for wallaby and possum.

I'm assured that possum is a wonderful meat but I admit to being a bit sceptical. I've read accounts of its being 'distinctive' and 'interesting' in old cookbooks and even worse and unmentionable from friends and others who have tried it.

Richard, however, has an explanation. Apparently there is a gland in a possum that needs removing very soon after killing. The possum meat needs to be hung and treated in a specific way for best results. If this is not done, the meat takes on an unpleasant taint. He has made a light curry with possum meat and visitors to his property were very enthusiastic about it, devouring it in no time.

And so I take heart about experimenting with it. The meat looks suitably anonymous in its shrink wrapping.

I've become more used to the idea of wallaby of late and have plans to make that into a Kangaroo Steamer, such as Lady Jane Franklin described and pronounced as 'very good' when attending a dinner at Port Arthur penal settlement.

I will mince some and make pasties and I'd like to make some jerky as well. Richard will provide me with meat as long as I want to experiment. There will also be, he tells me, a Taste of Bruny festival in November. Would I like to come along? Certainly, and plans are made to that end — I may even be able to demonstrate there.

June 4

The morning starts early with Robert picking the last of the rhubarb before he goes to work. It is starting to die down and Alistair would like whatever we can spare for cakes at Sweet Envy. It's hard to come by now, coming into the end of the season, but he will cook it up so that his exceptional Dexter tarts can continue to be enjoyed in his shop.

He needs curly-leaf parsley too and we harvest some for him. He is keen to get the roots when we dig the plants out soon. I could never understand the swing to flat-leaf parsley as it doesn't seem to have the flavour, let alone the texture, of the curly-leaf.

In recent days I'd been able to get a 10-kilo bag of pickling onions. I've really left the pickling of onions rather late this year, busy as we've been.

Now that I have them and with a hectic week to come, I have designated tonight for the task. Robert is the one who always peels the onions, usually outside on a breezy day, but the weekend was occupied with other things and so we must undertake this indoors tonight.

Robert, ever the boy scout of spirit, uncovers a pair of large goggles from the depths of the shed and stands bug-eyed, peeling for over an hour, until the task is complete, tear free.

The onions are duly salted and are to be left for two days before being preserved in vinegar.

For this year's batch I've decided to trial three different vinegar mixes. It's not that I don't like the recipe in *A Year in a Bottle* but I'd like to compare and maybe even use less sugar.

Traditional English pickled onions use dark malt vinegar with spices added, so this will be batch 1.

For batch 2, I will use a commercial spiced malt vinegar, lighter in colour and less pungent in flavour, but will still add extra spices.

Batch 3, I will use plain white vinegar. Cider vinegar could be substituted but the difference would be negligible, and besides, there's none in the pantry. White wine vinegar is another option, but this seems to vary in strength — I've had some that have been very overpowering and so usually steer clear of it except for in salad dressings.

Unfortunately it will be two months before I can taste the results.

Pickled Onions

BRINING SOLUTION
200g cooking salt
2 litres water (3 cups boiling and 5 cups cold)

1.5–2kg pickling onions, peeled

SPICED VINEGAR
7½ cups vinegar
20g allspice berries
20g peppercorns
a few cloves
1 bay leaf
¾ cup sugar
1 teaspoon grated fresh ginger

To make the Brining Solution, combine the salt and boiling water and stir until the salt is dissolved, then stir in the cold water. Allow to cool, add the onions and weigh down with a plate or similar and set aside for 24 hours.

The next day, make the Spiced Vinegar by combining the vinegar, spices, sugar and ginger in a saucepan and bring to just below boiling point. Cover the saucepan with a lid, then leave to infuse for at least 3 hours. Strain through a sieve. Set aside to cool completely.

Drain onions from the brining solution, rinse well and pat dry with a paper towel. Pack onions into sterilised jars to within 2.5cm of top of each jar. Each jar should contain 650g onions approximately. It's important to keep the proportions right so that there is enough vinegar in each jar to preserve the onions effectively.

Pour the cooled spiced vinegar over the onions, ensuring they are completely covered. Each jar should contain about 3 cups of the spiced vinegar.

If the onions float to the surface, place a crumpled piece of baking paper in the top of each jar and press into the vinegar, making sure there are no air pockets underneath. After a few days this can be removed as the onions will have absorbed the vinegar and should stay submerged.

Seal immediately and store in a cool, dry and dark place for 2 months before using.

Makes 1.5–2kg onions

By the time the onions are bottled I am well in the swing of this pickling and decide on a whim to pickle some eggs as well. I've used a dark malt vinegar so that they will resemble English pub-style eggs. These will be ready in a month's time. I lift the lid after a while, and like my quietly fermenting sauerkraut in the laundry, I hope it will taste better than it smells.

Pickled Eggs

This amount will fill a litre jar. Make sure that the lid is non-corrosive so that it does not react with the vinegar.

> *9 eggs*
> *3 cups vinegar*
> *12 peppercorns*
> *15 allspice berries*
> *1 stick cinnamon*
> *¼ teaspoon dried chilli flakes, optional*
> *a pinch of salt*

Hardboil the eggs and peel them. Set aside in the fridge while preparing the vinegar.

Place the vinegar and spices in a stainless-steel saucepan and bring to the boil. Reduce the heat and simmer for 5 minutes. Cool, then strain through a sieve.

Place the prepared eggs in a sterilised litre jar and pour the vinegar over. Seal the jar and leave for 3–4 weeks before using.

Makes 9 eggs

June 6

There's *another* book-signing today, this time at the ABC shop in Hobart. They are a jolly crew there and have set me up — much to my horror — in full view in the arcade walkway. Still, I've brought food along to share — dips made with various of my pickles and some fresh, warm spelt bread pulled from the oven just before I left home.

I add some jars of the melon chutney for people to take home, and fresh raspberry jam for the tasting. Some of that jam melon cheese too. I'll be interested to see what people think.

As I'm packing up to leave, a lady approaches with a teenage girl. She explains that she has come along especially to thank me for my books. I thank her, but she goes on to say that it is especially so in her case. Her lovely daughter has an intellectual impairment, she explains, and is in the process of moving into a situation of living independently. She has been successfully using my cookbooks, especially *The Complete Slow Cooker*, and can now confidently cook for herself. This is a huge step in acquiring the ability to managing independence.

The daughter, a beautiful, bubbly, happy girl, is quite articulate but with a discernible disability. She chats happily about the recipes she's tried and on Monday will make her first soup ever.

I am pleased beyond words that the books are useful in this context. I once wrote a book about disability, for which I can take little credit as people with a disability helped me enormously. The struggle to be treated equitably and appreciated for their individual abilities, rather than judged for evident disability, is an ongoing challenge.

Another issue is the move to live independently. If I write nothing else ever, I will be content that my books have proven useful at least to some.

June 7

The morning starts badly. I had window cleaners coming and wanted to bake a cake for their morning tea. Distracted as I was by some small matter, I left out the baking powder and the cake when it emerged from the oven was flat and colourless.

Furious with myself, I threw it in the chook pot and decided to make a Swiss Roll. When it came time to put it in the oven I realised I'd set the temperature to less than 100°C. The poor old Kenwood Chef had to do double time to keep on beating the eggs until the oven was ready. I've been advised by the repairer not to overwork the beater as it's quite aged now and parts are hard to get. Still, it soldiered on.

Finally I've turned a corner — it's the best Swiss Roll I've ever made. The boys obligingly ate it all, which was great. Here is the recipe — remember to overbeat the eggs as I did as it really seems to work very well.

Swiss Roll

3 eggs
½ cup sugar
½ cup self-raising flour
¼ cup cornflour
3 teaspoons sugar (extra)
½ cup raspberry jam
3 teaspoons icing sugar

Preheat the oven to 180°C. Grease a Swiss Roll tin measuring 25cm x 30cm and line the base with baking paper. Grease again.

Beat the eggs with an electric beater for 7 minutes, then gradually add the sugar, about 1 tablespoonful at a time, and beat for 3 minutes more. Meanwhile sift the flour and cornflour together. When eggs and sugar have finished beating, sift in the flour and fold in with a wire whisk until smooth. Pour evenly into the prepared tin.

Bake for 10 minutes or until golden and pulling away from the sides of the tin.

Place a piece of baking paper on the bench, slightly larger than the tin. Sprinkle with extra sugar. As soon as the cake comes out of the oven, turn out onto the sugared paper. Remove the baking paper from the baking tin if it has clung to the cake. Trim the edges and roll up, enclosing the new baking paper. Cool on a wire rack.

Heat the jam, unroll the cake, remove the paper and spread the surface with the jam and roll up again. Sieve icing sugar over the top.

Serves 6

Our friend David is coming to dinner and I decided to use some of the wallaby meat. There's a nice piece of topside among it, which I pot-roast on top of the wood heater. Redcurrants are a natural accompaniment, I think. I know that blackcurrants combined with wallaby is more usual, but the tart redcurrants seem to me to be a better option.

I am more than happy with the result — the wallaby is tender and succulent, and the sauce exceptional. Served on a sweet potato and King Edward potato mash, it is a very pleasing match.

June 8

Last night David brought me a bagful of feijoas. These are a most delicious fruit, every bit as aromatic as a quince. The jam is exceptional, the jelly even better, chutney not so much. It is one of those fruits so distinctive in flavour that it is a travesty to overpower it with vinegar and spices.

However if you have a glut and a mind for it, I've included a recipe that I once put together.

They can also be bottled and are really delicious this way, so I would go with this rather than the chutney.

Bottled Feijoas

Feijoas are also known as pineapple guavas. They have a unique flavour, and are very aromatic. They are low in acid and discolour quickly, so when preserving by bottling either lemon juice or tartaric acid should be added. For each litre of preserving liquid (see page 386), add 5g citric acid or 2 tablespoons lemon juice. Have the preserving liquid at the ready.

Working quickly, peel and slice the feijoas and place them in the jars. Pour the syrup over the fruit and seal the jar immediately (see instructions page 385).

Place in the preserver and fill to the base of the lids with cold water. Turn the preserver to 90°C and bring up to temperature slowly over 45 minutes and hold at this heat for 1 hour. If you have a thermostat-controlled preserver, this will happen automatically, just set to temperature and leave for 1¾ hours.

Feijoa Jelly

1kg feijoas, washed (but not peeled) and chopped
1 litre water
juice of 1 small lemon
4 cups sugar

Place the feijoas, water and lemon juice in a large saucepan and bring to the boil. Reduce the heat and simmer until the fruit is soft. Pour the mixture into a colander that has been placed over a large bowl or pot. Leave to stand for 20 minutes at least. Pour the resulting liquid through a sieve that has been lined with one layer of muslin or similar.

Place this final liquid into a saucepan and add the sugar. Bring back to the boil, stirring constantly, then reduce the heat to medium and cook until setting point is reached (see page 393).

Makes about 1.5kg

Feijoa Jam

1kg feijoa flesh, diced
juice of 1 large lemon

¼ cup water
900g white sugar

Place feijoas, lemon juice and water in a large saucepan and bring to the boil, stirring. Reduce the heat and simmer for 20 minutes. Stir in the sugar and bring back to the boil, stirring constantly.

Boil over a medium heat for about 25 minutes until setting point is reached (see page 393).

Makes about 1.5kg

Feijoa Chutney

1.5kg feijoa flesh, diced
250g onions, peeled and finely diced
500ml white vinegar
750g white sugar
1 teaspoon ground ginger
½ teaspoon ground cinnamon
1½ teaspoons salt
2 teaspoons cornflour, mixed to a paste with 1 ½ tablespoons extra white vinegar (optional)

Place all the ingredients in a large saucepan. Bring to the boil, stirring, then reduce the heat to medium—low and cook for 1½ hours or until a chutney-like consistency. If you think the chutney needs thickening just a little, stir in the cornflour paste.

Makes about 2kg

June 9

I've been able to get some fresh cumquats. At the local tomato farm there is a tree, its fruit being sampled by birds or falling on the ground. Owner Nick promised that I can pick some and now I have a small bucketful to process.

There are pink peppercorns too, the fruit of the Columbian pepper tree. The peppers in their pink husk are aromatic and ideal for sweet dishes as well as savoury. Apparently they are best dried and then crushed before using, and so they now sit on the table in the house, waiting for the warmth of the wood heater to do its work of dehydrating them.

Last evening was spent processing cumquats — the initial stages for marmalade, cordial and liqueur. The marmalade I think strongly resembles Seville Orange marmalade, quite astoundingly so. I've reduced the amount of sugar and water, and maybe this is the reason.

For those who like a milder-flavoured marmalade, add an extra cup of water during the soaking process and add an extra 250g sugar with the amount specified.

Cumquat Marmalade

500g cumquats, washed
1.25 litres water
juice of 1 large lemon
1.25kg sugar

Slice the cumquats finely, removing the seeds as you go; set those aside in a cup.

Place the cumquats in a large saucepan or jam pan and pour over the water and lemon juice. Place the pips in a piece of muslin and tie the top with a piece of cotton or string to make a bag. Add to the saucepan. Leave to stand overnight.

Next day, bring the mixture to the boil and simmer for 20 minutes, then remove bag of pips. Stir in the sugar and bring to the boil, stirring. Boil briskly for 20 minutes or until setting point is reached.

Leave to stand for 5 minutes, then pour into warm, sterilised jars and seal immediately.

Makes about 1.5kg

Cumquat Cordial

This cordial has wonderful colour and flavour. Serve 1 part cordial syrup to 4 parts chilled water or soda water for a refreshing drink.

> *1.5kg sugar*
> *1 litre boiling water*
> *1 tablespoon (rounded) citric or tartaric acid*
> *500g cumquats*

Place the sugar, water and acid in a large bowl and stir until the sugar is dissolved.

Chop the cumquats finely and stir into the mixture. (I use a food processor to chop them). Leave to stand until cool, then strain through a fine sieve, pushing down on the pulp so that maximum flavour is captured. Mix well.

Pour into sterilised bottles and seal immediately. Refrigerate after opening.

Makes about 2 litres

Cumquat Liqueur

> *600g cumquats*
> *500g sugar*
> *750ml vodka*

Prick the cumquats several times with a fork and place in a large jar.

In a large saucepan, heat the sugar and vodka together until lukewarm, stirring with a whisk as it heats. Be careful not to overheat. Pour over the cumquats and place a (non-reactive) lid on the jar.

Store in a cool, dark place for 6 months before using. The liqueur can be drained off and the cumquats served with ice-cream or as an accompaniment to a slice of cheesecake.

To make Cumquat Brandy, that almost universally popular tipple, substitute brandy for the vodka in this recipe.

Makes about 1.5 litres

June 10

A bright sunny day is expected, so the time is opportune to put more work into the garden. We have to be making some progress, surely, with all this work that is going into it. As we stand back and look and reflect on what the property was like when we came, we realise that indeed it is so. We have vegetable patches in various stages of growth and today we set out the first of the lines for the raspberry canes in the far paddock.

Under the warmth of the winter sun, with animals surrounding us, we really couldn't ask for a more idyllic existence.

The intense chill of the evenings now calls for a large pot roast for dinner. I need to write a column about warming winter food, so experiment with some of the remaining quinces and the apples that our neighbour at the Neck has provided.

It occurs to me that the lovely, sweet, earthy nuttiness of spelt would be a perfect match to the winter fruits. You can also use bottled apples and/or quinces in this recipe.

Winter Fruit Tart with Spelt Pastry

FILLING
600g quinces, peeled, cored and cut into 1cm pieces
450g apples, peeled, cored and cut into 1cm pieces
200g pears, peeled, cored and cut into 1cm pieces
½ cup water
sugar (to taste)

PASTRY
180g butter, melted
150g sugar
2 small eggs
125g plain flour
125g spelt flour
1½ teaspoons baking powder

Preheat the oven to 190°C. Grease a 23 cm tart tin.

To make the Filling, place the fruit in a saucepan with the water and bring to the boil. Reduce the heat and simmer until the fruit is just tender. Stir in sugar to taste.

If the mixture is too watery (which isn't likely) thicken with 1–2 teaspoons cornflour mixed to a paste with 1 tablespoon cold water.

To make the Pastry, whisk together the butter and sugar and then add one of the eggs. Reserve about 1 teaspoon of egg white from the second egg, and add the remainder to the batter and whisk again.

Whisk in the combined flours and baking powder. The pastry is quite moist, more like a cross between a pastry and a cake batter.

Spoon two-thirds of the batter into the base of the tart plate. Brush with the reserved egg white. Spoon the fruit over.

Place the remaining pastry into a piping bag and pipe lattice style over the top of the fruit.

Bake for 10 minutes at 190°C, then reduce the heat to 160°C and bake for 20 minutes more or until the pastry is golden.

This tart is delicious served with a dollop of Greek yoghurt drizzled with a little leatherwood or bush honey.

Serves 6

June 14

Today Robert and Nat are to do some chores around the farm and Stephanie and I will cook a massive dinner, as our friend David is staying for the weekend. Later in the day they decided to brew some beer, again with a view to providing drinkables on our sausage-making day in July.

Stephanie has spied my lemon tree. Last year the lemons were tiny but tasty, whereas this year there must be at least one hundred, all perfect specimens. She has a mind for making limoncello, the Italian lemon liqueur, and so picks 45 lemons for the several batches she has in mind.

The one disadvantage is that only lemon zest is used, steeped in vodka. The juice can be frozen but there is rather a lot so we set to inventing a recipe that might make better use of most of it.

Lemon sorbet is always good and we will certainly make some, but we are interested in something with a bit more longevity. Hence, lemon syrup.

Lemon Syrup

> *500ml lemon juice*
> *1.2kg sugar*
> *3 cups boiling water*
> *2 teaspoons citric acid*

Mix all ingredients together in a bowl until the sugar is completely dissolved, then pour into warm sterilised jars and seal immediately.

Makes about 2.5 litres

Dehydrated Lemon Slices and Lemon Powder

Lemon slices are very handy to have on hand and are nice added to a cup of black tea, or, as my nan used to serve them, in a cup of the strongest black coffee made with coffee and chicory essence.

However, by far their best use is to dehydrate the slices until brittle, then process to a powder that can be used to flavour cakes and savoury dishes such as curries.

Simply cut the washed lemons into 8mm slices, removing pips, and dehydrate either in a food dehydrator or the oven at 65–70°C.

Freezing Lemons

Lemons can be frozen whole very successfully. They are then much easier to zest and the juice yield is high. Just place in freezer bags and freeze for up to 12 months.

June 19

My desire for and the need to work with wallaby and possum meat is growing, probably due to my interest in the recipes of the colonial era.

The first recipe I try used a whole (small) wallaby roast. It was quite successful but I admit to tasting only a smidgeon. Next, pot-roasted wallaby topside pieces, cooked on the slow-combustion stove. Our friend who came to visit went into raptures over them, even though he'd been hesitant to taste the dish at first. It was good when I finally mustered the courage to taste it. Pasties came next and were very tasty — I even ate a whole one.

By way of wallaby, this just left the shanks.

'I hate shanks,' said Robert as I placed them in the slow cooker, he not being a fan of the slight greasiness of the dish when made with lamb shanks.

However, the wallaby shanks were lean and I wanted to trial the recipe, so I'm afraid he would just have to suffer it. When they were cooked, my goodness, they were sensational. None of the greasiness that comes with lamb shanks cooked this way. Even Robert was well pleased and sang their praises to others.

Roasted Wallaby

3 tablespoons olive oil
1 onion, diced
2 sticks celery, sliced
2 carrots, sliced
125g mushrooms, sliced
3 sprigs thyme
1 haunch wallaby
1 lemon, quartered
½ cup white wine
½ cup tomato sauce
½ cup water or chicken stock
1 teaspoon quince or redcurrant jelly or apricot jam
½ teaspoon stock powder or ¼ teaspoon salt
2 teaspoons cornflour mixed with 1 tablespoon cold water
   (optional)
salt and pepper

Preheat the oven to 120°C.

Pour the oil into a baking dish, add the vegetables and thyme, and place the wallaby on top. Squeeze lemon juice over and place the skins in the dish.

Cover the dish with foil and then bake for 2 hours, basting once or twice with the pan juices and re-covering with foil each time. Increase the temperature to 140°C and cook for 1 hour more.

About 45 minutes before the end of cooking time, pour in the combined wine and tomato sauce. Cover with foil and return to the oven.

When the wallaby is tender, remove from the pan and leave to rest, wrapped in foil.

Add the stock and jelly or jam to the pan and bring to the boil on the stovetop. Pour the mixture through a sieve into a small saucepan, pressing the pulp through as far as possible.

Add stock powder or salt.

Bring to the boil and then thicken if needed with some or all of the cornflour paste. Add salt and pepper to taste.

Serves 4–6

Wallaby Pasties

This recipe makes between 12 and 16 pasties, depending on the size of your pastry cutter. You can by all means halve the recipe, but the pasties freeze well and are delicious served hot or cold, making them a good item for a lunchbox or picnic.

You could used ready-rolled shortcrust or puff-pastry sheets instead of making your own, but the lovely buttery pastry is hard to beat and certainly worth the little extra effort of making it.

PASTRY
360g plain flour
1½ teaspoons baking powder
¾ teaspoon salt
180g butter, diced
about ⅓–½ cup cold water

FILLING
500g wallaby pieces such as topside
120g bacon
60g peeled turnip
60g pumpkin
2 small onions
1 apple, peeled and cored
½–1 teaspoon salt
60g butter, diced

Preheat the oven to 200°C. Line 2–3 baking trays with baking paper.

To make the Pastry, combine the flour, baking powder and salt and then rub in the butter with your fingertips until it resembles breadcrumbs (or use the food processor to do this). Gradually add the water until a soft dough forms. Put aside to rest in the fridge while making the filling.

To make the Filling, mince together the wallaby, bacon, vegetables and apple and then mix in the salt.

Divide the pastry in half and roll one out thinly on a floured surface, dusting the top of the dough with flour as well. Cut into saucer-sized circles. Repeat with remaining dough and reroll scraps to make more.

In the centre of each pastry sheet, place about ½ cup filling and top with a small piece of butter. Dampen around one edge of pastry and then fold over to enclose the filling, sealing edges well.

Place on baking trays and bake for 10 minutes, then reduce the heat and cook for a further 25 minutes or until the pastry is golden and the pasties cooked through.

Serve with tomato sauce, relish or chutney and fresh seasonal vegetables.

Makes 12–16

Pot-roasted Topside of Wallaby with Redcurrant and Pink Peppercorns

If you don't have pink peppercorns, you could substitute 6 Tasmanian pepperberries. Both can be purchased from herb and spice retailers.

800g wallaby topside, cut into large pieces
½ cup flour
¼ teaspoon salt
½ teaspoon sweet paprika
1 tablespoon vegetable oil

30g butter
1 onion, diced
1 clove garlic, crushed
8–10 pink peppercorns, lightly crushed
¼ cup tomato sauce
½ cup red wine
¾ cup chicken stock (or water with ½ teaspoon chicken or
    vegetable stock powder)
1 sprig rosemary
60g fresh or frozen redcurrants
½ teaspoon quince or redcurrant jelly
1 teaspoon Worcestershire sauce
salt and pepper

Toss the wallaby pieces in the combined flour, salt and
paprika.

In a flameproof casserole dish, heat the oil and butter
together over a medium–high heat and then brown the
wallaby pieces on all sides. Add the onions and garlic
and cook for 1 minute more, then add the rest of the
ingredients.

Bring to the boil, reduce the heat and simmer gently
over a low heat for 2–2½ hours or until the meat is
tender. Add salt and pepper to taste.

Serve over creamy sweet potato and potato mash with
steamed greens or beans.

Serves 4–6

Slow-cooked Wallaby Shanks

4 wallaby shanks
1 onion, finely chopped
1 carrot, halved and sliced
1 stick celery, sliced
1 tomato, diced

½ cup tomato sauce
¼ cup white wine
2 teaspoons soy sauce
2 teaspoons chutney
1 teaspoon orange or cumquat marmalade
a pinch of dried oregano
2 tablespoons orange juice
¼ cup water

Place all the ingredients in the slow cooker and stir to combine.

Cook on high for 4–5 hours or until the meat is tender. Add salt and pepper to taste.

Serve with creamy mashed potatoes and seasonal vegetables.

Serves 4

Possum Pies

An elderly friend for years teased me by saying that he ate possum regularly. I didn't believe him for a long while and never dreamed that one day I'd find myself inventing a recipe for just this dish.

It's taken me a bit to get to the stage where I can actually make these. It's a mental thing, I know, and it doesn't help that as I make them Charly looks at me with her big blue eyes with just a hint of a tear and says, 'Nan Nan, you didn't kill a possum, did you? They are so cute.'

My hasty assurance that I didn't isn't received all that well, but still, the meat needed to be cooked, and so it must be.

I was astounded at how light the meat is, and how delicate in colour, almost like chicken thigh in texture as well as colour.

FILLING
1 tablespoon vegetable or canola oil
2 teaspoons butter
700g possum meat, cut into 1cm cubes
2 teaspoons curry powder
1 onion, finely diced
1 carrot, diced
1 small parsnip, diced
about 1½ cups stock or water with 1 teaspoon stock powder
2 teaspoons soy sauce
1 teaspoon sweet chilli sauce
3 teaspoons apricot jam
1 teaspoon Worcestershire sauce
1 teaspoon chutney (any sort)
salt and pepper
2 teaspoons cornflour mixed to a paste with 2 tablespoons cold
      water

PASTRY
180g butter, diced
50g grated tasty cheese
360g plain flour
2 teaspoons baking powder
1 teaspoon salt
½–¾ cup cold water

To make the Filling, heat the butter and oil over a medium–high heat and sauté the possum meat until it changes colour. Add the curry powder and onions and sauté for 1 minute more, then add the rest of the vegetables and stir to coat in the curry powder and pan juices.

Add the stock, sauces, jam and chutney. Bring to the boil, then reduce the heat and simmer until the possum is tender, about 2–3 hours. Add salt and pepper to taste.

Thicken with some or all of the cornflour paste and then leave to cool.

To make the Pastry, place the butter, cheese, flour, baking powder and salt in the bowl of a food processor and process until the mixture resembles breadcrumbs. With motor running, add the water gradually until a ball of dough forms. Wrap in cling film and refrigerate for 30 minutes.

Preheat the oven to 200°C.

Divide the pastry in half and roll out on a floured surface until about 6mm thick. Grease 10–12 1-cup capacity pie tins.

Cut pieces of pastry to fit the bases and press into place. Brush the edges with water. Fill the pies almost to the brim with the possum mixture. Roll the rest of the pastry to make tops for the pies and fit into place, crimping the edges together well. Prick the top of each pie once with a fork.

Bake the pies for 8 minutes, then reduce the heat to 150°C and cook for about 10 minutes more or until the pastry is golden brown.

Makes 10–12

There is an interesting aside to this recipe. The staff at Veolia, Robert's workplace, have always been enthusiastic test-tasters. I figured a possum pie might be taking it a bit too far, but Robert assured me that a particular co-worker would be up for trying one. He was wrong. Although it was taken home with the best of intentions, the pie didn't make it out of the fridge. He simply couldn't bring himself to taste it, at least not in the short term.

One evening shortly afterwards he had to attend a dinner function for work. His wife, left at home and reluctant to cook dinner for one, found the pie in the fridge and decided that this would be an easy snack.

It was clearly marked with a pastry 'P' on top, but she thought that just stood for 'Pork'.

When her husband came home, they exchanged the customary conversation about what each had for dinner.

'I ate your pie,' she said, struggling to understand why her husband was by now doubled over with laughter. 'The pastry was delicious and the vegetables were lovely.'

'What about the meat?' he managed to stammer.

'Oh yes, that was delicious too, lovely and tender.'

Gradually the story unfolded and to this day I am not sure that his wife is speaking to him again.

However, it does demonstrate that the eating of some foods is mind over matter.

June 21

There's a book-signing this evening at Fullers bookshop in Hobart. I've been asked to make soup for the 80 people who are anticipated to attend. What is soup without a little bread, I think. Regardless of a pressing book deadline, I decide to bake this as well.

The best thing about book-signings is getting to chat to people about my recipes, but far more so, the opportunity to learn about their own treasured family recipes.

For tonight I've made a pumpkin, roasted onion and apple soup, which is very well received, thankfully. What is that special flavour, I am frequently asked during the event, and it is just the addition of an apple.

I learned about this when visiting a restaurant many, many years ago in the seaside town of St Helens. We had ordered pumpkin soup, but the flavour was so exceptionally good that I asked to speak with the chef. He was from the US and told me about the addition of apple. I have included it in my pumpkin soup ever since. It adds a subtle sweetness and fruitiness that enhances the appeal of the soup greatly.

Roasted Pumpkin and Apple Soup

1 tablespoon olive oil

1 tablespoon butter

1kg diced dark-fleshed pumpkin (peeled weight), cut into 4cm
*   pieces*

1 cooking apple (such as Granny Smith), peeled, cored and
*   diced*

1 large onion

1 litre chicken or vegetable stock or 3 teaspoons stock powder
*   with 2 cups water*

½ teaspoon salt

½ cup cream (optional)

⅔ cup grated tasty cheese (optional)

Heat the oil and butter over a medium heat and sauté the pumpkin, apple and onions until almost tender, taking care they do not brown (reduce the heat as necessary).

Add the stock and salt and bring to the boil, then reduce heat and simmer until the pumpkin is very tender. Purée in a food processor or with a stick blender. Stir in the cream and cheese and reheat but do not boil.

Serves 6

By way of chatting, a lovely lady told me about her experimentation with sweet potato soup. She found that the addition of a small pear gave a whole new depth and dimension of flavour to the soup.

This I will have to try, and I have great expectations of the result. I have used apple with sweet potato, but never thought of pear.

As I drive alongside the Derwent River on the way home in the dark, the fog known as Bridgewater Jerry makes its presence felt, swirling back and forth across the road. It's an eerie feeling and I'm considerably comforted by the presence of others travelling the same route. Our own road is well shrouded in very thick fog, yet as I approach the gate a large bird swoops mere centimetres from my windscreen and alights on the post next to the gate. It shows no fear whatsoever and I'm delighted to see it's a tawny frogmouth owl. At the Neck for a time we had one that used to come to our balcony rail each evening.

I think they are one of the most majestic birds, so ugly as to be beautiful, so serene as they watch you with their baleful eyes. I hope he remains and visits very often.

June 22

I've long been an enthusiast for checking in supermarket fresh-produce departments for fruit and vegetables that might be going at a reduced price. This need not mean that they are past their best or of inferior quality. Oftentimes it's just a matter of a product that has no huge appeal to the customers in that region.

Today I am lucky enough to find just such a treasure — a large bag of passionfruit: several bags, in fact. Now this is cause for rejoicing as the pulp is so incredibly tasty and delicious. For years I've wanted to try making passionfruit cordial. It would serve well as a coulis.

I read in a book once that if passionfruit pulp is heated above 35°C, it loses the intensity of flavour and the pips become extremely hard, almost unpalatable. (There goes the idea of preserving them by the old waterbath method as it would need to be brought to 80°C.) The book recommended just mixing equal parts of passionfruit pulp and sugar in a sterilised jar and shaking several times over the space of a day or so to dissolve the sugar. The pulp would then keep well, but as an added precaution, other recipes suggested adding a soluble aspirin tablet.

Actually, this aspirin-enhanced technique was once very popular but it is not recommended nowadays as many people are allergic to aspirin.

With all these facts I mind, I set to developing a recipe for a cordial syrup. The result was very pleasing. I will keep it in the fridge as it hasn't been heat-processed, and if you were lucky to have a very large amount,

I'd keep it in the freezer. It wouldn't actually freeze because of the high sugar content.

I plan to use it in a whole range of ways — as a coulis over cheesecake or pavlova — but within a day it is almost gone, devoured as a drink by visitors conscripted as test-tasters. A true sign of how delicious it was.

Passionfruit Cordial Syrup

1 cup passionfruit pulp
1 cup sugar
½ teaspoon citric acid

Mix all the ingredients together and allow to settle overnight. The next day, strain out the pips and pour into sterilised bottles and refrigerate.

Freeze if not to be used within 3 weeks.

Makes about 375ml

June 23

I never like to leave home during weekends, even if I don't have classes on a Saturday. It's our family time for those who can and choose to come. This weekend is to be the same. Robert has great plans for working outside, rotary-hoeing more of the far paddock to plant out yet more raspberry canes, as well as the loganberries and boysenberries we've extracted from the now largely untended garden at Eaglehawk Neck.

At breakfast, however, a minor disaster strikes. Robert's back 'goes' while he is simply eating breakfast and so any activity is all but impossible. While a day of rest would do him no harm at all, he is champing at the bit, with chores to do and animals to feed.

At 9 a.m. Stephanie and Nat arrive. They've heard of Robert's dilemma and before long barrowfuls of neatly stacked wood are at the door. It's a great excuse for a cook-up and Stephanie and I bake away, for hours, our favourite pastime.

Sunday sees them back again, this time to rotary-hoe the paddock, and soon Andrew, Emma and baby Hunter arrive for a visit. This is the best of days — with children playing happily outside, impervious to the cold as they run lightly clad among the sheep grazing contentedly on the grass in the enclosure by the house.

Tom the cat follows close, helping them pull apart the stones on the rock wall, seeking stray and interesting insects for Jacob's collection. He then goes to check progress with the hoeing and jumps in and out of the holes dug for the raspberry canes, being his usual mischievous self.

Della toddles along as best she can. She is getting quite old now and arthritis is getting to her. Her weight doesn't help either. She steadfastly refuses a kennel, shed or cubby house and insists on sleeping in her basket on the front deck each evening. At bed time we do the best we can by her and on especially cold evenings even give her a hot-water bottle. Stephanie has provided two discarded sheepskin car seat covers to line the basket and we cover her with woolly blankets (thermal) and hope she won't wriggle out. For a dog of little brain, she has finally worked out that to stay there till morning is a good option.

I'm pleased to see that a small kookaburra has come to live. He feels the cold too obviously as he sits huddled, head under wing, in the branches of the now leafless elm tree outside the kitchen window. He stirs from time to time to pull corbi grubs from the grass. Each evening now another — the mate-to-be, I expect — joins him. They spend an hour or so feeding together before night sets in.

June 25

In this, the week of the winter solstice, an icy chill has crept in. We have been here close on a year now and the changing of the seasons never ceases to amaze me — the chill of last winter, the bursting through of spring with a resounding blaze of green and blossom. The summer heat was a great shock after so many years of gentle heat by the ocean with refreshing sea breezes to mollify the senses.

However, I have come to love the extremes that we have experienced here, with the seasons so clearly marked.

This week has been a revelation to me — an eerie fog creeps up the valley each evening, enveloping the trees around the house in a misty shroud. Yesterday we held a gluten-free class, and with the slow-combustion stove warming the kitchen and many dishes filling the air with savoury and sweet aromas of baking, the view over the garden out of the window was nothing short of stunning as the mist swirled around the shrubs and vegetable beds, waxing and waning on its merry dance through the garden.

The fog, I suspect, is an extension of the Bridgewater Jerry. It is a frequent visitor from the Derwent Valley through to Hobart and its surrounds each winter. Perhaps one could complain about its icy fingers, but when you stand back a little way and watch it roll down the Derwent River, pitching its cloud into the air, tumbling over itself as it goes, the cold is all but forgotten, replaced with admiration of a phenomenon so incredibly beautiful.

The fog that creeps into our little corner at the head of the Molesworth Valley is no less ethereal. It envelops the house with its nebulous blanket. The sun that you know is somewhere above filters through the mist and spreads a gentle glow, outlining the trees as they peek out from the cloud. As the mist retreats, it often leaves in its wake, especially this week, a coating of heavy frost. As the sun breaks through, the grass, and indeed the sheep's backs, appear covered with myriad sparkling diamonds. Though I love the ocean and its wild and wonderful ways, I have never in my entire life experienced a scene more beautiful.

A hidden benefit to this is the promise of exquisite summer fruits to come: the intensity of the cold is a guarantee of superlative flavour that is valued and sought increasingly the world over.

June 26

There's another gluten-free class at the school today. Stephanie has coeliac disease and any straying from the prescribed diet causes her all sorts of digestive issues. It was for this reason that I wrote *From My Kitchen to Yours*, with its gluten-free recipes.

By 9 a.m. everyone has arrived and we start out with a classic raspberry jam and, soon afterwards, sweet chilli sauce. It may seem a strange thing to do, after all it isn't a preserves class, but my philosophy with gluten-free is to make the other elements in the dish so tasty and delicious that the fact you are deprived of wheat and other gluten slips into the background.

Homemade preserves are a wonderful standby in the pantry, at your fingertips to add flavour aplenty in a way that no commercial equivalent can.

I would especially recommend the two we are making, but encourage the participants to make homemade Worcestershire sauce at home if they can. It is simplicity itself to make — all you need to watch is that you don't use dark malt vinegar, which is not gluten-free. Cider vinegar is the best option.

Gluten-free Worcestershire Sauce

You can use virtually any fruit in this sauce — damson plums are classic and traditional, but I've used many varieties of plums, and also apricots, cherries and even a mix of tomatoes and apples to make up the weight.

> 2.5kg plums
> 3 litres cider vinegar
> 60g garlic, chopped (no need to peel)
> 60g salt
> 2 cups treacle
> 500g brown sugar
> 60g ginger, bruised (no need to peel)
> 45g cloves
> 15g whole allspice
> 1 teaspoon cayenne pepper

Combine all the ingredients in a large pot. Boil for 2 hours, strain and pour into warm sterilised bottles. Seal immediately.

Makes about 3.5 litres

The classes here generally develop a life and direction of their own and today is no exception. Blackberry meringue pie is on the menu, as is butter chicken, to be served with gluten-free naan breads.

We are to make pancakes, which can be shredded to make fettuccine, or used for lasagne sheets. Today we will make a tortilla bake, which uses pancakes rather than gluten-free pasta. While gluten-free pasta may have its place, I find it becomes stodgy and cooking it a hit-and-miss affair. For the minimal effort of making the pancakes, you get a far, far better result.

The pancakes freeze well and can be used in sweet dishes. For instance, simply sprinkled with lemon juice and sugar for that classic all-time favourite of young and old. They can be layered with stewed fruit and then cut into wedges to be served with gluten-free custard or ice-cream.

I also want to demonstrate how to make a gluten-free pastry that can be used for savoury pies and tarts. By now the sweet chilli sauce is ready, and though I've not had this on the menu, we decide to serve it with cream cheese and biscuits.

However, the cupboard is bare of gluten-free rice crackers. A perfect opportunity to trial the pastry as little savoury biscuits, then. It works like a dream — I haven't bothered to wash the food processor bowl after chopping the chilli sauce ingredients, so they have minute pieces of chilli through them, very tasty indeed.

A question was raised during class about gluten-free scones. Now, I'm not a fan of scones, never have been, and so I've not bothered to put a recipe together. I really expected that it wouldn't work. However, now would be as good a time as any to invent one. They were baked and pronounced very good, and even better served with fresh raspberry jam and whipped cream.

The class came to an end with a great feast. It was so good to meet people of similar dietary challenges and find a way to overcome them.

Gluten-free Scones

1½ cups gluten-free self-raising flour
1 teaspoon baking powder
a pinch of salt
1 tablespoon melted butter
1 egg, lightly beaten
¼ cup water
¼ cup cream

Preheat the oven to 180°C. Line baking trays with baking paper.

Mix together the flour, baking powder and salt until very well combined.

Make a well in the centre and then pour in the butter and egg. Do not mix yet. Combine the water and cream and then pour in almost all of this, holding about 1 tablespoonful back.

Mix the batter together and if more liquid is needed to make a soft dough, add the rest of the cream/water mixture.

Turn out onto a surface that has been dusted with gluten-free flour and knead briefly. Pat out to a rectangle about 2cm thick. Cut with a round scone cutter and place on the trays.

Bake for about 15 minutes.

Line a bowl with a tea towel and place the cooked scones in this and then fold the tea towel loosely over until ready to serve.

Makes 12–16 scones

Gluten-free Savoury Biscuits (Crackers)

180g gluten-free self-raising flour
½ teaspoon salt
90g butter, cubed
1 egg
about ¼ cup cold water

Preheat the oven to 160°C. Line 2 baking sheets with baking paper.

Place the flour and salt in the bowl of a food processor. Process the butter with the flour until it resembles breadcrumbs. (If you don't have a food processor, rub the butter in with your fingertips.)

Turn out into a bowl and make a well in the centre. Briefly whisk the egg and pour into the well, together with the water, using no more than ¼ cup at first. Mix with a metal spoon until smooth, adding extra water only if necessary to bring the dough together.

On a surface that has been dusted with gluten-free flour, roll out the dough until it's 6mm thick. (You will need to sprinkle a little of the flour on the dough before rolling also.) Cut into 5cm rounds and place on baking trays. Repeat with the remaining dough.

Bake for 8–10 minutes until golden. Once cool, store in an airtight container.

Makes about 30

June 27

Each Thursday there is a meeting of the firefighters down at the local fire station and whenever I can I like to bake a little something for them to enjoy at the end of their session. It's the very least I can do, given the fact that they give so much time, energy and commitment to the community during the fire season and beyond.

After the class of yesterday I have half a jar of last summer's preserved apricots. This apricot cake is an all-time family favourite, simple to make and never fails, even if gluten-free flour is used instead of wheat flour. It will be perfect, I think, as I am so busy at present. I'll top it up with frozen blackberries as well.

I rarely use self-raising flour, preferring to make my own with plain flour and baking powder, a simple thing by adding 2 teaspoons baking powder per cup of flour. Once the cake is mixed I lick the bowl as usual and discover it tastes very strange indeed. What could be the problem, I wonder?

Maybe it's just my imagination and it will be fine when it's cooked. However, as I watch it rise reassuringly in the oven, there is still a niggling doubt in my mind.

Terry the fire chief is coming to pick up the cake at 6.15 and by 5.45 it is cooked. It looks perfect, maybe a little darker than usual which is surprising, but nevertheless, all looks well. Thankfully that little voice in my head prevails and I cut off a little corner to sample it. Thank goodness I did! It tastes like sherbet gone wrong, salty, and the crumb had an alarming brown tinge.

I hate to imagine what the firies would have thought.

All that aside, there was no time to waste — I'd promised something for their supper, but what could possibly be done in the time? Scones to the rescue; by now I'd realised what had happened. The lid for the baking powder and the one for the bicarbonate of soda had somehow been switched in my clean-up of the cooking class yesterday.

So now as I make the scones I am thoroughly confused — which is which? Thankfully I do have a bag of self-raising flour in the pantry so there's only the risk with the one teaspoon of baking powder that needs to be added. With bated breath I make a combination of cream of tartar and what I think is bicarbonate of soda, as by now I'm thoroughly bamboozled, and the rush doesn't help.

By the time Terry arrives at 6.15 the scones are ready just in time with fresh jam and cream to go along with them. I am terrified what they will taste like — they look fine, but then so did the cake. I've

made a sample one but it will be hours before I can bear to taste it —
sometimes ignorance is bliss.

June 28

The day starts well with Terry returning the plates from the food I
prepared last night. He tells Robert that the scones were beautiful and
very well received. What a relief.

The day is spent on boring bookwork but still chickens need to be
fed, along with the ever more demanding sheep. I do remember, and
maybe it was an omen or prophetic, that friends of ours had once hand-
fed a lamb they called Bam-Bam. He grew to be a monstrous size but so
demanding that eventually he had to go the way of lamb chops.

I always seem to make the same mistake — I've come to the point
of spoiling these sheep and what I considered a kindness to them is now
an expectation on their part. They were a bit miffed this morning as I
didn't have many scraps to hand-feed them. I should have known that
trouble was in the air.

Sure enough, this afternoon when I take over the chooks' bread and
fat, several have forced their way into the chook pen. Not only have they
devoured all this morning's feed but everything else in sight, and they
are certainly not in any hurry to move out.

After some strategic throwing of food into the neighbouring
paddock, in the process sacrificing some of the chooks' dinner, I was able
to persuade all but one of them out. Now this straggler is Doris, the
strongest willed and most certainly the stupidest of this band of rebels. She
is always on the hunt for food. I chased her from one part of the chook
yard to the other, backwards and forwards. The more I chased her, the
more she stomped and romped and bucked, thrashing against the fence
of the chook yard. The now terrified ducks flew squawking into the wire,
the chooks over the fence, all thought of a comforting afternoon feed
erased from their minds in their panic. No eggs tomorrow morning then.

Eventually I hemmed Doris into my preferred pathway by cutting
off retreat with a wall of branches, stripped clean of their leaves by her

afternoon grazing. Puffed and bedraggled, I finally succeeded, but I've done it again — spoiled animals with kindness until they became brats on four legs.

I limped off towards the house with a twisted ankle, the discontented baaing of the sheep resounding in my ears, as if I had treated them ungraciously without cause.

June 29

The weekend will be a quiet one, with Stephanie and Nat having visitors stay for several nights. It's time to round up the last of the produce and 'put it down' before it spoils. There are quinces, apples, some straggly stalks of rhubarb and even some blackberries left from the gluten-free class.

Quite apart from the blackberry jelly I have in mind, I think a winter jam would be nice, lovely to serve with scones or pikelets, or simply on toast that's been cooked in front of the coals of the wood fire. It occurs to me that I've been doing a lot of combining of fruits this year. Better still I'll make a winter pudding — the family favourite of steamed jam pudding with rich and creamy custard.

Rhubarb and apple chutney will be good for adding to savoury dishes so this will be made as well.

Quince, Rhubarb and Apple Jam

300g quinces (peeled and cored weight)
400g apples (peeled and cored weight)
300g rhubarb stalks, cut into 1cm lengths
juice of 1 lemon
½ cup water
1kg sugar

Place the fruit in a large saucepan or jam pan with the lemon juice and water. Bring to the boil over a medium–low heat, stirring often. Simmer until the fruit is soft.

Add the sugar and bring to the boil, stirring. Cook over a medium–high heat until setting point is reached, about 20 minutes (see page 393). Pour into warm, sterilised jars and seal immediately.

Makes about 2kg

Rhubarb and Apple Chutney

> 2 cups finely chopped rhubarb
> 3 cups finely chopped apples
> 1 onion, diced
> 3 teaspoons finely grated fresh ginger
> 3 cups sugar
> 1½ cups cider vinegar
> 1 teaspoon salt
> 1 teaspoon mustard powder
> ½ teaspoon curry powder

Place all the ingredients in a saucepan and bring to the boil, stirring. Cook for 1 hour over a medium–low heat until a chutney-like consistency s reached.

Pour into warm sterilised jars and seal immediately.

Makes about 1kg

June 30

A phone call over the weekend has made me aware that Seville oranges are soon to be available. When making marmalade there is nothing better for that special bittersweet flavour and, as they are high in pectin, for a solid set. Sure enough, when I visit the fruit and vegetable market, there are plenty on sale, along with all sorts of other good quality citrus fruits.

I don't mind if a jam is a bit soft — it's good for filling the holes in crumpets as it's spread. However, in my opinion, marmalade needs to be set to a stable jelly. For this, Seville is simply the best. There are all sorts of delicious marmalades — some even incorporate carrot, which I don't fancy, though I guess it would give good colour.

For years, decades actually, I have used a really simple recipe. It calls for the mincing of the fruit, then boiling until the skins are soft, thereafter adding the sugar and boiling until setting point is reached.

This is one of those never-fail recipes, so long as the fruit is not too old.

However, at this premium time for marmalade-making, I've decided to put in a bit more effort and make fine-shred marmalade. I remember it almost being a competition between grandmothers and aunts as to whose marmalade had the best appearance, the finest shreds of peel, the best set. It was competitive to be sure, but seemed like fun nevertheless.

By all means use the easy method first listed here for an orange and lemon marmalade, but for sheer beauty on a pantry shelf, try the fine-shred method.

Any citrus fruit is nice made into marmalade: sweet oranges (such as Navel), blood oranges, grapefruit, tangelos and mandarins.

You can make lemon marmalade and add a little preserved ginger if you like. Lime is good, but I find it's best combined with a little lemon.

Marmalade can also be made from the skins of the fruit only, which is handy if you have used just the juice in everyday cooking. A recipe for this marmalade is to follow.

Basic Orange and Lemon Marmalade

500g oranges
1 lemon
1.5 litres water
1.5kg sugar

Put the fruit through a mincer or chop very finely. Place in a large saucepan and add the water. Bring to the boil and cook until the fruit is soft, about 25 minutes.

Add the sugar and bring to the boil, stirring until the sugar is dissolved. Continue to boil briskly for

25 minutes or until setting point is reached (see page 393).

Allow to stand for 10 minutes before pouring into warm sterilised jars and sealing immediately.

Makes about 1.5kg

Fine-shred Marmalade

500g citrus fruit of choice
1 lemon
1.5 litres water
1.5kg sugar

Remove the zest from the fruit, taking care not to include any of the pith underneath. Shred finely. Alternatively, use a zester. Place in a bowl with 2 cups of the water and leave overnight.

Next day, squeeze the juice from the fruit and add to a large saucepan or jam pan with the remaining water. Bring to the boil and simmer until the peel is soft.

Add the sugar and bring to the boil, stirring, then boil briskly over a medium—high heat until setting point is reached or until setting point is reached (see page 393).

Allow to stand in the pan for 5—10 minutes, then pour into warm sterilised jars and seal immediately.

Makes about 1.5kg

Seville Orange Marmalade

This is the recipe I have always used for Seville Oranges. However, you could apply the fine-shred method as in the previous recipe.

500g Seville oranges
1 lemon

1.5 litres water
1.5kg sugar

Put fruit through a mincer or chop very finely. Place in a large saucepan and add water and orange juice. Bring to the boil and cook for 25 minutes or until fruit is soft.

Add the sugar and bring to the boil, stirring until sugar is dissolved. Continue to boil hard for 25 minutes or until setting point is reached (see page 393).

Allow to stand for 10 minutes before pouring into warm sterilised jars. Seal immediately.

Makes about 1.5kg

Marmalade from Citrus Skins

600g citrus skins
600ml water
½ cup lemon juice
1 teaspoon citric acid
sugar

Mince the skins or slice very finely. Place in a bowl with the water, lemon juice and citric acid. Leave to soak for several hours or overnight.

Bring the mixture to the boil and then simmer until the skins are soft.

Add the sugar and bring back to the boil, stirring. Boil briskly over a medium–high heat until setting point is reached (see page 393).

Allow to stand in the pan for 5–10 minutes, then pour into warm sterilised jars and seal immediately.

Makes about 1.5kg

Whisky Orange Marmalade

550g oranges
juice of 1 lemon
1.5 litres water
1.5kg sugar
¾ cup whisky

Put the oranges through a mincer or chop very finely. Place in a large saucepan and add the lemon juice and water. Bring to the boil and cook until the fruit is soft, about 25 minutes.

Add sugar and bring to the boil, stirring until sugar is dissolved. Continue to boil briskly for 25 minutes or until setting point is reached (see page 393). Stir in the whisky.

Allow to stand for 5–10 minutes before pouring into warm sterilised jars and sealing immediately.

Makes about 1.5kg

Seville Orange Ice-cream

I was chatting one day to a lady in Alistair's shop Sweet Envy and the conversation turned to the virtues of Seville oranges. She told me she had made ice-cream with them, which she had served with a rich, dark mud cake.

She sent me the recipe a day or so later and it sounded very good. I've adapted it a little, adding some of the marmalade I'd made.

You could use any type of oranges and marmalade to get a similar result, but the flavour of the Seville is truly unique.

2 Seville oranges
3 egg yolks

100g castor sugar
600ml cream, lightly whipped
2 tablespoons marmalade

Finely grate the zest of the oranges and squeeze the juice.

Whisk the egg yolks with the castor sugar and add the zest and juice, along with the cream and marmalade. Whisk to combine, then churn in an ice-cream machine according to the manufacturer's instructions.

If you don't have an ice-cream machine, semi-freeze the mixture, then beat with an electric beater until thick and creamy, then pour into ice-cream trays. Cover the surface with cling wrap and freeze.

Makes about 650ml

July 1

A serious conflict situation has developed here. The ram that I've called Ramekin takes great exception to Tom's presence. Each morning and afternoon, when I go over for the afternoon feeding, Tom runs alongside. He often strays into the paddock with the sheep.

For some unknown reason, this infuriates the ram and he starts stomping on the ground, snorting in Tom's direction. The cat, never one to be fearful, goes over to the ram, head to head. It's a bit of a David-and-Goliath situation, but Tom with his agility is easily able to leap out of the way before actual contact is made. I think he secretly enjoys it.

I've had news of the alpacas Charlotte and Clarence. About two weeks ago at their owner's block of land, they were attacked by a dog. While Charlotte's injuries were only minor, Clarence's neck was badly bitten and he was close to death. The vet and Jordan have nursed him back to health. However, the fear is that if they return to the block, the dog will seek them out again. At the very least, and even if not, the alpacas will be traumatised.

I heard today that Jordan is thinking of bringing them back here and I am ecstatic. I have missed them terribly and now am much concerned for their safety. At the very least they would be safe here.

The sheep have been effective grazers of the paddocks, but the alpacas could settle into the far paddock and I could take feed to them each day. Besides, the sheep are now privileged enough to graze around the house during the weekend, so they have plenty of food to be going on with. They have turned out to be ever so helpful with those cape weeds, munching the tops off them so the battle has now turned in our favour.

Kerry the sheep owner has told Stephanie that within a day or two he will come to take Ramekin away. I will miss him but sometimes I don't like the look in his eye, and today he head-butted me as I turned away after feeding him. It's definitely time for him to move on to other pastures!

I noticed today that my Worcestershire sauce supply is not all that it could be. It's been so popular with all those who taste it that I've given little jars away left, right and centre, and now I won't have enough for winter.

I seem to recall that I made a mistake batch once, using too many apricots. That was also delicious, almost like a fruity barbecue sauce. I could use some of my bottled apricots to make more. I had someone give me boxes and boxes of apricots over summer in an effort to convince me that the Moor Park apricots were not superior to other varieties. While most were fine, one of the varieties did not bottle well; instead of holding their shape, they poured out the jar like a sludge and were terribly bitter, despite the sugar syrup in which they were bottled. However, this is of no importance when making sauce, and will save them going to waste.

Therefore, as in the recipes in *A Year in a Bottle*, as someone once pointed out, there is a Worcestershire sauce for every occasion.

Apricot Worcestershire Sauce

3kg apricots, fresh, frozen, bottled, even tinned will do
2.5 litres dark malt vinegar
500g brown sugar
1½ cups treacle
60g garlic cloves, roughly chopped
60 green ginger, roughly chopped
30g allspice berries
30g cloves
1 tablespoon salt

Place all the ingredients in a large saucepan or jam pan. Bring to the boil, stirring, then simmer for 2 hours, stirring occasionally. Sieve through a colander, pressing as much pulp through as possible.

Pour into warm sterilised bottles and seal immediately.

Makes about 3.5 litres

July 2

There are really strong winds here today, at a level we've not experienced before. The kookaburra that usually sits in the tree outside the kitchen window has disappeared, blown away, I suspect. He is a funny little bundle — in the cold fluffed up with his head under his wing. He shows less and less fear of us.

I've been conscious for several days now that there are still quinces left in the cooking school — the aroma greets me as I walk through the door. They've actually been there for about three weeks with no sign of rotting. I did think about feeding them to the sheep but that seemed such a lack of appreciation for such a wonderful fruit, so this morning I will use them to trial a recipe I was given at least two years ago.

A lady rang in to ABC talkback and asked me if I knew about making quince paste or cheese in the microwave. I didn't, so she kindly sent instructions to me.

I'm not a great one for cooking in the microwave generally speaking, but this recipe had me intrigued. First though, what did I do with it? I turn all the drawers, filing cabinet and folders out before I finally resurrect it. My study is a mess but that's a minor consideration as by now I'm really inspired.

I go through the recipe and requisite steps, making a few adjustments. The method will vary according to the wattage of the microwave, but it actually does work. It saves hours of stirring and the plopping, boiling mass spitting all over your stove, so it's well worth trying.

My steps and quantities are different from the original recipe, but the table-cum-worksheet is a good idea, so I have put one together here on a separate page for photocopying or printing off.

Be very careful with handling the dish during cooking as the mixture gets extremely hot.

Use the seeds and core from this recipe for quince jelly or use them as part of a sparkling quince fruit drink.

Quince Cheese in the Microwave

1.25kg quinces
juice of 1 large lemon
¼ cup water
950g sugar

Remove the cores from quinces — I found that the best way to do this is to cut them in quarters or eighths and then scoop them out with a sharp knife. Be sure not to include any of the 'gristly' section around the seeds as this will make your cheese grainy. You should have about 1kg flesh.

Cut into 3cm pieces (approximately) and place in a 2-litre heatproof dish with the lemon juice and water.

Cover the dish with cling wrap and cut a small hole in the top with just the tip of a small, sharp knife.

Cook in the microwave on high for 10 minutes. Remove and stir. Cover the top with a new piece of cling wrap, cutting a small hope in the top as before.

Cook in the microwave on high for 10 minutes more. Remove and then sieve, purée or press though a food mill. Return to the microwave, uncovered and cook for 1 minute.

Add the sugar and stir until dissolved. Return to the microwave and cook for 10 minutes. Remove and stir, then cook for a further 10 minutes.

Stir then cook for 5 minutes more.

Stir and spoon into small heatproof containers and seal immediately.

See below for the chart that helps keep track of these steps as you are making it.

QUINCE CHEESE IN THE MICROWAVE TRACKING CHART

Remove cores from quinces, chop the flesh (skin on) and place in a microwave-safe, heatproof dish with lemon juice. Cover with cling wrap.	
Cook on high for 10 minutes.	
Stir.	
Cook on high for 10 minutes (covered).	
Purée, sieve or press through food mill.	
Cook on high for 2 minutes (uncovered).	
Stir in sugar.	
Cook on high for 10 minutes (uncovered).	
Stir.	
Cook on high for 10 minutes (uncovered).	
Stir.	
Cook on high for 12 minutes (uncovered).	
Stir.	
Spoon into small heatproof containers and seal immediately.	

Well then there are those cores. I would recommend buying 2kg quinces
if indeed you've had to actually purchase them so that you can make
a respectable amount of quince jelly. Mind you, if you make a lot of
this quince cheese, you may have sufficient cores. Either way, the recipe
works really well.

Quince Jelly from Peels and Cores

1.5kg whole quinces, or peels and/or cores
or a combination
juice of 1 large lemon
water
sugar

If using whole quinces, wash well to remove the furry
bloom, then chop roughly. Add to a large saucepan
or jam pan with the lemon juice and enough water to
barely cover. Bring to the boil and simmer until the
quinces are tender.

Strain through a colander then strain the resulting
quince juice through a sieve lined with a double
thickness of muslin.

For each cup of liquid add 1 cup sugar. Bring to the
boil, stirring occasionally to dissolve the sugar, then
continue to boil until setting point is reached.

Pour into warm sterilised jars and seal immediately.

Makes about 1.8 litres

Sparkling Quince

This recipe makes good use of quince peels and cores and is a really lovely drink.

> *875g quinces, whole, cores and/or peels or a combination*
> *875g sugar*
> *1 lemon, chopped*
> *4.5 litres water*
> *180ml white or cider vinegar*

Wash whole quinces if using to remove the furry bloom, then chop finely. If using peels and cores, chop these also. Place with the rest of the ingredients in a food-safe bucket, mix well, then cover with a tea towel and leave to stand at room temperature for 48 hours.

Strain through a fine nylon kitchen sieve and pour into PET bottles and seal immediately. (Empty soft-drink bottles are ideal, or you can buy new ones from home brewing suppliers.) Store at room temperature.

The sparkling quince will be ready in 1–2 weeks. Open carefully — once it's developed its fizz, it's best to refrigerate it before opening. If you can't drink it all within a few days, it might be best to store the remaining bottles in the fridge. You can even store the bottles in the freezer (be sure to let a little of the liquid out so that there is room for expansion on freezing).

Makes about 4.5 litres

July 3

As is customary at this time of year, cauliflowers abound at farmers' markets and this is wonderful as mine are not ready yet. I really love to have cauliflower piccalilli on hand. Over the weekend I have purchased a real beauty — almost sparkling white and as fresh as can be.

This pickle is delicious served with meats, even on a cheese platter with pickled onions.

Cauliflower Piccalilli

700g cauliflower, cut into small florets
250g zucchini, finely chopped
60g green beans, sliced
2 large onions, peeled and finely diced
1 red capsicum, finely diced
¼ cup salt
2 cups sugar
2 cups white or cider vinegar
2 teaspoons mustard powder
2 teaspoons turmeric
2 teaspoons cornflour
2 tablespoons white or cider vinegar

Place the vegetables and capsicum in a bowl, add salt and mix well. Leave to stand for about 3 hours. Drain well.

Combine sugar, vinegar, mustard powder and turmeric in a large saucepan and bring to the boil, stirring until the sugar is dissolved. Add vegetables and bring back to boil and cook for 25 minutes.

If the mixture is too thin, mix cornflour to a paste with the extra vinegar and stir through. Cook for 2–3 minutes more.

Spoon into warm sterilised jars and seal immediately.

Makes about 1.5kg

July 4

The two younger daughters are coming today. For weeks now they've been looking forward to a toffee-making session. Stephanie has made several batches, as Courtney has been busy with university studies and exams, but finally they are set to make a big day of it.

I love to watch as they work and soon the air is fragrant with the aroma of toffees of several flavours and colours. A saltwater taffy is first on their list and soon the large hook on the wall is put to good use as Stephanie shows Courtney how to pull and stretch and twist the hot mass of sugar. I have a try and it's certainly fun, but strenuous. Courtney takes her turn and as the toffee cools, she cuts it into lolly-sized pieces for packaging in pretty little bags.

By the time they have finished, there are several delicious flavours — a raspberry cheesecake twist, peppermint, bubble gum and pineapple. There is an exceptional raspberry taffy that tastes like the Redskins that our children always loved, but this is so much tastier. We plan to sell some on the roadside stall at the gate, along with jams, cakes and baked goods.

Yesterday Robert, who has an eye for a bargain with fresh produce, bought me a red cabbage. Strange present, some may think, but to me it's a gem. I've been waiting to trial a recipe for pickled red cabbage and so I prepare this while the girls make toffee.

Pickled Red Cabbage

1 medium-sized red cabbage
45g salt
950ml vinegar
30g sugar
1 teaspoon ground allspice
1 teaspoon ground cloves

Remove the coarse outer leaves from the cabbage and cut out the tough core. Shred the cabbage finely. Layer with the salt and leave to stand overnight.

Next day, drain well and rinse. Place in an airtight jar.

Meanwhile, bring the vinegar, sugar and spices to the boil and then cool. Strain and pour over the cabbage.

The cabbage can be used after one week; it's best to use before 3 months or it will become soggy.

Makes about 1.5kg

We have had a potoroo inside the house paddock for some time now, despite the fact that the fences are supposed to be wallaby proofed. Anything that isn't surrounded by the unattractive chicken wire is decimated. I know he has to eat, but there is plenty of grass, surely, and so no need to attack my vegetables.

Tom is never very happy to see him. He becomes quite agitated, but as he is much smaller than the potoroo I'd thought nothing of it.

Sight of early this morning was Tom straddled on the back of the potoroo. Maybe he has sensed our antipathy towards it, or at least its presence in the garden. The potoroo, once he'd extricated himself from Tom's hold, actually went to the gate to indicate he wanted to go out, which is hardly surprising under the circumstances.

I'd like to think that was the end of it, but we've been through the gate ritual before. Our neighbour Terry has seen this potoroo standing patiently, waiting to be let out on more than one occasion. If we are out, he stops and opens the gate for it. Next day, it's back again and my vegetables, pansies and anything else remotely edible are gnawed to the ground even more.

Young Jacob is here today, along with Charly, and on their wanderings over the property they have noted that three potoroos are now in the home paddock around the house. No wonder the garden is suffering. Often we can chase them out with Jacob's help, but today we are all preoccupied and the men are at work, so Jacob takes it upon himself to lend a hand.

These potoroos can run (hop) like the wind and so are difficult to round up. Jacob, however, is very fleet of foot and soon he has picked one up, ready for Charly to open the gate so he can put it outside. Kind though their efforts were, the potoroo obviously took exception, probably still unnerved by observing its friend's endurance of Tom's playfulness this morning, and delivers a sharp bite to Jacob's thumb. Poor Jacob is mortified, as he can't comprehend why the wallaby would do such a thing when he was only trying to help.

July 5

Well, we have been here almost exactly a year now.

Today Jordan, the owner of the alpacas, has rung. Would it be possible for the alpacas to come back here? he asks.

Yes! I can barely contain my happiness — this will bring our year here to a very satisfactory conclusion. I've been very worried about the possibility of them returning to the block where they were attacked by the dog. This weekend will be their homecoming.

Jordan tells me that if there is anything positive to come from the whole dog attack experience, it's the fact that Clarence is no longer fearful of being handled. All the veterinary attention he has received over the past few weeks has diminished his fear of people.

I have a mind to make a barbecue sauce for the upcoming sausage-making day. This Saturday Elliott and several of his friends will come and use the cooking school as the space for one of their extended War Hammer battles. I will be able to bake pizzas by the score and more treats besides. The barbecue sauce will serve us well. After several hours of tweaking, at last I have a recipe that I find more than satisfactory.

Barbecue Sauce

You can use fresh, bottled or frozen tomatoes for this recipe, tinned even at a pinch.

½ cup orange juice
1kg tomatoes, chopped
300g onions, chopped
4 cloves garlic
1½ teaspoons salt
250g brown sugar
½ cup Worcestershire sauce
½ cup cider vinegar

Place all ingredients in a large saucepan or jam pan. Bring to the boil, stirring, and then simmer for 45 minutes. Purée or press through a sieve or food mill.

Return to the pan and bring back to the boil, stirring. Cook over a medium–low heat until a sauce-like consistency forms. (Keep in mind it will thicken a little on standing.)

Pour into warm sterilised bottles (wide mouthed) and seal immediately.

Makes about 1.5kg

I've been looking forward to Eliott's War Hammer day immensely. Each of the participants has been told to bring a few ingredients as toppings for the pizzas to keep their energy levels up for the day-long battle.

The game never ceases to amaze me with its intricate little figurines, painstakingly hand-painted, as well as truly fearsome alien creatures that seek to destroy them in a pseudo universe. The game seems to require intense concentration, several dice and tape measures as manoeuvres are carefully calculated to gain the best advantage.

The day progresses well with we girls in the house, Stephanie making cocktails, myself baking, and Robert and Nat and friend David working outside in the bitter cold, fixing fences and chopping wood. Robert is expanding the fenceline of the far paddock so the returning alpacas will have more room to themselves.

By early evening the game is finished, and I've had the best of days baking to my heart's content with many people to eat it all.

The snow is down very low on the opposite hill and before long it's falling on the grass here too. It's unlikely to settle but you can feel its icy grip as the temperature drops steadily by the hour.

Although it is very cold, from the comfort of the house warmed by the wood stove, it's a very pretty sight. The snow has even settled momentarily on the sheep's backs.

July 8

Amid the mêlée of the fifteen or so visitors that day we had the company of Andrew's dogs, Pepsi and Annie. These are two pretty little Cavalier King Charles spaniels who stay with us when Andrew and Emma go on holiday. They behave pretty well usually and love the open paddocks to run around in, but yesterday, perhaps the attention and affection they received from visitors went to their heads.

The issue is Tom, the poor cat. The last cat here, Ardy, had the dogs well under control: he simply had to raise a paw and they would cower in the corner. Tom, however, is the one who cringes and the dogs have realised their advantage. Last night they met in an almighty altercation at the back door, cat on the way in, dogs on the way out. They took off into the night after a fleeing Tom at breakneck speed.

I cannot even begin to explain my fury at them, unresponsive as they were to my calling to them to stop. I fear the worst — that Tom will bolt and return to the bush, never to be seen again, all because of these two foolish, rebellious dogs.

I race off after them in the dark, wielding the only tool to hand — a French breadstick that one of our visitors has brought for the animals. I am intent on giving them a scare by walloping the ground with it as punishment for being so disobedient. They seem to think it's a game. Looking back, I'm thankful it was so dark outside — a breadstick-wielding old woman, screaming like a banshee, chasing two little dogs may well have had the neighbours wondering what manner of person lives here.

The dogs at last came in unashamed, but one look at me sent them scuttling to their beds. Shutting them in the laundry was the worst punishment they actually received in the end as I'd calmed down considerably by that stage. The breadstick was a mess of crumbs — I'd pounded it on the grass threateningly as I chased them.

Today promises to be calmer. Food writer Jude Blereau, who has been referred to as the queen of wholefood cooking, is coming to visit with her friend Jean. They arrive in the late morning. We met at the Melbourne Food and Wine Festival a couple of years ago and became friends. Jude is in Hobart to launch and promote her latest book.

We have many things to talk about, not the least of which is that Jean has a passion for wild ferment, especially with whey, something I've wanted to experiment with for ages.

I tell her about my sauerkraut, explaining that I hope it is ready in time for the sausage-making day next weekend. I've had to put the sauerkraut outside, so offensive was its odour.

Jean kindly offers to take a look. Well, the sauerkraut is contaminated with leaves and twigs. Robert neglected to tell me that the lid blew off. So that's strike one. I'd neglected to give it due attention, removing the mould as it formed on top, and not monitoring the ambient temperature. So much for my carefully planned treats for next Saturday.

Jean asks if I have a cabbage on hand and I do, a magnificent specimen. She offers to show me how to make a successful sauerkraut. The proportion of salt to cabbage is around 2 per cent, she says, but she now judges primarily by taste.

This is the best way to learn — to be shown by an expert. She soon shreds a whole huge dish full of cabbage, laced with a little carrot and onion, and then mixes in salt until the mixture tastes, I think, like the saltiness of the ocean.

Greek yoghurt is quickly hung in a muslin bag to extract the whey and 4 tablespoons of this are added to the mix.

It is then left for about half an hour for the liquid to start to exude, and then Jean pounds the mixture with the end of a wooden rolling pin. This gives good texture in the finished product, she explains.

Soon it is packed into jars with instructions given for its care, and the news that it will be ready for the sausage-making day next weekend. So, a happy ending after all: there will once again be sauerkraut with homemade bratwurst on the menu.

As Jude and Jean leave more visitors arrive, and then Jordan with the alpacas. As the men settle them into their paddock we are pleased to see that Clarence's neck is healing relatively well. Perhaps they remember the shearing day here as Charlotte is very evidently summoning a spit to hurl in Robert's direction.

It will be interesting to see how they settle in by tomorrow. It is just as well Robert extended the far paddock for them as the night promises to be frosty and they have more shelter there under trees.

It's been a great weekend — I counted 27 visitors in all, and that's just the way I like it.

July 11

Today is the day I finally get to meet Gwen Pridmore (née Appeldorff). Chris Wisbey last week interviewed her for radio and gave me her phone number, suggesting we might meet.

Gwen lives in Collinsvale, a truly beautiful rural township not far from Berriedale in Hobart. I follow the twisting, winding road from Molesworth to the township and, like any traveller to this place, can not help but marvel as always at its incredible beauty. The short drive leads up and through the hilltops with exquisite views into the high valley floor below. The snow-capped mountains frame this lush green vale with its township of sloping-roofed houses that help to disperse the snowfalls of winter. On this frosty day, the sunshine accentuates the intrinsic beauty — it is breathtaking.

Gwen has lived here most of her life in a lovely cottage built by her father. She is 96 years old, soon to be 97. I've read about her, read her books and her recipes. What a privilege it would be, I had always thought, if ever I should meet her.

Her son Wally lives with her at present. I know him quite well from working at the Port Arthur Historic Site. He is an author in his own right, with books on Tasmanian history from almost every perspective. So this is another reason I look forward to visiting.

I had expected to meet a wizened little old lady, very feeble of frame. I was stunned to find her absolutely beautiful. If I look as good at 67 as she does at 97, I'll be very pleased indeed. Of course her mobility is somewhat limited, but not her mind. She shows me a cookbook with anecdotal historical accounts that she is in the process of writing. Her recipes contain all sorts of helpful hints for the novice or even more experienced cook.

While the way I write is similar in some respects, I hang my head in humility as her prose is so much more descriptive, written with a poignancy that makes my subjective writings mere scribblings by comparison. She has written all her life, she tells me, and perhaps even more so now as she has the time. Recollections of the past, the history of Collinsvale and beyond, knowledge that she holds guardianship of due to her long life, knowledge she is happy to share.

She also pulls out a drawer full of recipes she has collected over the years, treasured relics from the past when food was simpler, arguably tastier and certainly less pretentious. Astonishingly she allows me to take some home to look through and experiment with. I will guard them with my life.

No-one could ever say that Gwen has not led a productive life. She invites me to take a folder from behind an armchair — this contains her paintings, she tells me. What paintings they are — of the local region, the hills, the mountains and beyond to the lakes and ocean. Trees, flowers, earthenware pots — all have been captured by her artist's brush.

'You can take two large ones and two small,' she said, and I simply cannot believe it. I make my choice carefully: one of Molesworth, a kitchen scene, a vase of lilies and finally, the treasure beyond compare, a painting of the view from her kitchen window. Next week I will arrange to get them framed — I am enormously privileged to have them.

At last I must take my leave from her company and the lovely country cottage, but I'm invited to return. I will, and Gwen hopes to come with Wally to visit the cooking school before much longer. I hope to have her paintings framed and on the wall by then.

It is obvious that hers has been a life filled with fun and laughter from the time she was a child in the idyllic township of Collinsvale. She has many years left I'm sure — for anyone who has lived so well, happily and unselfishly, it is bound to be so.

July 13

For weeks Stephanie and I have been planning this sausage-making day and now it's finally here. Stephanie is far more organised than I could ever hope to be and has everything in place, checked and rechecked. Nothing is left to chance, no ingredient forgotten down at the house, as I am prone to do.

Stephanie has formulated the recipes and every person who comes along will be given the sheets to take away so they can make sausages at home.

There will be cocktails, based on homemade fruit liqueurs, Robert's homemade beer and stout, and non-alcoholic drinks galore, but the focus is the sausage-making. So much to learn, so little time.

It seems that about ten people are coming, more quite possibly, and all the meat has arrived. Rob of the quince tree has butchered a lamb, and Todd the butcher has provided sausage skins as well as an exceptionally good price for the pork and beef. He will help with the cutting of the meat, with his butcher's expertise.

By 10 a.m. almost everyone has arrived. Todd and his dad Pete sharpen knives and bone out the meat. The plan is to make several different types of sausages.

The day started with the early firing up of Carmichael, who is obliging today and doesn't smoke at all. The bread is mixed and set to rise in readiness for making finger rolls in which to serve the sausages. Dozens of scones are baked by 8.30 for morning tea.

I've planned for nibbles during the day — cheeses and pickled eggs, chillies and onions, quince cheese and a multitude of jams — blackberry and raspberry as well as blackcurrant jelly with clotted cream.

Rob has brought his large mincer, Elliott has lent us his, and we have two large mixers with mincer attachments. Stephanie has brought a formidably large and lethal-looking sausage-skin stuffer.

Before long the sausage-making is in full swing with all hands to the task. Meat and fat are cut to fit into the mincer, with proportions carefully weighed out, as are the herbs and spices to flavour them. We have opted for 25 to 30 per cent fat, which still seems high, but apparently at least this amount is necessary and far less than is used in most commercially prepared sausages. Still, all the ingredients are the best available — the meat from free-range animals raised on farms in the Derwent Valley.

Stephanie's sausage-stuffer has worked very well and everyone has taken a turn at the somewhat tricky process of filling the skins to perfection, so they don't split when cooked. Todd shows how to string them all together. So that the children can be involved with the whole process, they have ground up the herbs and spices with a mortar and pestle.

The home-cured bacon meantime has been roasted off in Carmichael, and done to a turn. Stephanie has cured hers with her usual recipe (see page 293), whereas I have used the quince jelly instead of maple syrup. Pete slices it for frying and it is beyond delicious, another perfect accompaniment to the (by now) multitudinous sausages.

By lunchtime several batches have been prepared and cooked for all comers to try. The neighbours have called in, as I invited them to, and a great feast is under way. The sauerkraut is a success, perfect for the bratwurst, and it's very good with the pork and apple sausages as well.

I stand back and observe the scene as I cook the sausages on Carmichael, and it is a cheery sight — friends and family working together with a common purpose, laughter and productivity going hand in hand to make a wonderful day. All who have come along get take-home packs. It's dark by the time everyone leaves and no-one wants any dinner.

With Stephanie at the helm of the mixing, several new recipes have been developed.

In all, during the day, we made eight different sausages: spiced lamb; lamb merguez; lamb, mint and rosemary; Mexican chorizo; bratwurst; pork and apple; Italian sweet (pork and fennel); and pepper beef (beef, Worcestershire and black pepper).

Stephanie is happy to share some of her recipes and supporting information here. Others she will teach in a specific class she will conduct in the cooking school in the not-too-distant future.

Sausage Basics

- Be sure that your sausages include a minimum of 25–30 per cent fat.
- Use the right amount of salt, at least 20 grams to every 1kg of meat.
- Make sure your meat is very, very cold, just off freezing is perfect. The fat can even be frozen. Warm fat does not mince well!
- Mix your meat mixture well to make sure you have a good texture and bind.
- Add ice-cold liquids when making the sausages as this distributes seasonings and gives a moister sausage.
- Cook your sausage slowly.
- You can use a sausage attachment on your mincer to stuff your sausages. However, the process of passing the sticky sausage mix through the worm drive heats up the meat considerably. You need to be very careful to keep everything cold so that the fat does not smear. If you are going to make sausages regularly I highly recommend purchasing a separate small sausage filler. We have a 3kg manual-crank stainless-steel one and it works a treat.

Master Ratio: Basic Sausage Recipe

2.5kg meat (minimum 25 per cent fat)
40g rock salt
1 cup ice-cold liquid
seasonings

Provided that you stick to the basic ratio you can make pretty much any sausage you like. Recipes for our three favourites follow.

Italian Sweet

2kg pork shoulder
500g pork back fat

40g salt
40g sugar
16g minced garlic
20g fennel seeds, toasted
8g freshly ground black pepper
20g Spanish paprika
200ml ice water
100ml ice-cold red wine vinegar

Lamb Merguez

2kg lamb shoulder, diced
500g pork back fat
40g salt
10g sugar
5g hot pepper flakes
20g minced garlic
200g diced roasted red peppers
5g freshly ground black pepper
20g Spanish paprika
20g fresh oregano leaves, chopped
120ml dry red wine
100ml ice water

Pepper Beef (Beef, Worcestershire and Black Pepper)

2kg beef rump (we use rump as we like the flavour)
500g pork back fat
40g salt
40–50g black peppercorns, cracked in a mortar and pestle
150ml Worcestershire sauce
100ml good quality barbecue sauce (see page 360)
40g rice flour or wholemeal flour

Mince the meat and fat together on a coarse mince, 6–8mm plate.

Mix the meat mixture with all the other ingredients and mince again on the same coarse plate. (If you like a coarser-textured sausage then just mix well. You do not need to mince again.)

Check that the mixture has formed a good bind. It should feel like a sticky hamburger mix.

Fry off a small amount and taste test. Add more spices/salt according to taste.

Stuff into casings. You can use either collagen or natural casings.

Makes 2kg

July 15

Today is my final day of diarising the happenings here on our little farm. It is the day when Clarence's neck wounds will be examined once more. With owner Jordan out of the state, it falls to his sister Kirsty to attend to dressing the wound. She is a lovely young woman who has an incredibly strong love of animals, and tells me she has nine cats she absolutely adores.

When she arrives, I tentatively ask if she needs help. The reason for my reticence is that this morning Charlotte delivered a mouthful of spit full into my face when the supply of apple I take for their breakfast ran out. I am sure it wasn't malice, perhaps just a small piece of apple skin she had to dislodge from her throat. However that didn't make the spatter with which my entire face was covered smell any better. I truly have never come across anything so foul at such close quarters.

So it was with some trepidation that I went to help Kirsty with Clarence this afternoon. I took along a plastic jug full of chopped apple to appease Charlotte. In the end it wasn't too bad, I merely needed to hold Clarence's collar while Kirsty attended to him. Charlotte was happy with her treat, though most of it spilled when Doris the sheep knocked it out of my hand in a desperate attempt to get some for herself.

I'd wondered if the alpacas could go into the paddocks with the sheep. Initially I was worried about Charlotte's tantrums — perhaps she would attack the pregnant ewes? However, the sheep and alpacas meet at the fence in a seemingly friendly fashion. This afternoon when I give each of the alpacas a handful of hay as a reward for behaving well, Doris eats some of the overhang directly from the side of Charlotte's mouth.

Kirsty explains that the alpaca was brought up with a sheep who became her constant friend. Through force of circumstance the sheep Barney could not move with Charlotte to her new home. So deep was her grief that Jordan purchased Clarence to keep her company. No wonder she is so protective of him, and why she tolerates the sheep so well. I think it's very likely that next weekend we will give them a trial run together. It will mean that the alpacas' story will have come full circle, happy again here at Shangri-la, as Jordan calls it, with the entire three paddocks to graze and roam in.

Epilogue

Bookings for our cooking school are now coming in thick and fast and it seems the dream will become a sustainable reality after all. The move here is becoming all that I hoped it would be and more. The building is a space where family can come and cook to their heart's content, teach what they like by way of cooking if they choose, or just have fun with food.

Nan's piano still sits resplendent in the school's dining room, alongside the old table where we all sit to enjoy whatever we've baked. On its keys I've placed a sign inviting any who would and could to play it any time they like. It's the best of days when a visitor chooses to do so. The sound of the melodies floating out across the property and down the valley is nothing short of magical.

Stephanie and I are running the school together now, which is an unforeseen and delightful experience. We have such great times and the people who attend the classes have all been wonderful, entering into the spirit of spontaneity as well as the more structured cooking plan.

The property has become a homestead for the family, geographically much closer to most of the children and so visited much more. It's warm and cosy and welcoming.

The orchard has received a lot of attention from Robert and Nat and the watering system is now in place to best effect, the area fenced in preparation for the next fruit season, and the vegetable gardens are thriving.

When my mother came to visit during summer, she said that as a little girl I used to make detailed drawings of a place I called 'fairyland', my ideal home. The pictures, she told me, looked exactly like this property, right down to the style of the house, with animals all around in the paddocks and fruit trees everywhere, so perhaps this move was destined to be.

I see the little gumboots at the door, a sleepy grandchild curled up on my knee for a bedtime story, the alpacas rescued and safe in their paddock, and the ewes very obviously soon to lamb. Tom the cat is now sleek, fat and content in front of the fire, and Della is snuggled up for the night in a lambs'-wool blanket with a hot-water bottle, and I really do think this move was meant to be.

All the things I value are here — the room to move, and the space to cook with family and friends in a wonderful community. The environment is breathtakingly beautiful and there is ready access to abundant and exquisite seasonal produce.

Life certainly couldn't get any better.

Recipes for the Fruit I Didn't Find This Year

There have been some fruits I've not had time to find this year, and among them is tamarillo. I find this a most unusual fruit, like half fruit/half tomato. The flavour has a hint of strawberry, a little citrus maybe, but also has undeniable undertones of tomato.

It's an attractive fruit and I was able to buy them at the Eaglehawk Neck market. I even bought some seedlings once and planted them beneath our bathroom window. Although the window was high off the ground, before long the tamarillos had grown to the point where the whole window was covered. They bore prolifically too, but in a moment of utter madness I decided I'd had enough of their shade and cut them down. I've regretted it ever since and hope one day to find more plants for the garden here.

In *A Year in a Bottle* there was a recipe for tamarillo jelly. I didn't at first say to peel them as I'd never found it necessary. Perhaps it was just the variety I'd been buying. I loved the little touch of earthiness added by the skins. However, bowing to the greater opinion, it is probably best to peel them. This is done by dipping them in boiling water for one minute, then plunging into cold water. The skins should slip off easily.

I've tasted a few tamarillo chutneys and relishes but have never found one I like, so have steered away from them.

However, here are the recipes for the jam and jelly, both of which are delicious.

Tamarillo Jelly

1.25kg tamarillos (peeled weight) chopped
juice of 2 lemons
1 litre water
sugar

To peel the tamarillos, dip in boiling water for 1 minute, then into cold water. The skins should peel off easily.

Place the tamarillos, lemon juice and water in a saucepan and bring to the boil. Simmer gently for 20 minutes until the tamarillos are soft.

Pour into a colander that has been lined with muslin and leave to stand for several hours if possible.

For each cup of liquid add 1 cup sugar. Bring to the boil, stirring, then boil over a medium—high heat until setting point is reached (see page 393).

Pour into warm sterilised jars and seal immediately.

Makes about 1.5 litres

Tamarillo Jam

2kg peeled tamarillos, diced
juice of 1 lemon
1.75kg sugar

Peel the tamarillos (as per jelly recipe above). Place the tamarillos and lemon juice into a large saucepan or jam pan and bring to the boil, stirring often. Simmer until the tamarillos are soft.

Add the sugar and bring to the boil, stirring. Boil over a medium–high heat until setting point is reached (see page 393).

Makes about 2.8kg

Blueberries

I really like to add blueberries to other berry jams as they keep their texture. They are especially good when combined with raspberries. The pectin level of blueberries is lower, so a slightly longer cooking time is called for.

Blueberry and Raspberry Jam

750g blueberries
750g raspberries
juice of 1 lemon
1.4 kg sugar

Place the raspberries and blueberries, water and lemon juice in a pot and bring slowly to the boil, stirring often. Cook for 10 minutes over a gentle heat.

Add the sugar and bring back to the boil, stirring. Boil briskly for 15 minutes or until setting point is reached (see page 393). Stand for 5 minutes, then pour into warm sterilised jars and seal immediately.

Makes about 2.2kg

Blueberry Jam

Blueberries make a delicious jam in their own right. Be sure to use the fruit very fresh as the pectin levels will drop rapidly the longer they are kept on the shelf.

1kg blueberries
¼ cup water
juice of 1 lemon
950g sugar

Place the blueberries, water and lemon juice in a pot and bring slowly to the boil, stirring often. Cook for 10 minutes over a gentle heat.

Add the sugar and bring back to the boil, stirring. Boil briskly for 20–25 minutes or until setting point is reached (see page 393). Stand for 5 minutes, then pour into warm sterilised jars and seal immediately.

Makes about 1.8kg

Bottled Blueberries

Blueberries are probably the only berry that I would bottle as the usual problem of seeds slipping between the rim of the jar and the lid, causing spoilage, is not a problem: the seeds are nicely contained in the quite firm outer skin of the fruit.

Use the basic bottling method (page 385). Bring slowly up to 80°C over at least 50 minutes, then hold at this temperature for 30 minutes. Alternatively, if you have a thermostat-controlled preserver, set to 80°C, then process for 1 hour and 15 minutes.

Freezing Blueberries

For free flowing spread on a tray and freeze. As soon as they are frozen, pour into airtight freezer containers or freezer bags.

Alternatively, for solid pack, place desired amounts into freezer bags or containers, allowing headspace, and freeze.

Kiwifruit

Kiwifruit is another thing I've not found. A friend at the Neck often has a huge crop, and would share the excess with us. I've tried all sorts of recipes, combining them with apples, but it's such a shame to do this as their flavour is dulled.

Some people think that a jam made with them is tasteless but I've found that if a little citric acid is added, this fixes the lack of flavour and difficulty in setting.

Kiwifruit Jam

1kg peeled kiwifruit, diced
1 teaspoon citric acid
900g sugar

Place the kiwifruit and citric acid in a saucepan and bring to the boil, stirring. Simmer for about 10 minutes until the kiwifruit is soft.

Add the sugar and bring to the boil, stirring. Boil briskly over medium heat until setting point is reached.

Pour into warm sterilised jars and seal immediately.

Makes about 1.8kg

Laurel Berry Jam

Laurel berries make a lovely jam. They are like tiny plums, deep purple in colour. The jam has an almost almondy flavour that is very nice indeed. Removing the stones is a bit tedious, but worth the effort.

1.5kg laurel berries, stones removed
3 cups water
1.75kg sugar

Simmer the laurel berry stones with 1½ cups of the water for 20 minutes, then strain, retaining the liquid and discarding the stones.

Place the laurel berries and remaining water in a large saucepan or jam pan and bring to the boil, stirring occasionally. Simmer until the berries are soft, then add the water from the stones and the sugar. Bring to the boil, stirring until the sugar is dissolved, then cook briskly over a medium–high heat until setting point is reached (see page 393).

Pour into sterilised jars and seal immediately.

Makes about 2.4kg

Persimmons

It was a few years ago now that I first spied a persimmon tree. As I pulled into the car park of a B&B in Launceston, the tree stood high on a grassy bank, almost devoid of leaves but with several brilliant orange fruit still hanging from its branches.

At breakfast next morning I asked if I could pick and buy some of the fruit, to which the response was I could take all I wanted, as it always just ended up falling on the ground.

With little more than a kilo to work with, I was able to develop a recipe for jam, which is in *A Year in a Bottle*. A little jelly was made also, just enough to serve as a tasty glaze for fruit tarts.

I've done some research on them since, living in hope and waiting until I can get my hands on more. They apparently freeze well, either just the pulp or whole.

I've read that in Japan many of the varieties (and there are over 1000) are peeled and the fruit is suspended on string by the stems and then dried in the sun.

The purée is said to be very nice and can be used as the liquid component in cakes.

They are quite high in tannic acid, but if they are used ripe, this disappears during cooking.

So, until I have access to more, here are the mere two recipes I've been able to develop so far.

Persimmon Jam

1kg persimmons
juice of 2 lemons
1 cup water
sugar

Chop the persimmons and place in a large saucepan with the lemon juice and water. Bring to the boil, stirring often, and then simmer for 10 minutes or until the persimmons are tender.

Press the mixture through a coarse sieve or food mill. For each cup of the resulting purée, add 1 cup sugar.

Bring to the boil, stirring, then cook over a medium—high heat until setting point is reached (see page 393).

Makes about 1.5kg

Persimmon Jelly

It's best not to work with more than 1.5kg fruit at a time.

1.5kg persimmons
juice of 1 lemon (per kg fruit)
sugar

Chop the persimmons and place in a large saucepan or jam pan with the lemon juice and barely cover with water.

Bring to the boil and then simmer until the fruit is soft.

Pour the mixture into a colander lined with muslin, collecting the juice underneath. Leave to stand for several hours if possible.

To each cup of the resulting liquid, add 1 cup sugar. Bring to the boil, stirring and then boil briskly over a medium–high heat until setting point is reached (see page 393). Pour into warm sterilised jars and seal immediately.

Makes about 2 litres

Regarding Produce

For best results use fruit that is as fresh as possible. Varying stages of ripeness can be tailored to different preserving methods.

For bottling: Use just-ripe fruit that is still firm.

For jam and jelly: Fruit that is fresh picked and just ripe, or a mixture of slightly under-ripe and fully ripe, will give really good results. This is because the pectin levels are higher in fruit that is barely ripe. When you use a mixture, you get the pectin boost from the slightly under-ripe and the full flavour from the fully ripe.

For cordials: Ripe fruit is fine for cordials, in fact better as the lower pectin levels help to prevent the cordials from gelling (this can occasionally happen with fruits high in pectin such as currants, especially if the mixture is boiled too hard).

For chutneys and relishes: Ripe fruits are fine to use.

Basic Methods

Preserving (Bottling) Fruit

The times specified in the recipes for different fruit are those that make for the best retention of nutrients and optimum presentation in the jar.

There is no need to sterilise jars before preserving by this method, though they should be scrupulously clean. They are sterilised during the bottling process.

For many years, decades even, there was only one type of preserver available, the faithful Fowlers. Although I use Fowlers Vacola bottles, many types of jars are available nowadays. However, take care to ensure that any jars used are guaranteed heat-safe over the amount of time required for preserving. Make sure that replacement sealing rings for bottles are readily available.

Always remember to use fruit in premium condition and check that all utensils too are scrupulously clean.

The basic procedure for bottling fruit is as follows:

- Wash and rinse the bottles, ring and lids.
- Prepare the preserving syrup of choice (see over page).
- Place the rings on the bottles, ensuring that the ring is not twisted.
- Prepare the fruit and pack neatly into bottles.
- Fill the jar to the top with the prepared preserving liquid.

- Place lid evenly on jar, then the clips to secure. Alternatively, if using screwtop jars, screw the lid on as usual, then release a quarter of a turn.
- Place jars in preserver.
- Fill preserver to just below the lids with cool water.
- Set to the required temperature (either those specified in this book or those in the preserver's manufacturer's instructions).
- Remove from preserver and stand on a wooden board.
- Allow to stand undisturbed until completely cold (approximately 24 hours).
- Remove clips if used — the bottles should be sealed. If not, store in fridge and use within three days.
- If using screwtop jars, screw the lid down tightly immediately after processing, while still hot.

Preserving Liquid

The liquid can be water, fruit juice or sugar syrup. Sugar quantity in syrups can vary according to personal taste. In the case of gooseberries, however, a light syrup is often recommended to prevent the shrinkage or shrivelling of the berries.

Light syrup	1 part sugar to 4 parts water
Medium syrup	1 part sugar to 2 parts water
Heavy syrup	Equal parts sugar and water

For many years, and still to this day, some people choose to bottle fruit by placing the filled jars in their conventional ovens. The method is to place the prepared jars of fruit (with lids, rings and clips or even with screwtop jars) in a baking tray filled with 3cm water in a moderate oven for an hour. Food authorities no longer recommend preserving in this way. For effective preservation the core temperature should be at least 85°C in each jar.

Another more recent method of bottling fruit is to use a microwave oven. Although some people find this effective, food authorities do not recommend it. There are many factors that can affect this process, for instance: the wattage of the microwave oven; and whether or not other appliances are being used in the home at the same time, even if there is moisture on the turntable.

An additional factor to consider is that with microwave ovens even distribution of heat is not always guaranteed, which in turn means that the core temperature of all bottles may not reach the required 85°C.

Sterilising Jars

It is essential that preserving jars and bottles are sterilised, unless bottling with a preserver or making sparkling fruit drinks, before any products are poured into them. A simple method for doing this is:

- Wash the bottles and lids in hot soapy water, rinse and place upside down on a clean cloth or dish drainer to drain.
- Place on a tray in a cold oven.
- Turn oven to 110°C. When the oven reaches this temperature, turn off the heat and leave the bottles for 10 minutes.
- When cooled to warm, they are ready to pour in your jam, jelly, cordial or pickles.
- Simmer lids in boiling water for 2 minutes, drain and use dry. (I speed this up by using my blow dryer on high temperature — it then only takes a couple of minutes.)
- To sterilise muslin for jellies, cordials and the like, place in a small pot, cover with boiling water and simmer for 2 minutes. Drain and dry.

Making Jam, Jelly and Marmalade
Pectin

Pectin is a natural substance in fruit which, when boiled with the correct amount of sugar and sufficient acid, reacts to form a gel. This is the building block for jams, conserves, jellies, fruit pastes and cheeses.

Several factors can help maximise pectin when making jam:
- Use fruit that is just slightly under-ripe.

- Don't use fruit that is very ripe; save this for cordial, relish or chutney (even then, not too ripe).
- Use fruit that has only recently been picked. Pectin levels drop significantly the longer the fruit has been on the shelf.
- Freezing fruit for jam lowers the pectin level.
- Combine a fruit with low pectin with one that is high in pectin (see following tables).
- Acid helps release the pectin in fruit. For this reason it is important to add the lemon juice or citric acid from the outset wherever possible.
- Keep in mind that the amount of pectin can also vary with the season. For example, in a wet season blackberries (and other berry fruits) contain more moisture, which results in less pectin per volume of fruit.

Here is a simple test to ascertain pectin levels in the fruit you are using:

- Simmer the fruit with a little water until it is soft.
- Place one teaspoon of the fruit juice from this mixture in a heatproof glass.
- When this has cooled, add 3 teaspoons methylated spirits, shake gently, then leave to stand for one minute. A translucent jelly–like substance will have formed.

The following table will give an indication of the results and how to match these to the proportion of sugar that should be used.

Testing for Pectin Levels in Fruit

Evidence (jelly-like clot)	Pectin level	Quantity of fruit pulp	Quantity of sugar
1 firm clot	High	1kg	1.25 kg
2–3 less firm clots	Medium	1kg	1kg
Many small clots	Poor	1kg	750g

The following table gives an indication of pectin levels of many of the fruits used for jams and preserves:

Pectin Levels of Various Fruits

Poor	Medium	High
Bananas	Apricots	Cooking apples
Cherries	Blackberries	Crabapples
Elderberries	Blueberries	Cranberries
Figs	Eating apples	Currants: red, black,
Guava	Grapes	white
Kiwi fruit	Greengages	Damsons
Mangoes	Medlars	Gooseberries
Melon	Nectarines	Grapefruit
Mulberries	Persimmons	Lemons
Passionfruit	Plums (most varieties)	Limes
Peaches	Tomatoes	Oranges
Pears		Plums (some varieties)
Pineapple		Quinces
Rhubarb		Rosehips
Strawberries		Raspberries
		Loganberries
		Tangerines
		Tangelos
		Mandarins

At times it may be advantageous to add pectin to jams and jellies made from fruit with low levels of pectin. In this case use a liquid pectin stock (see page 390).

Adding Extra Pectin

If you have made jam and it has not set, you may want to boil it up again and add extra pectin. There are several ways to do this, and it's good to add extra acid as well, as acid helps extract and maximise the effect of pectin. Pectin powder can be purchased through Green Living Australia www.greenlivingaustralia.com.au/homepreserving_pectin.html. Alternatively, there are jam setting agents available at supermarkets.

For a batch of jam that is comprised of, for instance, 1.5kg raspberries and 1.5kg sugar, pour the jam back into the saucepan or jam pan and bring to the boil. Mix together 2 teaspoons pectin powder with 50g sugar and 1 teaspoon citric acid. Whisk this into the jam and boil briskly for 5 minutes, then test for set, cooking for up to an extra 5 minutes, though this should not be necessary.

If you are making a jam with a fruit that you know to be low in pectin, then you can pre-empt the issue by making pectin stock as below.

Pectin Stock

1kg gooseberries, whitecurrants or cooking apples such as Granny Smiths
3 cups water

Combine gooseberries, whitecurrants or apples (or even just the cores) with water in a large saucepan. Bring to the boil and simmer for 45 minutes. Strain through a colander, then the resulting liquid through muslin (two thicknesses).

For each kilo of fruit, add 1 cup pectin stock. Freeze any excess pectin stock in small containers.

Makes 1 litre

The Role of Acid

It is important that acid levels are sufficient in the fruit for optimum setting of the jam, jelly, paste or cheese.

Fruits that are low in acid include:

- eating apples (i.e. sweet varieties)
- elderberries

- figs
- kiwifruit
- lychees
- mangoes
- medlars
- melon
- nectarines
- passionfruit
- peaches
- pears
- pineapple
- quinces
- strawberries
- sweet varieties of cherries
- tomatoes

When using these fruits it would be advisable to add 2 tablespoons lemon juice or 1 level teaspoon citric acid for each 2kg fruit. Remember to add this at the outset. An alternative is to combine these fruits with high acid fruits such as:

- cooking apples
- crabapples
- cumquats
- currants — red, black or white
- damson plums
- gooseberries
- grapefruit
- greengages
- lemons
- limes
- mandarins
- oranges

Reducing Sugar in Jams

For jam to keep well on the shelf, it is necessary to use 66 per cent sugar to the volume of fruit — i.e. 660g sugar to 1kg fruit. Even then it is essential to use fruit in prime condition, not over-ripe.

However, if you choose to reduce the amount of sugar, you can lengthen the jam's shelf life by processing by the water-bath method (e.g. in the Fowlers Vacola or a similar preserving outfit). To do this, the jam must be totally cooled and have the lids screwed on then released a quarter of a turn. Place the jars in the preserver, then fill to the bottom of the lids with cold water. If you have a thermostat-controlled preserver, set to 77°C, turn on and leave for 1 hour. If your preserver is not thermostat-controlled, bring slowly to this temperature over about 50 minutes, then hold at this temperature for 15 minutes. Remove jars carefully from preserver and screw lids down tight.

You can make sugar-free jam by simply stewing fruits together until mushy. If you add some apple and/or pear it will sweeten it to some extent. Allow to cool and add a natural sugar-free alternative sweetener. Store in the fridge for up to 2 weeks at most. Do not process by the waterbath method as the alternative sweetener can become bitter. Some people add grape, apple or pear juice concentrate to sweeten jams. Keep in mind that the natural sugars in these products are already concentrated.

The filled jars of jam can also be frozen, or freeze the jam in small freezer containers. Allow a little space in the jar or container for expansion.

Savoury preserves (relishes, sauces, chutneys) can have their sugar content reduced as well, but again this may mean a reduction in shelf life.

To extend their shelf life, process, as described for jams, at 83°C for 1½ hours for a thermostat-controlled preserver, or if not, bring to this temperature slowly over about 50 minutes, then hold at this temperature for 45 minutes.

Again, also as for jams, freeze in small jars or containers. Refrigerate after opening.

Testing for Set in Jams and Jellies

There are three main methods for testing for set/thickness/gel:

- **Insert a sugar thermometer** into the mixture: when the mixture reaches 105°C, the sugar reacts with the fruit and acid to form the pectin gel, which means that the setting point has been reached. (Be sure the thermometer does not touch the base of the pot.)

- **Flake test**: collect a little of the mixture with a metal spoon. Allow to cool a little, then tilt the spoon on its side. If the jam is ready it will fall from the spoon in a sheet, rather than form liquid drops.

- **Wrinkle test**: put 2 teaspoons of the mixture on a cold saucer, then place in fridge for a few minutes. Run your finger through the cold jam; if the surface is quite firm and wrinkles, the jam has reached setting point.

Making Jam (Stovetop Method)

- Prepare the fruit according to the recipe instructions. Most fruit will need to be washed, with the exception of very soft fruit such as raspberries.

- Some fruit such as apricots, peaches and nectarines will need to have their stones removed.

- Plum stones can be removed before cooking, or they can be removed as they rise to the surface during cooking, or sieved out through a colander after cooking.

- Place the fruit in the saucepan with the specified amount of water and lemon juice (see individual recipes for recommended amounts).

- Cook, stirring occasionally, until the fruit is well softened. Apricots should be stirred more often as they tend to catch. Grease the base of the pan to help prevent this or add four to six stainless steel forks — it diffuses the heat and prevents catching.

- Remove the fruit mixture from the heat and stir in the sugar.

- Return to the heat and bring back to the boil, stirring to ensure that the sugar is dissolved before the mixture boils.
- Boil steadily until setting point is reached (see page 393).
- Remove from the heat.
- Allow to stand in the pot for 10 minutes before pouring into warm sterilised bottles.
- Seal immediately.

Microwave Jam
Smaller batches of jams can be made successfully in the microwave using the same basic principles as for that prepared on the stovetop. For jams, cook the fruit in a microwave-safe bowl on high until soft, then add the sugar and boil the mixture until setting point is reached. Bottle the jam and seal immediately.

Fruit Jellies
- Prepare the fruit as for jam.
- Add the lemon juice and enough water to barely cover. Berry fruits need much less water.
- Bring to the boil and cook until the fruit is softened and has released its juice.
- Strain first through a colander, then the resulting liquid through a double thicknesses of muslin.
- For each cup of liquid add 1 cup sugar (this amount can be reduced to two-thirds of a cup if desired, particularly for lower-pectin fruits).
- Return the mixture to the heat and bring to the boil, stirring to ensure that the sugar is dissolved before boiling point is reached.
- Cook steadily until setting point is reached (see page 393).
- Do not stir in the scum that rises to the surface. Remove with a slotted spoon or put a few small pieces of butter on the surface to help prevent scum forming in the first place.

- Remove from the heat.
- Pour into warm sterilised bottles and seal immediately.

Cordials

Homemade cordial syrups are a great way of using excess fruit. If you can't handle large amounts of produce at any one time, simply make up a smaller batch and freeze the rest of the fruit until a later date.

- Place the fruit in a pan with the specified amount of water.
- Bring to the boil and cook until the fruit is soft.
- Strain first through a colander and then the resulting juice through two thicknesses of muslin.
- To this liquid, add 1 cup sugar to each cup of juice (this may vary with some recipes).
- Bring to the boil, stirring.
- Cook for one to two minutes until *just* simmering.
- At this stage in some recipes citric acid, tartaric acid or vinegar is stirred in until dissolved.
- Pour into warm sterilised bottles and seal immediately.

Fruit Pastes and Cheeses

- Prepare the fruit as for jam and place in a saucepan with very little water (see specific recipes) and lemon juice.
- Cook until the fruit is very soft.
- Strain the mixture through a sieve or food mill.
- For each cup of fruit pulp, generally add 1 cup sugar unless the recipe specifies otherwise.
- Bring back to the boil, stirring to completely dissolve the sugar before the boiling point is reached.
- Cook over a medium–low heat, stirring frequently, until a paste is produced. Towards the end of cooking the heat may need to be reduced to very low.

- To make a fruit cheese the mixture should be cooked for a longer time. It is ready when a wooden spoon dragged through the mixture leaves a clear trail across the base of the saucepan.
- For pastes, spoon into warm sterilised jars and seal immediately. Store in a cool, dry and dark place.
- For fruit cheeses, pour the mixture into foil-lined slice tins to a depth of 2cm and leave to set. When completely cold, cut into squares and store between layers of baking paper in an airtight container.

Savoury Preserves

Chutneys, Pickles and Relishes
- Prepare the fruit and/or vegetables according to recipe instructions.
- In some cases brining of the fresh produce will be recommended.
- Cook for time recommended in recipe or until desired consistency is reached.
- Pour into warm sterilised jars and seal immediately.

Clear Pickles
- Brining of vegetables is generally recommended (each recipe has its own instructions for brine) to extract some of the vegetable's natural juices, allowing the vinegar to penetrate and preserve effectively.
- Prepare the vinegar and spice mixture.
- Generally, the method is to place the brined vegetables in sterilised jars (in some cases after briefly cooking them) and pour the vinegar over. Some recipes call for the vinegar to be cooled before covering the vegetables in this way, in others it should be used hot.
- It is essential that the vegetables are submerged in the vinegar mixture. If they float to the surface, place a piece of crumpled

baking paper in the top of the jars and press down into the vinegar. After a week the paper can be removed and the vegetables should remain submerged. If not, replace the paper and leave for another week.

- Seal immediately.

Sauces
- Use a similar method as for chutneys and relishes. However, it is important to note that the ingredients and methods for individual recipes will result in a more liquid consistency.
- Strain sauces after cooking, return to the heat and re-boil.
- Pour into sterilised bottles and seal immediately.

Thickening Savoury Preserves
If relishes, chutneys, pickles and, occasionally, sauces need to be thickened, this is best achieved by making a thin paste of cornflour and vinegar. (A mixture of cornflour and water is not advisable as it could introduce a contaminant at the late stage of cooking, which may affect the product's shelf life.)

Arrowroot can be substituted for the cornflour, but if this is boiled for even only a short time, there is a risk that it may break down and lose its thickening quality.

Flour and vinegar paste can be used, but this can make the savoury pickle taste a bit chalky, so cornflour is my preferred option.

Dehydrating
Dehydrating food is an excellent way to preserve fruits, vegetables and even meats.

This form of preservation removes moisture from the foods so that bacteria, yeast and moulds cannot continue to grow; it also slows down the enzyme action that causes foods to spoil. Any produce that is to be dried should be very fresh and of the highest possible quality.

Three primary methods can be used: oven-drying, a dehydrator and sun-drying. Sun-drying can be a little tricky sometimes (and a humid climate is not really conducive to sun-drying), therefore only the first two methods will be discussed here.

If using the oven, the temperature needs to be held at a steady 60°–65°C for effective dehydrating. An oven thermometer is highly advisable to ensure that the temperature remains consistent at all times. Leave the oven door slightly ajar to allow moisture to escape and rotate the trays to ensure even drying of the entire batch.

A food dehydrator is a good investment as it allows the temperature to be controlled easily. Follow the manufacturer's specific temperatures and times for different types of food.

Dehydrated foods should be cooled, then tightly packed and placed in airtight containers such as small glass jars, plastic containers with tight-fitting lids or freezer bags.

Store dehydrated foods in a cool, dark place. For safety, I store these containers in the fridge or, if not to be used within 3 weeks, in the freezer. As another safety measure, check the dehydrated foods occasionally. If there is any sign of mould growing on the food, throw it out immediately.

Dehydrating Fruit

Some types of fruit such as cherries, blueberries, grapes and plums need to have their skins made more porous due to a waxy coating that will prevent moisture from escaping. To treat the skin, dip the fruit in boiling water for 1 minute, then pat dry with paper towel.

Other types of fruit can be sliced to a thickness of 1cm.

Pre-treatment is recommended to prevent loss of vitamins and discolouration. Here are three different methods:

- Mix 1 tablespoon lemon juice with 1 cup water and sprinkle over the fruit as it is prepared.
- Make a sugar syrup from equal parts of sugar and water. Add the fruit and simmer for 1 minute. Remove the fruit with a slotted spoon, then drain well, rinse carefully and pat dry.
- Soak in fruit juice or nectar.

Depending on the type and/or thickness of the fruit, dehydrating time will be between 6 and 36 hours.

To reconstitute dried fruits, add 1 cup fruit to 2 cups water, allow to stand for 2 hours. The fruit can then be stewed if desired.

Fruit Leathers

Fruit generally needs to be stewed then puréed for fruit leathers. Very little, if any, sweetening should be used as the fruit's natural sugars concentrate as the leather dries.

However, if you feel some sweetener is necessary, it is preferable to use honey as sugar has the potential to make the dried fruit leather brittle. About 2 teaspoons to 500ml purée should be ample.

Spread the fruit purée on baking paper-lined trays and place in the oven, or alternatively, spread the purée on special fruit leather trays and transfer to the dehydrator. The fruit leather is ready when there are no sticky spots evident. To test, tear a small piece of the leather. If no liquid is exuded, then dehydration is complete.

Remove from the trays and roll while still warm.

Vegetables

Most vegetables need to be blanched before dehydrating to slow down the enzyme action that causes the vegetables to spoil. Exceptions to this include mushrooms, capsicum, mushrooms, onions and okra.

Vegetables often need to be sliced. Depending on the vegetables, the slices need to be 8mm for effective drying with a consistent result. Exceptions are peas and corn.

For best results blanch the vegetables in boiling water or steam for the same amount of time recommended for freezing, then plunge into ice water, drain and pat dry.

Spread vegetables in a thin layer on baking trays and placed in the oven or dehydrator. There should be room for the circulation of air between the trays. Dry vegetables at a minimum of 60°–70°C, for anywhere from four to 15 hours.

To test for dryness, place a piece of vegetable on a board and tap with a hammer — the dried vegetable should shatter.

To reconstitute for cooking, soak the vegetables first. For each cup of dried vegetables use 2 cups water and soak for about 2 hours.

Herbs and Spices

It is important to pick herbs that are in the very best of condition and are pesticide-and insect-free. The newest leaves will have the most flavour, as will leaves picked in the morning. Once a plant has started to flower, the leaves will have less flavour and this may result in a measure of bitterness once they are dried. Flowers, such as chive flowers and rose petals, can also be dried. Again, these should be in full bloom and used very fresh.

Before drying shake the leaves or flowers to remove any insects or dirt particles, then wash and pat dry.

Spices such as pepperberry must also be fully ripe for optimum flavour after dehydrating.

Herbs are not suited to oven-drying. They can be dried in a food dehydrator at 35°C. Alternatively, tie in bundles and hang in a cool, dry place, or put in brown paper bags in a dark cupboard.

Freezing

Fruit

Fruit should be frozen when just ripe and in prime condition as soon as possible after picking.

Preparing Fruit

Work with only small amounts of fruit at any one time to prevent spoilage. It is best not to add spices to fruits before freezing as their flavour is greatly diminished.

Generally, frozen fruit will be of better quality if it is frozen with dry sugar or sugar syrup (though this is by no means a necessity). Fruit to be used later in preserves should *never* have sugar added to it before freezing.

Sugar Syrup

The quantity of sugar can vary according to taste and the type of fruit used.

250g sugar
2 cups water

Combine sugar and water in a saucepan and bring to the boil, stirring until the sugar is dissolved. Allow to cool before use. For each kilo of fruit, use about 1 cup cold syrup.

Dry Sugar

Use 250g dry sugar for each kilo of fruit. Mix the sugar carefully through the fruit before packaging for the freezer.

Fruit such as apples, apricots, peaches, nectarines are inclined to discolour during preparation and/or freezing. There are three methods to help prevent this.

Ascorbic acid powder: Obtained from good home-brewing shops, this can be added to the fresh fruit, fruit purée or sugar syrup. For fresh fruit, mix ¼ teaspoon ascorbic acid powder with ¼ cup cold water and stir to dissolve. This amount can be mixed through 1kg of fruit before placing in containers or bags and freezing. If using a sugar syrup to cover fruits for freezing, add ½ teaspoon ascorbic acid powder for each 4 cups syrup.

Citric acid or lemon juice: Mix 1½ teaspoons citric acid or 3 tablespoons lemon juice for each litre of water. Dip the fruit, drain well and pat dry with paper towels before freezing.

Steam blanching: place fruit in a steamer basket over a saucepan of boiling water. Cover with a lid and steam for 3 minutes.

Packaging Fruit

Freezer burn is caused by exposure to air while in the freezer, resulting in the product drying out. It affects the texture of the food and to some extent the flavour. It does not make the food unsafe, but makes it dry, leathery and discoloured. Cut these portions out of food before using. To avoid freezer burn, expel all air from the packaging.

Fruit can be frozen in freezer bags or containers. For freezer bags, place the fruit in the bag, allow 1.5cm headspace for the fruit to expand, and insert a plastic straw into the space around the fruit. Squeeze the neck of the bag in around the straw and suck out the air, remembering to allow for the headspace (this is necessary as the fruit expands as it freezes). Remove the straw, pinching in the top of the bag, and fasten immediately with the bag tie. For containers, fill with fruit to within 1.5cm of top, then cover with the lid.

For free-flowing product, fruit (whole, sliced or diced) can also be tray frozen. Place prepared fruit on a tray in a single layer, sprinkle with sugar (optional) and pack into bags or containers as soon as it is frozen (extended exposure will result in a loss of moisture). In this case it is not necessary to leave headspace. Place the bags or containers in the coldest part of the freezer. Allow 2.5cm around each package for faster freezing. Once the food is frozen, the packages can be packed tightly together.

Frozen fruits will keep from 8 to 12 months when stored at −18°C or lower. (It is highly advisable to buy a fridge/freezer thermometer so that this can be monitored — the cost is minimal.)

For future jelly-making, cook fruit and strain off the juice by the usual jelly-making procedure, then freeze the liquid in containers. The fruit jelly can later be prepared by thawing this juice, adding sugar and boiling till the setting point is reached.

Vegetables

Use very fresh vegetables in prime condition, not over-ripe or under-ripe produce. It is best to work with only small quantities of vegetables at any one time.

Blanching Vegetables for Freezing

It is necessary to blanch most vegetables before freezing. To blanch effectively, bring 5 litres water to a rolling boil. Place the prepared vegetables in a single layer in a wire basket and immerse in the water. No more than 500g of vegetables should be blanched at any one time. Place the lid on the pot. Blanching time is counted from the time that steam comes out from under the lid.

Vegetables may be steam blanched. Bring 3 cups water to the boil in the base of a pot. Place the prepared vegetables in a wire basket above the water and place the lid on the pot. The time needed for steam blanching is longer than that of the boiling water method and is not suited to all types of vegetables.

Herbs do not need blanching, with the exception of basil, which should be blanched for 1 minute only.

Plunge the vegetables into ice-cold water, then drain thoroughly and pat dry. Cool thoroughly before packing for freezing.

Packaging Vegetables for Freezing

There are two ways that vegetables can be packed and subsequently frozen.

Method 1

- Pack the drained and dried vegetables into portion-sized freezer bags.
- Allow 1cm headspace to allow for expansion as the vegetables freeze.
- Make sure that as little air as possible remains in the bag. This can be achieved by inserting a plastic drinking straw into the filled bag, then pulling the neck of the bag in with your fingers. Suck out as much air as possible. Pinch the neck of the bag tight as the straw is removed and secure with the twist tie for the bag.

Method 2

- For free-flowing vegetables, spread the blanched and dried vegetables in a single layer on a tray and freeze quickly. Pack into bags or containers as soon as they are frozen through.
- There is no need to leave any headspace as the vegetables are already frozen.

Placing the Packaged Vegetables in the Freezer

Allow space of 1.25cm around each freezer bag or container until the vegetables are completely frozen, after which they should be packed together tightly. No more than 10 per cent of the freezer should be used for adding the packed vegetables.

The temperature in the freezer should be a steady −17°C or lower. Check with a fridge/freezer thermometer.

Vegetables under these conditions can be stored for up to 12 months.

Cooking Frozen Vegetables

Cook in a little boiling water for about half the time it would take to cook them from fresh.

Troubleshooting Chart

Bottled (Preserved) Fruits

Difficulty	Comment or Cause	Cure/other advice
Fruit risen in jars	Don't worry too much — it usually means there is a good seal Fruit might have been over-ripe Fruit packed too loosely Apricots, nectarine, peaches and plums are particularly susceptible as they are sensitive to heat. Ripe fruit can push some of the liquid out of the bottle, sometimes leaving the top portion of fruit uncovered. If the jar is sealed, the fruit is still edible. A heavy syrup can tend to make the fruit rise The temperature might have been a bit high or has risen to that point a bit too quickly	It's best to use fruit which is just ripe or slightly under-ripe for best results in appearance Make sure the jars are packed tightly Leave the bottled fruit to stand for 2 weeks undisturbed, then turn the jar on its side and shake gently in a short, sharp jerking manner — this makes the syrup move between the pieces of fruit which will then be distributed more evenly in the jar. Repeat this as needed.
Darkened fruit in the top of the bottle	The heat may have been a bit high or brought to heat too quickly, scorching the fruit Fruit is left uncovered in the vacuum space Jar may not have been filled to the rim with syrup	If the jar is sealed the fruit is fine, though for appearance purposes it's best to discard the discoloured fruit Fill jar brimful with syrup

Difficulty	Comment or Cause	Cure/other advice
Cloudy syrup after bottling	Small pieces of fruit suspended in the liquid — fruit may have been over-ripe so that minute pieces break off Hard water may have been used (the minerals can cause this cloudiness)	Use fruit that is just ripe or slightly under-ripe The liquid will most likely clear after standing for a week or two
Jars didn't seal when preserved	The rubber ring may have been twisted Old rubber rings may have been re-used Fruit seeds, pips or skins may have slipped under the lid of the jar Thermometer might be faulty on preserver Not high enough temperature or insufficient preserving time Rim or lid of jar may be damaged	Use fruit immediately. Refrigerate the jar of fruit or pour into containers and freeze. Use new rings each year or at the very least make sure that re-used rings are in very good condition I tend to freeze, rather than preserve, berries for this reason Check jars and lids before using
Mould on top of fruit	Use of: • over-ripe fruit • fruit with bruising of flesh Seal has been compromised during processing • Tiny hole in cover • Damaged rim, rubber ring, or lid	DISCARD! Next time: Use freshest possible fruit Check jars and lids before using
Fruit fermented	Preserving time too short Temperature not high enough Damaged rim or lid of jar Rubber ring twisted	DISCARD!

Difficulty	Comment or Cause	Cure/other advice
Flesh of fruit discoloured while waiting to bottle	Can happen with pears, apples, quinces, bananas and feijoas	When preparing, drop fruit into a solution of 2 tablespoons lemon juice (or 1 teaspoon citric acid) to 2 cups water
Fruit covered with small bubbles after preserving	These are not air bubbles but a kind of oil exuded from the skins	They will disappear over time
Cracks in skin of plums after bottling	Skins are sensitive to heat	Packing the bottles tightly will diminish the visual effect of split skins

Prick each plum with a fork (twice) before placing in bottle |
| Air bubbles in finished jars (amongst fruit) | Fruit packed too tightly | Ease out air pockets by sliding a knitting needle or long slim knife down the inside as syrup is poured in |
| Seal on bottle broken during storage | Over-ripe, damaged or bruised fruit

Preserving temperature too low

Not preserved long enough

Chip or crack in bottle

Twisted or damaged rubber ring

Chipped rim on bottle | DISCARD! |
| Liquid oozes out during processing | Fruits packed too tightly

Temperature brought up too quickly

Air bubbles not removed during processing | Ease out air pockets by sliding a knitting needle or long slim knife down the inside as syrup is poured in

Overall — doesn't really matter as long as jar has sealed |

Jams, Jellies, Conserves etc

Product	Problem	Cause	Comments
Jam	Not setting	Too little pectin Incorrect balance between pectin and acid Insufficient cooking time	Add lemon juice and re-boil Add commercial pectin according to packet instructions Cook for specified time or until setting point is reached
Jam	Too dark	Poor-quality fruit Cooked too long, so sugar has caramelised	Use fruit that is *just slightly* under-ripe for maximum pectin level, flavour and colour
Jam	Fruit has risen	Jars too hot Jam not allowed to settle before bottling	Leave until completely cold, then fold fruit through evenly, top with baking paper dipped in brandy Allow jam to stand for 10 minutes before pouring into jars
Jam	Crystallisation	Too much sugar in proportion to fruit Not stirring often enough (undissolved sugar) Lack of acid in fruit Over-boiling Sugar not dissolved when mixture brought to the boil	Add lemon juice at outset Ensure sugar is dissolved before boiling point is reached again Add 30g butter per 1kg fruit (after boiling for some time)

Product	Problem	Cause	Comments
Jam	Mouldy on top	Damp or poor-quality fruit Insufficient boiling Covered while warm Stored in a warm, unventilated and/or damp place Too much water added to the mixture Jars were wet	Cover jam when piping hot Place a bowl of lime on the shelf where jams are kept Ensure sterilised jars are completely dry
Jam	Fruit tough	Insufficient cooking before sugar was added	Test taste fruit before adding sugar As an alternative, use conserve method: layer sugar with fruit. Stand overnight, then cook until setting point is reached
Jam	Fermented	Poor quality or over-ripe fruit Insufficient cooking Not enough sugar Cover not airtight Incorrect storage	DISCARD!
Jam	Hard or dry	Over-boiling Stored in too warm a place Cover not airtight	Use screwtop lids
Jam	Syrupy	Insufficient boiling Over-boiling to beyond setting point	Test regularly until setting point is reached

Product	Problem	Cause	Comments
Jam	Poor flavour	Too much sugar Over-boiling Over-ripe fruit Under-ripe fruit Boiling too slowly	Use fruit in prime condition that is just ripe
Jam	Poor colour	Poor quality fruit Fruit not softened sufficiently before adding sugar Boiled too slowly to setting point Stored in bright light	Use best quality, just-ripe fruit Soften fruit well before adding sugar Boil briskly to setting point (over medium-high heat)
Jelly	Cloudy	Sugar or fruit or jelly bag not clean Jelly bag was squeezed Boiled too fast as setting point was reached Jelly bag still contains some residue, or if new, some minuscule pieces of fibre from the fabric (e.g. flannel) Scum was stirred in	Wash fruit well, use good-quality sugar Wash jelly bag and scald before using Remove scum from surface with slotted spoon For smaller streaks, add small knobs of butter to disperse
Jelly	Dark on surface during storage	Stored in too warm a place Stored in too light a place Stored too long (this often occurs with apple and other light jellies due to enzyme action)	Store in a cool, dry, dark place

Product	Problem	Cause	Comments
Jelly	Thick and syrupy but not set	Insufficient pectin	Add lemon juice: 1 tablespoon to 1kg, then re-boil for 5 minutes. Alternatively, add commercial pectin and boil for 10 minutes more
Jelly	Set in preserving pan before bottling	Acid content too high	Combine with lower acid fruit
Jelly	White streaks	Scum stirred in Scum not removed carefully before bottling	Add a few small knobs of butter to disperse small pieces of scum Remove large pieces of scum with slotted spoon
Jelly	Not setting in large jars	Too slow in cooling process	Use smaller, even-sized, similar-shaped jars
Jelly	Air bubbles	Jelly poured too slow or fast into jars Jelly not poured down inside surface of jar Boiled too fast as setting point was reached Allowed to stand too long before bottling	Pour jelly down inside surface of jar Bottle within 5–10 minutes of cooking
Conserve	Fruit doesn't stay whole	Fruit not mixed with sugar and left to stand long enough Cooked too long	Leave combined sugar and fruit to stand overnight at least
Conserve	Shrinks in jar	Seal faulty Storage conditions too warm	Store in a cool, dark, dry place. Place freezer bag over lid and secure with a rubber band

Product	Problem	Cause	Comments
Conserve	Air pockets	Too cool before pouring into jars	Allow to stand no more than 10 minutes before bottling
Marmalade	Cloudy	Too much pith included (this will always happen if whole fruit is minced) Scum stirred in	Ensure pith is removed Remove scum with slotted spoon
Marmalade	Peel rises to surface	Jars too hot when marmalade is poured into them Mixture not allowed to stand before bottling	Allow sterilised jars to cool to warm before pouring marmalade into them Allow marmalade to stand for 10 minutes before bottling
Chutney	Shrinks in jar	Over-boiled Not covered tightly enough Stored in a warm place	Cook only until chutney-like consistency is reached with no clear vinegar liquid remaining After bottling, place a freezer bag over lid and secure with a rubber band
Chutney	Mouldy	Poor quality fruit and/or vegetables Insufficient vinegar Under-cooking Use of unsterilised jars Use of damp jars	DISCARD!
Chutney	Liquid on surface	Insufficient boiling down of mixture	Cook until no free-flowing vinegar liquid is evident
Flavoured oils	Cloudy	Flavouring contains too much liquid (e.g. onions)	Use quickly or it will become rancid

Product	Problem	Cause	Comments
Flavoured oils	Rancid	Incorrect storage	DISCARD!
		Faulty seal on bottles	For future reference:
		Oil came into direct contact with sunlight or heat	Basil oil: remove herb from oil after 2 weeks
			Garlic oil: use within 2 weeks (keep refrigerated during this time)
Pickles	Not crunchy	Not salted long enough	Ideally soak in brine for 24 hours
		Brine too weak	
		Vinegar quantity or acetic acid level insufficient to preserve adequately	
Pickles	Hollow	Raw ingredients too mature	Use freshest produce possible
		Vegetables kept too long before use	
Pickles	Dark in colour	Iodised salt used	Use cooking salt
		Too many spices	Use whole spices in a muslin bag
		Ground spices used	
		Dark vinegar used	Use bottled or filtered water
		Brine made with hard water	
Pickles	Vegetables or fruit rise to top	Vinegar takes a little time to penetrate vegetables	Place a piece of crumpled baking paper in jar, leave for 1 week, remove
			Repeat if necessary
Pickles	Pale or bleached	Jar exposed to light during storage	Store in a cool, dark place
Pickles	Soft and slippery	Salt or vinegar solution not strong enough	DISCARD!

Product	Problem	Cause	Comments
Pickles	Garlic looks green	Not uncommon	Blanch garlic before use
Pickles	Green spots on pickled onions	Caused by fermentation of a harmless substance	Okay to eat: I remove the outer spotted layer as often the rest of the onion is usually unaffected
Pickles	Fermented or mould visible	Too little sugar Cooking time too short Salt/vinegar solution too weak Cooking equipment not clean Incorrect storage Decayed or bruised fruit or vegetables used	DISCARD!
Pickles	Unpleasant odour	Pickles are spoiled	DISCARD!
Sauce	Separation on storage	May not have been cooked long enough so that it still has a watery appearance Tomato sauce: breaking down of pectin gel	Shake to restore smoothness
Sauce	Dark on top	Tomato sauce is susceptible to this: lids may not have been airtight	Cover lid with a small freezer bag, secure with a rubber band or dip completed bottles in sealing wax

Acknowledgements

Extra special thanks must go to our daughter Stephanie and her husband Nathaniel, without whose efforts, elbow grease, true grit and support the school would never have happened so soon, if ever; for their ongoing fixing of equipment, gardening, painting and endless scrubbing and cleaning to bring the school building and surrounds to what it is today.

Of course thanks must go to my husband Robert, who shared my vision for the school, and for his support in setting up and extending fruit and vegetable gardens and for taking on an ever-growing menagerie of farm animals.

Thanks to son Elliott for his help and advice on electrical issues.

Thanks also to son Andrew for his help with the plastering.

In fact huge thanks to all our children for their support and encouragement for the cooking school venture.

To the cheery tradespeople who joined in the spirit of the thing as they carried out their specialised work, from carpenters, plumbers, electricians, to tilers and more besides.

Thanks also to the fruit- and vegetable-growers and meat producers of the Derwent Valley and beyond in Tasmania for their passion in producing such exquisite product that is an absolute joy to work with.

As always, thanks must go to Chris Wisbey for his encouragement through the writing of the books, which has now extended into the setting up of the cooking school. The seeds of all this were sown in his Jams and Preserves talkback so many years ago.

To the wonderful and supportive team at ABC Books/ HarperCollins: Amruta Slee, Foong Ling Kong, Kathy Hassett, Nicola Woods, Matt Stanton, Mark Higginson and Robert Winter.

And finally, thanks most definitely should go to all those who have attended classes in the school, for the time you spent with us and the cooking experiences we've shared together, for the sense of fun and camaraderie. We've learned a lot from you and loved your company.

Index